Living with Enlightenment

A JOURNEY OF LOVE

Brad Laughlin

CoreLight

CoreLight Publishing
223 North Guadalupe Street #275
Santa Fe, NM 87501 USA
www.CoreLight.org

Library of Congress Control Number: 2019904741

ISBN: 9781931679138 paperback
ISBN: 9781931679145 ebook

Editor: Mae Naude www.maenaude.co.za
Cover Artist: Canyonland Dreamtime, Leslie Temple-Thurston www.corelight.org

Design/Formatting:
Pickawoowoo Publishing Group www.pickawoowoo.com

Printing and distribution:
Lightning Source (USA, UK, AUS, EUR).

First Edition: March 2019
This paperback edition first published in 2019

To my beloved Leslie

Table of Contents

Preface

SELF-DISCOVERY

When we believe we are the ego, or personality, we miss out on so much. We limit and compartmentalize everything and end up believing that our spiritual life is separate from everyday life—from our work, money, relationships, sexuality, body, nature and the world. Yet it is possible to adopt a different perspective. We can integrate all aspects of worldly life into our spiritual journey and discover that our worldly life *is* our spiritual journey. The intention of this book is to support this integration.

The commitment to know the truth of who we are leads us on an extraordinary journey of discovering, evolving and becoming our own inner divinity. The journey is the path of Self-discovery. *Self* with a capital *S*, as opposed to *self* with a lower-case *s*, implies the essence that we truly are, beyond the confines of the ego—not something separate and outside of us, but within us.

The word *ego*, so closely linked to *personality, identity, role* and *self,* will be used interchangeably with these terms throughout the book. It is made up of our thoughts, feelings, memories, habits and physicality. Using the ego's lens, we create a frame of reference though which we view, interpret and construct both ourselves and our world. This lens, or mirror, reflects our constructed world back to us. For many the surface is equated with the reality. For a growing number, this is not sufficient.

Transpersonal Autobiography

My personal journey of Self-discovery over the past thirty years has been an amazing and unanticipated adventure. I have not only received more inner fulfillment and spiritual wealth than I ever could have imagined, but also I have been given more rewarding work, more material abundance and a more intimate, fulfilling relationship than I had ever hoped. My life partner, Leslie Temple-Thurston, and I have lived and worked together for the past twenty-five years and share an intimacy and love that is deep, ancient and abiding. Our unconventional love relationship is at the heart of the story you are about to read.

In 1993, we co-founded the non-profit organization, CoreLight, based on her teachings of non-duality, unconditional love and spiritual enlightenment. We have co-taught retreats and workshops worldwide and have co-authored books which have been translated into several languages. Tens of thousands of people have attended our events, and over a thousand have trained in our courses, from which a deeply committed base of teachers, healers and change agents have realigned their lives in the principles of non-duality and unconditional love.

I began writing this story as a self-healing exercise because in the past few years Leslie has started to experience memory loss. While grieving the gradual loss of my beloved, I have found writing the memories of our time together to be a profound support—a kind of *transpersonal autobiography*, if you will. In telling the story it is possible to fully embrace it, release it and recognize that we are not our memories. Memories—whether painful or pleasurable—are aspects of the egoic self, which is not who we truly are. Ultimately this process is about transcending the personal self and awakening the awareness of Self.

We learn who we are through our relationships with everyone and everything we encounter in the cosmos—transpersonal experiences. Because my relationship with Leslie was critically important in my journey to Self, she is featured as the central character here.

Each chapter offers a personal story, illustrating transpersonal truths. While these are stories of Leslie's and my personal adventures, they contain universal motifs, which transcend the personal, offering themes that apply to all. Just as our story is unconventional, every-one else's journey is also unique, and this exemplifies the universal principle of unity in diversity—one of the primary experiences we all incarnate on Earth to have. Together the stories form a map, navigating a conscious path to realization of the Self.

THE SPIRITUAL WARRIOR

At this pivotal moment in human evolution, Leslie's and my unwaver-ing objective has been to train a corps of spiritual warriors to enter the new paradigm of heart-centered consciousness. This involves moving beyond feelings of victimization and escaping from polarized thoughts and behaviors. When enough people step into love and unity consciousness, our fragile blue planet, poised on the brink of catas-trophe, will experience unprecedented healing and transformation. The purpose of this book is to facilitate that shift in each of us and to support readers in finding true balance and peace in life.

An emerging balance between masculine and feminine is integral to this paradigm shift and will be explored throughout the book. As the new era of balance is birthed, we create greater peace, healing and harmony, both inwardly and in the world. This process involves opening the heart—weaving generosity, compassion and love into the tapestry of our world.

As courageous spiritual warriors, we move forward, choosing balance and love—feeling love, expressing love, receiving love and becoming love—and then putting our love into action.

NOTE ON FORMAT

In this book I have made extensive use of dialogue, rather than reported speech, to communicate interactions between myself and others—primarily my discussions with Leslie. In so doing, I hoped to bring an intimacy and immediacy into the text so that the reader could hear, not only my voice, but the voice of significant others. Although I have followed the style of dialogue used in novels, I have not used quotation marks. Instead, the dialogues are in italics. The reader's attention is also drawn to the fact that important teachings are indented and boxed.

Acknowledgments

First and foremost, I thank my beloved Leslie for providing me with the map, the compass and the inspiration for my journey. Your light and love, my dear, have touched each and every page of this book. We are in an eternal embrace which nourishes my soul.

I would like to acknowledge my editor, Mae Naude, who so wisely and lovingly helped midwife this book. Her brilliant insights and compassionate guidance were invaluable sources of inspiration. Finding common threads in my stories, she helped weave the many themes into a holistic tapestry. I will always feel grateful to you, Mae, not just for your impeccable editing skills but also for your nurturing friendship through enormous challenge.

My gratitude also goes to Andrew Harvey for his inspiring mentorship and loving friendship over the past few years. You made this version of the book possible.

A simple thank you is not a strong enough way to express my gratitude to two dear friends and soul sisters: Kellyann Conway, whose saintly nature and devoted care have made writing this book and continuing CoreLight's work possible; and Lina Berntsen, whose enlightened perspective and loving friendship planted the "writing seed" and nurtured me through the most difficult chapter of my life.

I extend deep and heart-felt appreciation to all of my friends who generously volunteered to read, and reread, the various drafts, and to Jenny D'Angelo for inspired proofreading and encouragement. Your honest feedback and astute discernment helped shape so much of this work. Thank you for your time, courage and insight.

I am indebted to every character mentioned in this book and to all my dear soul friends, named and unnamed, who have been such radiant sources of love over the years and who have supported me on so many different levels.

Boundless gratitude goes to the entire CoreLight community, past and present—big-hearted donors, enthusiastic volunteers, dedicated employees and others. Without your generosity and devotion this book and CoreLight itself would not be possible. You are too numerous to mention here, and you know who you are. I thank you from the bottom of my heart.

Last but certainly not least, I thank my parents, Jim and Sandi Laughlin, for the beautiful, nurturing, empty beach nest in Naples, Florida, and the extraordinary gift of quiet alone time to write and begin a journey of healing.

Prologue

THE END OF SEPARATION

We are at the end of a great Age. The 5,000–6,000-year cycle known as the Age of Patriarchy is completing now, and a new paradigm of heart-centered consciousness is birthing. At this pivotal moment in human evolution, we are moving out of what many call a system of separation.

The system of separation—what it is and how to transcend it—is described in detail throughout the book. For now, suffice it to say that it is a system characterized by imbalances such as: tyrants vs. victims, haves vs. have nots, and superiority vs. inferiority, to name just a few. These polarities reinforce and exacerbate the self's erroneous belief that it is separate, autonomous and disconnected from the whole—from other people, nature and the Earth. Our connection, humanity and love are diminished. The resultant feelings of isolation, power-lessness, despair and meaninglessness bring further imbalance, and a negative feedback loop ensues.

In seeking a way out of this trap, we have tended to project our own power onto charismatic leaders, politicians, celebrities, religious leaders and gurus. Of course, this idealization reinforces our sense of pow-erlessness and helplessness, which we secretly resent and hold against them. We set them up for failure by hoisting them onto pedestals built on the shaky foundation of our projected veneration and then, when they fail to live up to our expectations, we self-righteously depose them. By finding balance and owning our own realities, we move from the old paradigm to the new.

THE TEACHER-STUDENT RELATIONSHIP IN THE NEW PARADIGM

In the old paradigm the teacher was venerated, and the students projected their power and authority onto the teacher, abdicating their own responsibility. The relationship was characterized by a superior-inferior dynamic in which the teacher assumed the role of the powerful, all-knowing authority, while the students were required to be obedient, passive and sponge-like. The path of learning was rigid, linear and formulaic. It trapped us in a limited paradigm, encouraging conformity and a disempowered, myopic worldview. Because of this imbalanced dynamic, the word *teacher* has taken on negative connotations, and some have thrown the baby out with the bathwater by rejecting the need for any teacher at all. This is an unfortunate and short-sighted reaction because it is the nature of, rather than the notion of, teaching that needs changing.

In the new paradigm the teacher-student relationship is more balanced, reciprocal and egalitarian in nature. It is more about sharing information, encouraging students' leadership and empowering their personal authority. Teachers and students walk the path together, acknowledging that we are all learning and growing. The journey is dynamic, fluid and circular. It is a *process of becoming* rather than a *destination or a goal*. While teachers have a certain level of subject mastery enabling them to speak with authority, they are not perfect and don't have all the answers. At times it is okay for everyone to be together in the unknown, in uncertainty and in formlessness. This fosters humility and wisdom in the teacher and empowerment in the students. As soon as the teachings become dogmatic, rigid or predictable, they lose their value.

In the new paradigm there is no rulebook. The rigid rules have changed into flexible principles that keep responding to a changing reality in search of a dynamic balance. Teachers can point the way and offer tools, guidance and inspiration, but students think for themselves, listen to their hearts and follow their own inner truth. In this new form of the relationship, we are all moving towards the knowledge of who we truly are—our own authentic Self.

THE NEW PARADIGM OF THE HEART

There are many names for this Great Turning. Some call it shifting from the third dimension (or third density) into the fourth dimension (or fourth density). Astrologers call it the end of the Age of Pisces and the dawning of the Age of Aquarius. For the purposes of this book, it will primarily be referred to as moving out of the system of separation (or duality) into a new paradigm of heart-centered consciousness.

This is not a swinging of the pendulum to bring about ascendancy of one side of a polarity; it is a balancing between the masculine and feminine, between the mind and the heart and between spirit and matter.

When we begin to live in balance, we birth a new world inside us—a world characterized by unity consciousness. Qualities of the heart, such as tolerance, respect, compassion, love, forgiveness, peace, nonviolence, generosity, gratitude and wisdom, are genuinely valued. This is true power—the power of the Self.

In this new paradigm of the heart, we use power in a non-polarized way. We do not project it onto authority figures and indulge in power games with tyrants, saviors, rebels and victims. Those games have brought us to where we are now—corralled at a cliff edge.

There is a way out. It is a path many are discovering. It is walking the middle way, the way of balance between the extremes, the way of opening the heart. It is the journey of the spiritual warrior.

This change is upon us now. While many still have both feet in the system of separation—the world of either-or, black-and-white and right-and-wrong—some are starting to lift one foot and move it forward into the new paradigm. Many others already have the front foot firmly planted in the new paradigm, have lifted the back foot and are shifting their weight forward. When enough of us start living the new paradigm, it will be birthed in the world. The tide is turning. The wave has momentum.

What direction are you choosing in your life and in the decisions you make?

Why not choose love?

Part One
The Quest for Meaning

CHAPTER 1

Following the Heart

❦

Please do not give blood today if in the last ten years: 1) you have had a blood transfusion, or 2) you have used intravenous drugs, or 3) you are a man and have had sex with a man. You may have the life-threatening disease, AIDS, and should visit your doctor immediately for testing.

It was 1985, and I received this alarming information in a Red Cross brochure I was given at the blood drive. Shocked to my core, reeling with confusion and fear, I made my way home in stunned silence.

Oh my God . . . I could die.

Incredulity and denial gave way to reluctant recognition of this very real possibility, and I broke down into uncontrollable tears. I felt so ashamed, so alone and so destitute.

A few weeks prior I had seen the news that macho movie star, Rock Hudson, had announced he was gay and dying of AIDS—a shocking revelation that stunned the world. The media was quick to fan hysteria about a mysterious *gay plague*. With little understanding of the cause, it was seen as a curse with no cure. Reports of mass deaths and predictions of an escalating pandemic gave rise to public panic, including talk of quarantines. But I hadn't considered that I might also have the disease. After all, I was only twenty-three years old.

Grieving the potential loss of my yet unlived life, I tried to negotiate a way out.

> *God, if you get me through this, I promise I will dedicate my life to you. I will do whatever you want me to. I will live fearlessly and will serve you in whatever way you ask.*

There's nothing quite like facing death to motivate divine pacts.

In retrospect I see this as the beginning of my journey of Self-discovery. This initial step is perhaps the most important one we take on the journey in consciousness. *Know Thyself* as the Delphic Oracle says. Until we begin to face ourselves and wrestle with the inner, subconscious self, progress on the spiritual path remains limited.

Up until that time my energy was focused on mastering a socially acceptable mask. Because I desperately needed external approval and was so afraid of disapproval, I had created an elaborate and impenetrable façade to hide a taboo which was beyond imagining in the culture in which I was raised: I was attracted to men.

This was an unmentionable truth in suburban America during the 1970s. In the era of my youth and puberty, male role models were macho, unyielding and vehemently heterosexual. Nobody dared speak about homosexuality or bisexuality, except in the context of mental illness or social reprobates. Until high school, I had never even heard the word *gay*. Calling a boy *gay* was the worst possible insult, like *fag, sissy, pansy*—or *girl*. What an indictment of our culture's misogyny—the hatred and fear not just of women but of the yin side in men too.

Believing I was the only one who had these feelings, I felt totally alone, like a freak of nature.

Confused and terrified, I hid that part of me from the rest of the world—and from myself. I thought if I denied it, it would go away, and one day everything would be okay. I dated girls, played sports, got good grades and did everything in my power to fit in. I compensated by overachieving and living for the praise and approval of others, believing that if I could just be the best athlete and the smartest, most popular kid in school, everyone would love me and life would be fine. Meanwhile, inwardly I harbored shame, worthlessness and self-loathing.

After graduating from college, I moved from the East coast where I had grown up, to Los Angeles where I found work as an engineer. The newfound freedom that came from a steady paycheck and living on my own in a big city was incredibly liberating. I secretly began exploring my sexuality, going to great lengths to ensure that none of my friends or family would discover my terrible, shameful secret.

I did get tested for HIV/AIDS. Several angst-filled days were spent soul-searching and reaffirming my pact with the Divine while I waited for the results. Overjoyed with relief at the news that I was HIV-negative, I began a new chapter of my journey, committed to discovering what the Divine wanted of me. So began the journey to reconcile the agonizing division inside me. It was the beginning of my consciously opening to the yin energy.

Jump and the Net Will Appear

Although stable and secure, working 9-to-5 for a corporation felt soul-destroying, and my free spirit wanted to soar and explore life in fun and creative ways. In truth, I wanted to become an actor and had already begun taking classes in Hollywood at night, after work. Over many months and with the encouragement of a gifted teacher, I gradually built confidence in my ability. Although I believed that earning a living doing it would be impossible, I considered taking the leap. Trying to honor my new commitment to live fearlessly, I wrestled with the difficult decision—either stay in a miserable job to earn money for safety and security, or jump off the edge of the familiar into the great unknown to follow my heart.

Eventually the desire to follow my heart outweighed the fear of failure, poverty and loss. I plucked up my courage, quit my job and plunged into the pursuit of an acting career full time.

Many chase this dream, but it's a world where 1% of the actors reap 99% of the rewards. Although I was fortunate to land my first job on the very first audition—a television commercial for a Japanese beer— most of the time I was desperately broke. Struggling for money amidst the many dry spells, I took a night job as a valet at the Beverly Hills Hotel, parking cars for the rich and famous. Fortunately, with that supplemental income and a few more commercials and TV jobs, I managed to pay the bills.

What fun those years of exploration and adventure were. Feeling happy and fulfilled in a creative, adventurous life, I knew I had made the right decision in following my heart and jumping off the cliff. And because the money came, I felt supported by the universe.

The spiritual principle I learned through this experience (although at the time I wouldn't have called it spiritual) has been one of the most valuable on the journey of Self-discovery. It involves trusting the heart when we are guided to let go of an old self in order to become true to the Self.

When the heart calls us to do something, it is vital to listen because the universe speaks to us through the heart. If we take the leap, it's a universal truth that money and resources will show up in support.

Jump and the net will appear.

The challenge is that we usually have to demonstrate faith and jump off the cliff without knowing how the support will come. Most times we stand at the edge of the cliff, fearfully look down, see the ground very far below, imagining free-fall and a painful end, and say, *No thanks! I'll jump after the hands show up to catch me. Show me the support first, then I'll jump.* But it doesn't work that way. The invisible hands come out to catch us *after* we jump in pursuit of our truth.

We face these decisions every time we come to a fork in our life's path. Will we heed the call of our heart or choose the path of safety, security and least resistance? The growing unrest and discomfort with the status quo are inner calls to adventure, which can be both scary and thrilling. Taking the leap requires discernment, courage and faith— all qualities of the heart. These are skills of the spiritual warrior, which take time to develop, and with practice and patience lead to the realization of the Self.

WHAT'S THE MOTIVATION?

This above all: to thine own self be true,
And it must follow, as the night the day,
Thou canst not then be false to any man.
—William Shakespeare, Hamlet

Despite the excitement of the acting adventure and my commitment to live fearlessly, I was still hiding my sexual orientation and living a dual life. Little did I realize how pursuing an acting career would support me in resolving my internal conflict.

Being an actor requires insight into human behaviors and motivations. In order to play a role, you have to understand the emotional life of the character and recognize what motivates the character's behavior. To achieve this you really have to understand your own internal world. How else can you expect to know another person if you don't know yourself? With my characteristic bias for action, I decided to make a thorough study of what was happening inside me.

I bought dozens of books on the subject of homosexuality—spiritual, psychological, historical, academic and more—and started journaling extensively about my feelings. Exploring my strong desire for approval and fear of disapproval, I gained a lot of understanding about the need to conform and please in order to feel accepted. Many anguished nights I fell asleep fearing eternal entrapment in my dark, terrible secret.

Eventually after months of confronting the truth, I made a commitment to get very real.

> *Why are you so damn afraid of disapproval? It's your life, and you need to live it without worrying about what other people think!*

Taking a long, deep look in the mirror, I knew I had reached a tipping point. The desire to live a more transparent life in integrity outweighed the fear of facing rejection and the ridicule of others.

Making appointments with a long list of friends and family, I began the process of full disclosure. In the course of about a year, I had come out of the closet to everyone on my list, and more.

For the most part people responded with varying degrees of acceptance. Interestingly a few of the friends whom I thought would be understanding were not, and others whom I thought might be intolerant were accepting. It didn't matter. I had reached the point that I knew I would be okay no matter how others judged me.

The main lesson was that in being truthful, I opened a door for others to explore their own truths, values and judgments. They could choose to walk through the door, continue on the journey as my friend, or not. It was their choice, not mine. By keeping that door closed, not only was I hiding, stagnating and suffocating, I was denying others an opportunity for growth. My transparency supported my own development as well as that of those around me—a win-win situation.

As all of this unfolded, an old part of me dropped away and a new self emerged—more confident, independent, courageous and self-aware. Living a more transparent life brought a freedom and happiness I had not previously known. With this newfound liberation I started questioning what I really wanted to do with my life.

As my inner world expanded, the enthusiasm for pursuing an acting career diminished. I recognized that my motivation for it had been fueled by the old desire for approval. I realized that to feel fulfilled by the business, I'd have to be driven by something other than approval, fame or fortune. Furthermore, having fulfilled certain predetermined goals, I was beginning to feel a sense of completion with that chapter. It was time to find another cliff.

Deepening in self-examination, I began recognizing a passion for the exploration of spirituality and consciousness. Having no idea how to pursue it, I decided to consult Ginny, my local priest.

> *You should think about going to divinity school and getting a master's degree. Yale has an excellent program and would be good for you.*

As soon as she spoke the words, something clicked inside. Knowing immediately it was right, I felt very excited and inspired by the idea.

I decided to go to graduate school not to become a priest but rather to get a Master of Arts in Religion, to fully explore the religion in which I was raised and to learn more about spirituality in general. Even though I didn't know exactly what I was looking for, I knew that this was the next step on the path, and I sincerely hoped I would find some answers.

Within a few months I had applied and received the acceptance letter to Yale Divinity School. I bade farewell to my agent, manager and friends and headed for Connecticut. Jumping off this cliff had been easier than before—practice and passion were already paying off.

CHAPTER 2

Moving from Religion to Spirituality

✑

If God is good, and if God is all powerful, then why is there suffering and evil in the world?

It was the fall of 1989, and this mind-bending question was posed to the class by our theology professor at Yale Divinity School.

I had no immediate answer, and the conundrum made me ruminate uncomfortably for quite some time. I experienced an unexpectedly challenging emotional reaction to the question (known as *theodicy*[1]), and after wrestling with a lot of childhood concepts about God and writing a lengthy paper on the subject, I concluded that something about what I had been taught in church just didn't add up.

This was compounded by the irrefutable details, offered to us during church history class, confirming that the church was a hierarchical organization which had historically focused on gaining power and money. Furthermore, the excessively intellectual nature of our classes left my mind feeling twisted like a pretzel. Virtually every minute was spent in my head, and although it was a course in theology, my heart and spirit were starved.

The master's program was generating more questions than it answered, and some of the answers it did offer were causing uneasy shifts within me. Confronted by the limitations of the church as well as the exceedingly cerebral academic environment, I made the decision not to return to divinity school after the first semester.

Although the program was not fulfilling, the silent evenings that I spent in a small, round chapel in the corner of the basement of the main building were magically rewarding. Sitting peacefully, usually alone, in the quietude of that sweet sanctuary, I prayed, contemplated, gazed at the candles on the altar and emptied my mind of all thought. There I could simply be. Amidst the intense workload and overwhelming pressure, the tiny chapel was a place of reprieve and solace and a balm for the soul. I went there to escape the madness, to feel my peaceful, inner center and to come just a little closer to *finding the divinity inside me.*

Some Bible passages assisted in my growing understanding that God was not an old bearded man sitting on a throne in some antiseptic corner of the universe, but rather something *within,* something beyond the mind:

> And the peace of God, which passes all understanding, shall keep your hearts and minds through Christ Jesus. (Philippians 4:7)

> Be still, and know that I am God. (Psalm 46:10)

What I learned at divinity school was that I wanted an *experience* of God, not just a cognitive understanding of the concept, and it was in the stillness of that little round chapel that I began to know a *peace which passes all understanding* and to catch a glimpse of a higher truth.

JESUS

The teachings of Jesus had always drawn me to Christianity. Although his message was eventually coopted and edited by the church's founding fathers and used to control the masses for the benefit of the few, one can still find timeless, eternal truths in what remains.

Because there is so much dogma associated with Jesus, I like to think of myself as a *salad-bar* Christian: I take what I like and leave the rest behind. If we swallow all of the dogma, even what we sense is a bit off, we are practicing Church-ianity, not Christianity. And surely the essence of Christ's teachings should be at the heart of the faith.

As a child, the exclusivity of Christianity never made sense to me. I always wondered how it could be that only those who accepted Jesus as the one and only savior would go to Heaven. *What about all the kind, loving people in the world who were born into non-Christian cultures? How could they be excluded just because of their location?* I was also perplexed by the notion that we were sinners by virtue of the fact that we were born human and that we needed to be saved from ourselves. In my young mind none of this added up.

Later I came to understand that the savior archetype is an aspect of the old, hierarchical, patriarchal paradigm. The self-sacrificing savior/martyr is neither the essence of Christ's teaching nor an ideal to be emulated. Instead it is a polarizing concept that keeps us locked in the system of separation. These words may sound highly offensive and even blasphemous to many devout Christians, and if so, I apologize. My intention is not to offend or to demean anyone's religious beliefs. However, because the savior archetype, tied to its victim polarity, is one of the main knots in consciousness holding back human evolution, it is essential to open it up and shine a light on it now.

This important theme is explored in Chapter 23, Moving Beyond Victim Consciousness, but for now it is essential to highlight that in order to have a savior, one must be a victim who needs to be saved. However the inherent inferior-superior split in the victim-savior relationship is destructive. Defining oneself as an unworthy victim is disempowering. Victim consciousness traps us in a pattern of projecting our power and worthiness outside of ourselves, onto people and organizations such as charismatic leaders, governments and religious institutions. However, as we begin to explore our own inner divinity, we realize this is not the truth of who we are. We are not victims. In fact we discover we are immensely powerful, worthy and creative beings.

> If we leave the dogma, the savior archetype and the Bible's patriarchal language at the salad bar, the Jesus who remains is an important role model for all modern-day spiritual warriors.

Jesus is an embodiment of purity and heart-centered consciousness who inspired untold masses. As a child I aspired to live by his beautiful example of love, compassion, forgiveness, peace and nonviolence. These practices always made sense to me. *After all, if everyone were to live this way, wouldn't the world be a much kinder, gentler, happier place? Isn't that what everyone wants? If so, why is it that so many people don't practice them? Why do those who profess to be Christians feel it is okay to go to war? Why are those who do practice them considered inferior, weak and powerless?*

> *You have heard that it was said,* An eye for an eye and a tooth for a tooth. *But I say to you, Do not resist one who is evil. But if anyone strikes you on the right cheek, turn to him the other also.... Love your enemies and pray for those who persecute you. (Matthew 5:38–44)[2]*

Many of the world's most revered heroes and most powerful leaders have lived by these words and found forgiveness in their hearts for their persecutors: Mahatma Gandhi, Martin Luther King Jr., Nelson Mandela and Malala Yousafzai, to name a few. These men and women are certainly not powerless or weak—helping to overturn corrupt, unjust, entrenched structures and governments against all the odds and inspiring entire nations by their heroic actions. The transformational visions held by these leaders were thought by others to be impossible. Yet their lives demonstrate that apparent miracles can become reality through the power of loving, peaceful, non-violent and forgiving actions.

JESUS ON FAITH

Jesus' message about faith always resonated deeply with me:

> *Therefore I tell you, do not be anxious about your life, what you shall eat or what you shall drink, nor about your body, what you shall put on. Is not life more than food, and the body more than clothing? Look at the birds of the air: they neither sow nor reap nor gather into barns, and yet your heavenly Father feeds them. Are you not of more value than they? And which of you by being anxious can add one cubit to his span of life? And why are you anxious about clothing? Consider the lilies of the field, how they grow; they neither toil nor spin; yet I tell you, even Solomon in all his glory was not arrayed like one of these. But if God so clothes the grass of the field, which today is alive and tomorrow is thrown into the oven, will he not much more clothe you, O men of little faith? Therefore do not be anxious, saying, 'What shall we drink?' or 'What shall we wear?' For . . .* your heavenly Father knows that you need them all. But seek first his kingdom and his righteousness, *and all these things shall be yours as well.* [Emphasis mine.]

Therefore do not be anxious about tomorrow, for tomorrow will be anxious for itself. Let the day's own trouble be sufficient for the day. (Matthew 6: 25–34)[3]

When I was in divinity school, in my late twenties, I could not have explained why this passage struck such a deep chord inside my being, but life experience has since revealed the truth of this profound wisdom. For our modern, materialistic culture, which relies on money for virtually everything, this is one of Jesus' most important teachings. It serves us incredibly well and is a powerful, foundational lesson on the path of Self-discovery that runs as a theme throughout this book. As spiritual beings, immersed in a consumer culture, we are perfectly placed to practice our faith in divine support. As the words on each US dollar should remind us, *In God We Trust.*

Understandably, most people struggle to live by Jesus' simple words of faith. Flooded by stories of misfortune—people losing their homes, contracting terminal illness or experiencing cataclysms—it is difficult to believe unshakeably in divine support. When we experience personal tragedies and catastrophes, the world does not seem supportive. We feel like victims of circumstance and tend to blame life or God. We feel Jesus' advice might apply some of the time but that divine support is just too inconsistent to rely on in any permanent way. Some may feel his sermon on faith is naïve, airy-fairy or religious non-sense. I once counseled someone who was in debilitating fear of losing his job and steady paycheck, and I made the innocent blunder of quoting the above Bible passage in an attempt to comfort him. He scoffed sarcastically, *Well, the lilies of the field didn't have a mortgage to pay!*

Unfortunately in our modern world, having faith only in the almighty dollar is all too common.

To understand this passage it is important to define what is meant by *seek first his kingdom and his righteousness, and all these things shall be yours as well.* This does not refer to searching for some heavenly realm belonging to a patriarchal Sky God in the clouds, separate from Earthly reality, or to following a bunch of religious dogma pertaining to right and wrong. Leaving the possessive masculine adjectives at the salad bar, one begins to see that instead it refers to walking one's own path of Self-discovery.

Jesus is saying that when we make this journey of conscious evolution our priority, all our needs are met. When we seek the truth of who we truly are and awaken to our own divinity by serving the greater Self, our needs are met in the most amazing ways. I know many (including myself) for whom experience has borne this out. Not only are material needs taken care of, such as money, food, clothing and shelter, but other forms of abundance come to us as well, such as meaningful relationships and satisfying work—usually in more fulfilling ways than we could have ever dreamt possible. Even amidst adversity we feel held and loved by nurturing, invisible hands, and we know everything is going to be okay.

> Having faith is about overcoming fear—a skill which can be learned. We are not born with it full-blown, manifesting like an avatar hovering above a lotus blossom. Rather, becoming courageous on the journey of life is the adventure we incarnated for. It is a practice. Through experience we grow into ever-deepening faith, step by step by overcoming fear.

When we embrace this practice consciously and willingly, we can have more fun and learn to play the game of life much better. In Chapters 8, Synchronicity; 16, Work and Money; and 19, Greased

Grace, we will explore examples of this principle of moving beyond fear and strengthening our faith muscles.

JESUS ON UNITY CONSCIOUSNESS

The light of the body is the eye: if therefore thine eye be single, thy whole body shall be full of light. (Matthew 6:22)

This mysterious passage always baffled me. *Why would Jesus speak about making your eye single?* It reminded me of the Cyclops and made no sense. The various simplistic interpretations I had heard, for example about single-minded focus on a goal, never felt right either. However, it finally made sense after I left divinity school and began to learn about the ancient mystery-school teachings of non-duality, of which Jesus was certainly a master. This important esoteric message is both metaphoric and literal. The metaphor refers to seeing the world of duality, the system of separation, through *two* eyes. When we evolve beyond duality and into unity consciousness, we will see through a *single* eye.

Beyond the metaphor, his words are a reference to the anatomy of the human subtle body, which is metaphysical—beyond the physical, visible only to clairvoyants. We will explore the anatomy of the subtle body more fully in Chapter 13, Samadhi. For now, suffice it to say there is a place between and above our two physical eyes, right in the middle of the head, where two subtle energy currents merge to a single point. It is the seat of unity consciousness in the body. Interestingly the pineal gland, which is related to the retina in many ways, is one of the physical organs in the center of the head corresponding to the metaphysical single eye. When we learn to access this mystical place, we experience unity consciousness, and as Jesus says, we become illuminated.

Much of this book is dedicated to exploring this very aspect of our evolutionary journey—how we move from duality into unity consciousness. Jesus has given us a clue by referring to our anatomy.

Jesus also offers an unmistakable message about reconciling the dualities of the world and entering unity consciousness in the gnostic *Gospel of Thomas*:

> When you make the two into one, and when you make the inner as the outer, and the upper as the lower, and when you make male and female into a single one, so that the male shall not be male, and the female shall not be female: . . . then you will enter [the kingdom]. (Saying 22)

There are many examples throughout the Gnostic Gospels[4] of the union of male and female as a symbol for the ultimate experience of unity.

The Gnostics were early Christian mystics whom the orthodox church considered heretics. Some of their manuscripts were discovered in 1945 in a desert cave in Nag Hamadi, Egypt, concealed for close to two millennia. These Gnostic Gospels indicate that several of Jesus' disciples were women and that Mary Magdalene was his companion and closest disciple. The texts, which include many revelatory, esoteric teachings by Jesus and his disciples, emphasize both the masculine and feminine aspects of the Divine as well as the doctrine of reincarnation. These teachings were removed by the orthodox church's founding fathers.

Elaine Pagels, in her popular book *The Gnostic Gospels*, notes several striking differences between the New Testament and the Gnostic Gospels:

> Orthodox Jews and Christians insist that a chasm separates humanity from its creator: God is wholly other. But some of the

Gnostics who wrote these gospels contradict this: self-knowledge is knowledge of God; the self and the divine are identical.

Second, the "living Jesus" of these texts speaks of illusion and enlightenment, not of sin and repentance, like the Jesus of the New Testament. Instead of coming to save us from sin, he comes as a guide who opens access to spiritual understanding. But when the disciple attains enlightenment, Jesus no longer serves as his spiritual master: the two have become equal—even identical.

Third, orthodox Christians believe that Jesus is Lord and Son of God in a unique way: he remains forever distinct from the rest of humanity whom he came to save. Yet the gnostic *Gospel of Thomas* relates that as soon as Thomas recognizes him, Jesus says to Thomas that they have both received their being from the same source:

Jesus said, "I am not your master. Because you have drunk, you have become drunk from the bubbling stream which I have measured out.... He who will drink from my mouth will become as I am: I myself shall become he, and the things that are hidden will be revealed to him."

Does not such teaching—the identity of the divine and human, the concern with illusion and enlightenment, the founder who is presented not as Lord, but as spiritual guide sound more Eastern than Western? Some scholars have suggested that if the names were changed, the "living Buddha" appropriately could say what the *Gospel of Thomas* attributes to the living Jesus.

MEDITATION

After leaving the master's program, I began to explore world religions, including Hinduism and Buddhism. Within a few months I learned to meditate and began to have life-changing, mystical awakenings. I found the experience of the Divine I had been searching for.

If praying is talking to the Divine, then meditating is listening to the Divine. It is the practice of relaxing, letting go and keeping the egoic mind occupied with simple concentration techniques. In doing so, we open to something beyond the conscious mind. We enter the eternal present moment—a place of extraordinary spiritual power, simplicity and freedom.

Through meditation, I realized that God is not a being separate and outside, and I experienced what mystics describe as *our own inner divinity*. In the deepest sense of the word, I felt I had come *home*. Knowing that the practice would become a permanent companion, I sensed it was going to lead me on the adventure of a lifetime.

I still consider myself a salad-bar Christian at heart, yet in the great restaurant of faith, I have learned to find nourishment in all religions and traditions, opening to receive universal truth from any source. There are many paths home.

CHAPTER 3

Building Your Light

&

Let's meditate together. Please close your eyes and relax.

A numinous, dignified woman with striking features had taken her place in the teacher's chair—her dark hair and eyes set off by clear, porcelain skin, high cheekbones and strong jawline. She looked to be in her forties, but possessed an ageless quality that lent an air of mystery, grace and timelessness to her striking appearance.

While vacationing in Los Angeles in June 1991, I was invited by my friend, Tom, to join his meditation class at the East-West Center in Culver City. He didn't give me any details about his teacher, Leslie Temple-Thurston, or what to expect, and I was rather neutral about the idea. However, I enjoyed Tom's company, and was always ready for a new adventure in meditation.

Speaking with extraordinary calm, poise and a lovely British South African accent, Leslie put on some gentle, soothing music. She talked us through a guided meditation, and I easily dropped into a deeply relaxed state, focusing on the sound of her comforting voice. Soon I sank into an exceptionally still serenity.

I had been practicing meditation for about a year and had had some profound experiences; however, there was something extremely different about this meditation. Even though my eyes were closed and Leslie was at least twenty feet from me, at some level of awareness I could *see* and *feel* her non-physical body moving around the room, working with each of us in consciousness. This was totally new to me, but I understood she was somehow filling us up with light and healing energy. I was amazed that something like this was possible and that I was able to feel it.

> *How can this be? How extraordinary!* I thought, trying not to break the concentration of the meditation.

We were like an orchestra and she, simultaneously, the conductor and musician—*playing us* like sonorous instruments while she performed the healing work. Our job was just to relax, to be receptive and to allow this phenomenal, energetic therapy to take place.

With my inner sight I witnessed her moving energy around the room performing healings on each person. Although her physical body never left the chair, she made several passes around the room, working repeatedly on individuals at ever deepening levels.

Although astounded, I also felt at ease with it, as though it were the most natural thing in the world. There was such lightness and grace to the healing work that I completely relaxed into it, surrendering to the peace and warmth spreading throughout my body.

When my turn came, I was aware that Leslie was building a beautiful, radiant light in the area of her heart. Inwardly I saw it growing in intensity. About the size of a beach ball, it was made of ecstatic love energy and was luminous like a brilliant, miniature golden sun.

What happened next is, like all powerful spiritual experiences, difficult to describe in words. It was something like the scene in the film

Cocoon, where the young man, who is in love with the beautiful young extra-terrestrial, asks what making love is like on her planet. She tells him to stand on the other side of the pool, about twenty feet away. Then she builds an intensely radiant ball of golden white light in her heart and sends it rocketing out, ricocheting around the room and into him. An explosion of light in his chest reverberates through his whole body and completely takes his breath away. He is stunned and enters an ecstatic, orgasmic, transcendent state. Glowing and speechless, he can only smile in a stupor of delight.

Well, almost the same thing happened to me that night, except it wasn't sexual at all. And Leslie's ball of golden white light didn't ricochet all over the room; instead like a swarm of luminous bees, it zoomed at high speed directly from her heart into mine. My breath was taken away, siphoned out of my lungs. Stunned by the sheer ecstasy of the experience, I felt an intensely radiant sun glowing inside my chest, and the most beautiful and exquisite love energy permeated my whole being. It was a spiritual bliss like I'd never known before. I was so drunk on light and love that I could not move or speak or even think. I could only smile and radiate, just like the young man in the movie.

The meditation ended at some point, Leslie gave a talk on a spiritual subject, of which I have no memory, and then she suggested the group take a tea and cookie break. Everyone else stood up, went to the kitchen and started chatting, but I remained rooted to my chair, shocked at how functional they all seemed. I opened my eyes and saw Leslie still seated in her chair, looking at me, patting the seat next to her.

Come and tell me about your experience.

Quite disoriented, I slowly rose, walked over to her on unstable legs and sat down.

I could FEEL you!

Yes, that's how it works.

Her simple statement and warm, loving smile comforted me. Apparently this was Leslie's everyday reality. Speechless at the events that had just unfolded, I mutely reveled in the spiritual bliss and inner stillness, which were the result of her energy transmission.

> *In the East it's called* shakti, *which is a Sanskrit word for the healing energy I transmit. Shakti is usually associated with the feminine, and I offer it as a gift to others for their spiritual upliftment. I direct it through my hands, gaze and voice.*

We spoke for a few minutes about the transmission of shakti; how seeing, feeling and managing energy is part of the spiritual journey and how important it is to become aware of energy. She assured me that the more I practiced meditation and worked on clearing my consciousness the more sensitive and attuned I would become and the more I would be able to see, feel and manage my energy.

Elated beyond measure, I floated to the car after class, and Tom drove home. Feeling tingly and sparkly all over, the edges of my physical body seemed to stretch beyond the boundary of the skin. I was a new person. Some old part of me had dropped away, and a different, more expansive consciousness was emerging.

I knew I needed whatever it was that Leslie offered. She was the spiritual teacher I had been praying to find. That night I offered a prayer of profound thanks to the universe and fell asleep feeling immensely blessed.

The following morning I resolved to return to Connecticut, pack my things and move back to Los Angeles to study with Leslie.

IMPECCABILITY

There is a direct equation between the general condition of your physical world and the power of your spiritual life. They correlate. For example, if your physical world is disorderly and unclear, or if you're lazy and don't take care of business, or if you're flaky and never quite complete projects, then you do not have what it takes to reach higher states of consciousness—not in your current state. All of this tends to interfere with your ability to meditate and your growth toward higher consciousness. There just isn't sufficient power in your system to get any lift-off. When you lack personal power, it's very difficult to advance, whether in the world of spirit or in the world of careers and relationships.[5]

In less than a month I was back at the East-West Center listening to Leslie share her profound wisdom with our little group. She was answering many of my unspoken questions about how to find my inner divinity while living and working in the world.

To manifest your dreams, you need spiritual power more than anything. I use the word power *here interchangeably with* light, awareness, energy *and* intelligence. *It takes a great deal of spiritual power to reach the superconscious states. Indeed, it takes a great deal of power to change yourself. But, of course, it is possible.*

No matter whether your aspirations lean toward growth in the material or the spiritual, you have to work at developing power. It would be a mistake to think you're stuck with yourself the way you are. Anyone can change. All that's needed is a desire and a willingness to apply yourself.

Most people, when they begin this study, simply do not have enough power. This is why there is the need for impeccability—with impeccability you can change into someone who has the right amount of power for anything.

In mystical terms the attitude which we call impeccability means the ability to use, direct, manage and store energy perfectly. It goes beyond a moral or ethical way of conducting one's life. The meaning is much deeper, more structural, in fact much more all-encompassing. When practiced, it will lead to greater changes in your life and subsequently to a greater dissolution of the separate self.

As human beings we do not use energy properly—at least, in the terms of the mystic, that is. A mystic is one who is pursuing divine understanding and experience; it is what you are becoming.

The human system is one of limitation. It has well-defined parameters. There are social, political and cultural mores which are used to define it. Definitions, by their nature, tend to be fixed, rather than fluid and flexible. However, these limitations are in the mind and are of the nature of unconsciousness. In other words when you perceive limits, you suppress awareness about the infinite alternative. The vastness of the totality is hidden from view and only a small range of awareness is available to you at any given time—hence the tendency in humans to age rapidly and die.

From the moment of birth, you have been told that you and the things around you are a certain way. You were told this again and again—so many times that it imprinted itself onto your awareness field, and you had no choice but to believe it. Now the mystic by comparison, which is what you're all becoming, is not governed by these traditional, cultural, and social ways of seeing. He or she has given up all attachment to these traditional parameters and has adopted different guidelines to define his or her life.

This is not to say that the mystic will flaunt his or her alternative beliefs or have a flagrant disregard for the laws of the land or anything like that. It's always an act of impeccability to exhibit common decency and to have respcect for all things. Rather, what I mean is that the mystic has given up all meaningless rituals—meaningless being the operative word—and all actions which drain his or her energy instead of building it. The mystic is choosing to live a life which is more fluid, more spontaneous and far more practical in a very real sense. The mystic opts for impeccability as a parameter or guideline.[6]

I loved it when Leslie referred to us as mystics. Studying world religions, I resonated deeply with the mystical branches' teachings of love and wisdom: Christian Gnosticism; Islamic mysticism, or Sufism, of whom the ecstatic poet Rumi is most famous; Hindu yogic masters, such as Paramahansa Yogananda; and the esoteric wisdom of the Jewish Kabbalah. Mystics access highest truth and passionately seek direct, personal experience of divinity. I was surprised that Leslie's advice about how to become a mystic was so practical and grounded.

In order to become impeccable, you have to review your whole life from time to time. As you gain momentum and begin to change, it's good to take stock occasionally, do a complete systems analysis of everything in your life and then work out a plan based on the results.

It's important to write it all in your journal where you can see it in black and white so you can access it. The act of writing brings your awareness from the realm of ideas and locks it into the physical world in the form of the written word. There is tremendous power in this— power that you can access anytime. It's a way of bypassing the all-too-regular human forgetfulness.

One part of the plan should be a loosely defined, long-range plan with a broad scope, reflecting the big picture of your aspirations. It's a skeleton-structure, establishing your commitments to yourself over the long term. Then also make a short-range plan; perhaps a year is good. In this, put more detail and definition.

It's better to design the plans according to the changes and states of mind you seek in your life rather than designing something too solid. For example, "I will have a pink Mercedes next year," is an inappropriate form of design.

Keeping your design focused on the states of mind you wish to achieve is more powerful. For example, if you ask for light, intelligence and awakening, you will most likely get them, and by having them, your whole world will be transformed.

Let Eternity decide the outer form of what you're asking for. Whether the car will be this color, or the house will be on that street isn't really relevant. Eternity will work out the details. If you focus on the rigid form, you may inhibit the manifestation, and not get what you want. Rather ask for qualities and values instead of a quantified value. You would reap wonderful rewards if you had great creativity, impeccability, inspiration, concentration and clarity. You can do anything you want with these qualities. So forget the pink Mercedes and the house on Broadway, and opt for your own perfection.

Now both of these plans should be based on your intuition of where you could be if your awareness *were in top form—because that's where you're heading. The plans should not be wishful thinking. Based on your present level of awareness, choose a time frame that feels realistic. Realistic plans have a better chance of working, and you would be amazed at how powerful they are in unfolding your direction and your destiny.*[7]

Leslie's very sensible guidance reminded me of many New Year's resolutions. In retrospect I realized I had rarely received coveted material goods but always received qualities of character that benefited my well-being if I'd asked for them.

You have to examine all of your routines and habituated behaviors in minute detail. Most are like an old security blanket that you've schlepped around since childhood. The payoff is that there's a certain security in repeating yourself. Perhaps it makes you feel grounded, comfortable or safe. Most people use routines to create structure and security, but the mystic doesn't worry about that. The mystic uses fluidity, change, light and impeccability as his or her structure—things that propel us forward toward higher levels of consciousness. These faster vibratory states of awareness are clearer, more concentrated, more empowered and make more energy available to us.

As Don Juan outlined to Carlos Castaneda in Journey to Ixtlan, *it is important to disrupt your routines. When you do habituated things, you're usually not conscious. For example, you may have a routine of driving to work a certain way every day. If so, it's a habit, which means you've become structured and stuck. A simple thing like driving to work a different way now and then would disrupt the routine and help you to become more present and aware.*

Routines have a way of making us feel stale and bored with life. Those qualities do not lend themselves to developing light and power. If you are feeling bored, you are not managing energy impeccably. Being creative on a moment-to-moment basis inspires you and fires up your sense of adventure. When you feel perked up, you have more light. It's a simple equation.

It's also important to discern between stale habits and freeing habits. For example you may find that meditating and exercising every morning at the same time feed and free you. Some habits may free up mental space for you to focus on something new. For example, if you had to rediscover how to dress yourself every morning, without any habitual behavior, you would probably never leave the house. Practicing impeccability, we become very conscious of unconscious and habitual behaviors. In this way we own them, rather than being owned by them.

Most importantly, you must make careful note of the behaviors that seem to have no real value toward raising your state of wellbeing and luminosity. Moderation in all things is a good rule of thumb. Any behaviors which cause you to abuse yourself, your body, your mind or your spirit must be slated for change. And this need not be a major production. It can be worked out sensibly and gradually over a period of time as you develop the inner power of your being.

Next is to look at all the things that drain you in more subtle ways. For example, your thoughts can drain you. If you're especially subject to negative thoughts and feelings, such as worry, guilt or shame for example, this is an enormous drain on your luminosity.

Another way to develop personal spiritual power is to offer oneself in selfless service. Service done impeccably develops tremendous power. Perhaps in the beginning it's not possible to engage in service with an impeccable attitude. You may find yourself in resistance to unconditional giving; that's to be expected.

Unconditional giving is not the norm within human experience, and service is seldom offered perfectly. But it's certainly better to offer imperfect service than none at all. It's a wonderful opportunity to practice generosity and compassion and to examine your motivations.

Eventually as you become a perfect giver, you develop enormous spiritual power and light. Giving frees you from avoidances and withholdings. It moves you from the paradigm of service to self to that of service to others — and this is critical if you want to experience the Self.

Service eventually leads to the dissolution of the separate self—a perfect giver can extend beyond the self's limits and leave the system of duality. Selfless means being beyond the old limited self. This is a critical aspect of living impeccably.[8]

Journaling

Although I had already integrated journaling into my daily practice, Leslie's insights reinforced its value. She often said to us that if you want to wake up, journal. There were many practical reasons for this.

Keeping a journal of your spiritual experiences is essential if you want to develop impeccability and increase your power and light. Preferably, it should be typed and include photographs or other memorabilia to remind you of the beauty and joy of your spiritual experiences. In it, record all visions and insights you have both in and out of meditation. It is the place for all realizations and transcendent experiences.

Essentially your journal is for any experience of an uplifting and revealing nature—which can happen anywhere and at any time. Spirit has a way of seeking you out, opening you to an experience of her presence and taking you beyond the norm of life—often when you least expect it. Maybe she's testing you to see how alert you are. Who knows! This could happen in the supermarket or on the freeway. A great symbol—the freeway of life. On the freeway of life, Spirit could overtake you at any time. Would you see her? Or would you be so spaced out, or bored, or stoned, that she's nothing but a blur? What sort of car would she be driving do you think? An old Honda perhaps, or maybe a sleek new Lexus? Maybe if she cuts you off, you'd get angry and yell obscenities at Spirit. Then what? Well, it could happen. Then you would be mad at yourself for missing a great opportunity. Be prepared, always!

It's a strange phenomenon of human consciousness that we are not able to accommodate these sudden insights into more expanded realities. The ego has a way of discarding anything it can't categorize. It also discards anything it can't explain according to its own limited belief. As a result, many of our most profound and truthful mystical experiences are filed away in an unmarked grave—a great loss of awareness and of course spiritual power. The mystic desires to open the doorway into these other levels of consciousness, but must be very alert to catch the opening before it closes again. The advantage of journaling is that you lock the experience into the mind and make it physical by verbalizing it.

So be apprised: The journal is a formidable way of storing power and shifting your limited reality. It really works to speed up the changes. There's a lot of effort required in keeping an impeccable journal, but it really pays off.

There's another phenomenon: We tend to fool ourselves into thinking we can remember all the details of the vision or spiritual experience. In the moment, we believe we will. Spiritual experience can be so vivid that we feel certain we can capture the memory forever—retaining all of its subtle feelings and realizations. Alas, this just isn't so. An experience that seemed so intense and immediate soon fades, and the treasure of its visit is lost in the sands of time. Eventually like the Red Sea it will close over—robbing it of its intensity.

As you write, something interesting happens: The experience expands and deepens. Unexpected detail and information appear, from the subliminal reaches of your mind. It becomes a multifaceted, multidimensional learning experience. As you write, hidden truths emerge and you add profundity to the experience. This is one of the major rewards of taking the time and trouble to write. Your experiences become vastly expanded. If you're in search of power, this is one of the places to find it.

Another advantage is that the power you store in this manner is easily accessible to you at a later date. When things are difficult, you can revisit your journal and re-collect the happier and more progressive times. There is a power stored in the words. This power floods your awareness and renews your aspiration and inspiration. Furthermore that power is not lost by your using it—it's not like paper used up in a flame but rather like a muscle which becomes stronger with frequent use. The power you've stored adds to you in that moment yet remains, even more powerful, on the page. So the next time you hit the rapids on your journey down the river of life, it's there to support you and re-establish your balance.

Keeping an impeccable journal has even more hidden advantages: The depth and breadth of your power of expression increase enormously. Your vocabulary increases. Your ability to string sentences together is greatly enhanced. You become very lucid and able to express yourself in subtle ways. And as you do that, the subtlety of your feelings increases enormously. This is a path from the gross to the awakening of more subtle feelings and states of mind. Developing a vocabulary to express those subtle states of mind moves you forward on the path.

The creative ability to express yourself powerfully and truthfully through the written or spoken word is a tremendous asset in worldly endeavors. It adds a quality of excellence and clarity to all of your business and social relationships. It gives credibility and poise to your personality. This impeccability in turn brings success. The success further develops your spiritual power by giving you the confidence needed to let go of your old, conditioned self. It's a cycle of enhancement in every direction.[9]

WHAT DRAINS YOU, WHAT FEEDS YOU?

I loved the incredibly pragmatic and down-to-earth nature of Leslie's teachings. I had come wanting to learn how to experience more light and was pleased that the lessons did not cloud the waters with vague impracticalities.

Identify the things that give you energy. Things that you enjoy and that increase your light are important to practice. These things are usually uncomplicated and could include the addition of colors, plants and music in your life. Something simple like showering, which clears the aura and washes away negativity, is most helpful especially at the beginning and the end of the day. It's also helpful to shower before you meditate. You'll have a higher meditation with more light and clarity.

Also identify the things that drain your energy. For example, too much sleep, eating incorrectly or indulging in too much small talk with your neighbor depletes you. Small talk is often gossipy, narcissistic and without heart, and when you've finished, you feel weary, you start yawning and you're uncomfortable because you've taken a loss of energy. The impeccable spiritual warrior avoids small talk. It's an activity which people do simply to pass the time. The mystic does not indulge in passing the time. Everything the mystic does counts.

Spend time alone as well, particularly in nature. If you don't know how to be alone, begin practicing and developing the ability. When you are alone, silently doing something that builds your light, you'll find yourself able to turn inward.

I also recommend keeping a clean, tidy house. Your home is important; it's your sanctuary. You renew yourself there. Ask yourself what your house does for you. Do you groan when you walk through the door, perhaps seeing the mess you left behind? If that's the case, then you're reminding yourself of your own laziness, insensitivity or distractedness. Or perhaps when you walk through the door, you sigh peacefully and relax into the perfection of your highest frequency.

You can fix your house up in a very simple, essential way—the less the better actually. Do away with all the clutter. The clutter only reminds you of the past. Most of it is rooted in all your old attachments. Play around with your environment. Change it when your mood changes and when you want your energy to shift. Change is good. Get used to it. Don't be afraid of it. We're on a path of growth, and we want to make friends with change.

So, too, it's a good idea to do away with all your old, worn clothes. Have a garage sale or take them to the thrift store. If you wear old clothes, you will look and feel old and worn. Take the money from your garage sale and purchase something fresh and new.

It's also good to do an analysis of your relationships and make changes where they're needed. If there are issues in your intimate relationships, make a note of them and work on them over time. In terms of our mystical understanding of the here and now, there is no reason that we need to drag old attachments along with us. Get your relationships cleaned up.

Take time to analyze the motives for your actions. Sometimes they're held in your unconscious, and you don't even know they're there. Do you have a conscious understanding of why you do things? Try to find the underlying motivations and not live by habituated routines.

Lastly, be sure to do enough exercise and stretching. Any of the martial arts, hatha yoga, Tai Chi, various forms of cardiovascular exercise and stretching are all good—anything that will bring flexibility, poise, balance and concentration through the body, mind and emotions. The benefits are really far reaching.[10]

Aim to eliminate the things in your life that drain you and do more of the things that build your light. Managing your energy impeccably is the very foundation of the path of Self-discovery. This practice is essential if you want to build your spiritual power while living and working in the world or to manifest your worldly dreams.

After absorbing Leslie's practical, no-nonsense wisdom, I began making changes in my life—not in a dramatic, impulsive way, but quietly, subtly and over time. One notable example is that I immediately thought of three friends with whom I had been spending a lot of time—Ralph, George and Betty (not their real names). Ralph was a cynical atheist, George an indifferent hedonist and Betty . . . Betty and I had complicated financial and romantic entanglements. Although I enjoyed being with them in various ways, I usually felt drained after spending time in their company. Ralph and George took every opportunity to ridicule my spiritual journey. Even though their barbs were supposedly in jest, they felt like invisible darts poking holes in me.

I decided to spend less time with them and this opened space for new friendships, more in keeping with *the new me*. I realized how much better I felt being around people with whom I resonated and even emulated in some ways. As my relationships changed, I was able to let go of unwanted parts of my personality, old behaviors and habits—and the world reflected the new me in the form of more uplifting friends and fulfilling opportunities.

After just a few months of practicing the impeccability guidelines, I moved to a new apartment, which had a cleaner, higher vibration, and I noticed an instant increase in my level of energy and light. My meditations were higher, my dreams and spiritual experiences more profound, and I was happier than ever before in my life. This trend continued. As I became happier, I practiced being more impeccable and in turn had more spiritual experiences—a positive feedback loop which continues to this day.

I didn't realize how these changes were just the beginning of discovering who I truly am—an aspect of the journey about to open to whole new levels.

Do you want to know what it's like to feel the presence of God, unity with all things? Do you want to experience the end of separation, going beyond all polarities, beyond the boundaries of your personality, beyond all the self-imposed limitations that have bound and hemmed you in all your life? Do you have enough determination, motivation and will to go beyond all of that? Beyond verbal knowledge even? Beyond your limited mind, beyond the confines of the ego? Do you really want to feel the presence of God? It's very subtle, very intense.[11]

CHAPTER 4

Who Am I?

❦

Excuse me, but some people are not in their bodies. Please return to your bodies, and I will wait to continue the discussion.

Leslie was addressing our little class of a dozen or so, and I knew she was talking to me. While she was giving a spiritual discourse, I was having my first, spontaneous, out-of-body experience. I had been meditating so deeply and become so relaxed that I just completely let go of the physical body. Feeling as light as air and floating on the ceiling, I was looking down from above at my body in the chair.

How can she know what's happening to me?

Surprised and slightly embarrassed, I reluctantly willed my consciousness back into my body, which was sitting in the East-West Center in Culver City. Gravity oppressed my unencumbered, carefree spirit, disappointed with having to stop levitating.

In our modern world the journey of Self-realization is very much about embodying the spiritual energies. It is about bringing the light right through into the physical, material plane—into the body, into our careers, money, relationships, sexuality and so forth. We are not here to disconnect from the body and the world. Most of us have had many lifetimes in monasteries and living on mountaintops where we sequestered ourselves and devoted our lives to the pursuit of Spirit, which was very important to do. But now we are here at one of the densest, most materially oriented, fastest-paced times ever on Earth, and we've chosen to be here to marry spirit with matter. It's as though we are giving ourselves the ultimate test, to put all that spiritual practice into action—with a high degree of difficulty.

I sensed the truth of this, and knew I was up for the challenge. *But what does this really mean in practice?*

In subsequent weekly classes over the next many months, Leslie spoke extensively about the *how-to* part, which was her mastery. In addition to living impeccably, Self-realization involved balancing, healing and clearing the human ego.

I want to talk with you about your identity. Who are you? When someone asks you this question, you normally reply by saying, "I am . . . " fill in the blank. I am an artist. I am struggling for money. I am someone with dark hair, brown eyes and medium height. You give a physical description, and you might share your likes and dislikes. I am someone who likes fine food. I like to travel. I like to dance. I don't like the color blue. And so forth.

But those are just activities and a description of your form; they are not who you truly are. All of these things that you take as your identity—your physical appearance, how you earn a living, all your preferences, your beliefs, thoughts and emotions and so forth—all of these constitute the human ego. It is an overlay. It is your patterning. And you are much, much more than the limited human ego, or personality patterning. You are the Self. You are pure awareness, pure consciousness, the All That Is.

The ego is just a structure, just a container for your consciousness, a vehicle in which the Self, the larger you, moves through life so it can have experiences and learn lessons.

It's like tea in a cup. Your consciousness is the tea, and your ego is the cup, which contains the consciousness. At death, the cup breaks, but the consciousness still exists, just in a different form; the tea is still tea, but it's not held in the cup anymore.

When we come into this world, the soft clay of our being is molded and imprinted by our parents, teachers, the media and others around us, and we begin to develop patterns in consciousness, likes and dislikes, fears and desires and so forth. When our parents encourage and reward us, we learn what is judged as good and what gets approval. When they scold and punish us, we learn what is judged as bad and what gets disapproval. This process is the formation of the ego, which is synonymous with the personality. It varies from person to person, culture to culture, and country to country. All of our wounding and traumatic experiences, all of our fears, desires and fantasies, all of our judgments about good and bad, all of this is bound up in the ego.

There are many variations on the same theme, but it is all the imprinting of the human ego. Every human on the planet has one. Some egos are more streamlined, refined and heart-centered than others. Some are denser and pricklier. But we all need an ego to be able to live here and have experiences and learn lessons.

It is similar to cars. All cars are different, but they all provide a mechanism to move us through life. A VW and a Mercedes have different chassis and even the engines are slightly different, but both run on the same principle. This is true of humans too. We all look different and have different patterning, different likes and dislikes; in fact, no two are alike. But we all have an ego.

The ego is both a blessing and a curse. On the one hand it provides a vehicle through which we can live on this exquisite emerald-blue planet and have these amazing and wonderful experiences as humans. On the other, the ego also limits us tremendously. Although we can't take a large family vacation or go off-roading in a tiny sports car, there is nothing stopping us from adapting or upgrading the vehicle in which we travel. Furthermore, we don't cease to exist while we are in the process of changing cars.

In truth at one level of our being, we are vast, timeless and eternal consciousness, but when we incarnate into a human life and take on an ego, we forget who we truly are, and we begin to identify as the ego. We think it's who we are.

We are like sausages! The vast consciousness that we truly are gets crammed into these tight little skins, which can feel awfully uncomfortable, cramped and limiting at times. There's a part of us that wants to burst out of our skin and be free of the confinement of the ego and the body.

And we feel so separate in the ego. In fact the ego is a central component in what is called the system of separation. *It's where we believe we are not connected to anything else around us and live in isolation. In the system of separation we believe we end at the boundary of our skin, and everyone else begins at the boundary of their skins. We believe we are not connected to each other or to nature or to plants or to animals or to the Earth or to anything.*

Yet in reality none of that is actually true. We are all connected. Science is even proving that nowadays. Reading quantum physics is like reading a page out of the ancient Vedas. At one level of reality there is no separation, and we are all one with everything. You and I are not separate from each other. We are not separate from the Earth and nature. We are one with each other and one with the Earth. This is what's known as unity consciousness, *or* non-dual consciousness. *At that level we know that the world, as we have been taught to see it, is not real; it is an illusion.*

It's as though we live most of our lives in a box. And we scour around inside the box, and we examine all the details inside the box, until we start to get a little bit bored and fed up. We know there's nothing left inside the box for us to discover. So, we gather up our courage and lift the lid of the box a little bit—just a crack to see what's out there. And it scares us, so we quickly close the lid again!

Then eventually we gather our courage some more, and we lift the lid again, but this time a little bit higher and for a little longer. We begin to see what awaits us outside the box before we close the lid again. And this process repeats itself for a while. Until eventually, we are ready to take the lid completely off the box, open it up and step out of the shadows and into the light of day.

This is the process that leads to Self-realization and to discovering who we are beyond the small, limited ego. It's a journey of clearing away the many layers of the ego, all of the personality patterning that we have built up in the course of our life, which keeps us locked into limitation. Like peeling an onion, we peel a layer at a time until eventually we've peeled all the way down to the core, which is our essence, our true Self.

Humans are like pack rats when it comes to holding onto things in the mind and emotions. This old but excess baggage tends to replay in the mind and emotions, often consciously but mostly subconsciously, just below your surface awareness. When you try to find your spiritual Self by becoming quiet and meditating, you find that these thoughts and emotions just beep and beep constantly. Try as you might, you cannot shut them off. They will not shut off until you have taken the time to clear out the old stored stuff that is the source of the thoughts and emotions. Clearing the ego helps remove the clutter and make way for the presence of oneness and unity to be felt—so palpably that eventually you will feel it right down into your body.[12]

Because clearing the ego involves digging around in our subconscious and unconscious mind, it is like shining a light into the dark places and dispelling the shadows, and this is why it is also referred to as shadow work.

It takes some time to do this work, but the good news is that it is not an infinite process. It may have taken you your whole life to pack your suitcase full of stuff, but it will take you a lot less time to unpack it.

And you'll feel so good when you do it! You'll feel so much lighter. It's like the Indian Saint, Sri Aurobindo, said, "You can only go as high as you are willing to go low." If you clean out your basement, you can ascend beyond your current ceiling. Your meditations are much higher when you've gone down and cleared out the shadows in the basement.

Every week for many months, I absorbed Leslie's words and let the information sink in deeply. It was a balm to my soul. At some profound level of my being, I resonated with the truth of her words, and I began to examine myself closely to see where I was locked into an identity. I wanted to know who I was beyond the 29-year-old, gay, white male, who had grown up on the East Coast and been an actor in Los Angeles. *Who would I be if I let go of the whole story?* I made a deep commitment to Spirit to do the work of discovering who I truly was.

In 1991 not many spiritual teachers were talking about shadow work, but Leslie was a pioneer. She had dedicated her life to this journey of clearing the ego, which included shadow work, and I was immensely grateful that she was sharing her knowledge. I look back on the many years of practicing it and realize what balance and clarity it has given me and how it expanded my consciousness. Clearing the shadow prepares us to face life's many challenges and to reach new heights on the journey of Self-realization.

> *When you do this shadow clearing, you begin to see that you are not who you thought you were. You are not the personality or the body or your thoughts or your emotions or your memories. You do not identify as being those things anymore. You do not identify with the ego. You begin to wake up and see that you are the Self. You are pure awareness—vast, eternal, timeless consciousness.*

In addition to seeing Leslie in class one night each week, I was also listening to her set of audio recordings called *The Marriage of Spirit*, which outlined techniques for clearing the ego. This was the *how-to* part, the *reconciliation of opposites technique,* which is based on ancient methods she had streamlined and simplified for the modern world— tools she used for her own spiritual awakening.

The Marriage of Spirit techniques are simple journaling methods one can do in the privacy of one's home, which are tremendously helpful in clearing the ego. They integrate three philosophies: 1) *Jnana yoga*[13], the yoga of the mind, also known as *Advaita Vedanta*, ancient Hindu teachings of self-inquiry based on non-duality; 2) the ancient principle of the reconciliation of opposites; and 3) spiritual psychology.

In 2000, many years after initially learning about The Marriage of Spirit, I co-authored a book with Leslie on this subject, *The Marriage of Spirit—Enlightened Living in Today's World.*[14] Two of its three primary tools—polarities and squares—are presented in Chapters 10, The Witness and Polarity Processing, and 12, Squares, and are incredibly effective, simple and speedy for clearing the ego.

THE EGO IS NOT THE ENEMY

Although some may feel that obliteration of the ego is necessary in order to achieve spiritual awakening, this is not the case. There is nothing inherently bad about the ego, and feeling that there is comes from those parts of us stuck in judgment and polarized perception—internalized parts such as the *critical parent* or *wounded child*. Shadow-clearing is not about annihilating the ego, and if we think we have to kill the ego to find our spiritual selves, we are missing the point. After all, to live in a human body on planet Earth, we need an ego. It is the vehicle we use to move through life.

On the path of spiritual transformation, the ego doesn't cease to exist but instead morphs continuously. As Saint Paul said, *I die daily*[15], meaning that the self or ego is repeatedly reborn to become more refined. But the ego is programmed to fear its death, and we often use this as an excuse not to do the egoic clearing work. All change requires the shedding of what previously existed, and life on Earth is about inescapable change. Practicing self-inquiry is an opportunity to assist the ego in its ineluctable destiny of change. If Saint Paul were alive today, might he say instead, *I morph daily*?

If we ever get caught up in self-judgment and the need to annihilate the ego, it is important to stop and take a big step back. The critical thing to remember in this instance is that the overall purpose of the egoic clearing work is about love—loving ourselves, loving others, loving the Earth and ultimately becoming love.

We need not beat ourselves up about the personality patterns we observe habitually playing themselves out. For example, instead of chastising ourselves for a knee-jerk anger reaction when someone cuts us off in traffic, we can learn to witness, from a stance of love, what is happening. This allows us to analyze and heal the conditioned aspects of the personality that arise. In psychology the dark side of human nature is often called the *shadow*, a term coined by the famous Swiss psychiatrist and psychotherapist, Carl Jung, not because it is bad or wrong but because it is made up of all the qualities of the personality that we would prefer to hide. When we keep the shadow hidden, it festers like a wound and grows with time. In contrast when we open and process the shadow, it heals and evolves into more enlightened qualities, allowing the ego to expand into a more loving, healed and whole self.

The ego is not the enemy, and the goal is not to attack and obliterate it. The process of clearing the shadow is a path paved with acceptance, love and enlightened change. The end result is not just about being able to love ourselves and others but to become love itself. This brings magic to life, and we open to absolute joy. Joy is the highest fulfillment of the spiritual path. In the final analysis if we could live in that state all the time, there would be no need to do any egoic clearing work. Living in love and joy is the ultimate, glorious attainment of this journey in consciousness.

The question then becomes: *Do I choose to die once in terror or be reborn repeatedly on the journey of conscious evolution?*

CHAPTER 5

Love and Generosity

❧

I give light freely because it is priceless.

The most generous person I had ever met, Leslie offered everything she did as a gift of service and didn't charge a fee. Although she never had expectations about others giving back to her, students donated as they were able. Not earning much money at the time, I offered my time outside of work, usually on weekends, as a reciprocal gift of service.

In those first weeks and months of studying Self-discovery with Leslie, I was finally getting answers to all my spiritual questions and regularly experiencing my own inner divinity. As the flames of my passion for Self-discovery were fanned, I wanted to know everything about her and how she worked with energy, and therefore, I spent every moment I could with her.

Most weekends were spent at her apartment in West Los Angeles doing whatever I could to support her, and inevitably we'd have time afterwards for a discussion about spirit. Receiving so much spiritual wisdom from Leslie, I was certain I was getting the better end of the deal. Typically I'd spend a couple of hours running errands or helping around the house, and then our spiritual discussions lasted the better part of the day and into the night. In her magnanimous and generous way, I think many of the service projects, which she could have easily done herself, were excuses she created to allow her students opportunities to receive the spiritual wisdom and shakti.

As her students we felt incredibly blessed and fortunate, and although she never required or expected anything in return, there was a natural desire to reciprocate in some way. Giving without thought of reward is part of a system she called *living in a flow*, which is one of the cornerstones of her teachings. When you live in a flow of generosity, you live a life of abundance—you always have what you need, and the universe provides for you in amazing and often unexpected ways.

Living life in a flow of generosity was something very new to me. I'd heard in church about the principle of giving without thought of reward but had never actually met anyone who was a living embodiment of it. Observing Leslie's example stopped me in my tracks. It forced me to question my preconceived notions about giving and receiving and kindled the desire to understand more about my motivations related to selfishness and selflessness.

I learned from Leslie that practicing generosity is a way of transcending the ego. Because the human ego fears death, one of its patterns is selfishness. Getting our needs met ensures our own survival, but when we practice generosity, we shatter that pattern of selfishness and break through those walls of ego. Generosity defies the egoic pattern of selfishness. In the act of giving we are affirming our connection with other human beings and life forms outside of us, acknowledging that we are not separate. It bridges the gap that seems to separate us, and in the act of giving we experience our connectedness, even if only to a small degree. This in turn opens us to unity consciousness.

Giving and generosity are qualities of the heart. As we practice generosity, we also develop other heart states, such as empathy, love, compassion and forgiveness. As our heart-centeredness grows and develops, so does our desire to give and be generous, which then becomes a self-reinforcing feedback loop of heart-centered consciousness. Living in the heart is one of the first steps out of the ego. It helps us to transcend the system of separation and instead feel at one with the rest of the world. Whenever you are feeling stuck, depressed or disconnected, watch what happens when you practice generosity. The act of giving can bring unparalleled joy and can have you walking on air for days.

Always an advocate of selfless service, Leslie encouraged us to practice generosity by doing community service projects from time to time and by giving money to the homeless and to charity.

Even if you are down to your last five dollars, it's better to give it away to a homeless person than to hang on to it or to try to use it for yourself. The best investment you can make is in practicing generosity because not only are you helping others, but also it will always come back to you.

When you give, the ego fears you will simply lose what you have, and you'll be empty inside. But because nature abhors a vacuum, more will always come in to replace it—often multi-fold.

When you are serving others, a torrent of grace floods your life, and magic happens. By making the welfare of others a priority in your life, Spirit meets you more than half way and provides for your own needs better than you could ever imagine yourself.

Love multiplies; it never divides.

As practitioners of the art of giving, we are on an ever-expanding, ascending spiral of spiritual power, which leads eventually to the realizations of the mysteries of the universe, way beyond the boundaries of the past, and into the light of faith.

THE HEART OF THE MATTER

Love and Truth are the most powerful forces in the universe. Because of this, it's important for a spiritual seeker to cultivate the heart. The heart is like a beautiful garden. In most people, unfortunately, the garden is not really clear or pure, and its beauty is hidden through lack of care. Overgrown and clogged with weeds, the garden has to be fully cleared before its real glory may be seen. The weeds need to be pulled and the trees trimmed so that the clear perfection of the environment is evident to all. Then you may take walks there and enjoy all of the magnificence. Eventually, you will be able to invite others to walk there with you.

It's important to be able to distinguish when you're in your heart and when you're operating from the system of separation rather than from the heart. When you live and act from the heart, it's surprising how beautiful the world is and how filled with love everything seems to be. You, as a student of heart, will be able to smile more often and won't be as vulnerable.

This study I'm taking you through is like a boot camp for the heart. When one lives established in the heart, life is lived "at the heart of the matter," which is at the heart of everything, at the Source, more harmonious with existence and less in conflict with it. If you are in your "me-ness," feeling and believing that "I, I am important. I have to take care of number one," ultimately, you will be unhappy because there will always be other "mes," both in your head and in the outside world, saying "I, me, I," and of course you won't hit it off with them.[16]

In the first few years of studying with Leslie, she created The Spiritual Warrior Training course[17] for our small group of about a dozen students in Los Angeles. It included several audio recordings, which I would play in an endless loop in my car. The course was specifically designed to help us to embody the spiritual teachings while living and working in the world. The core message was about love—specifically about *becoming love*.

We are running out of time. You're not getting any younger, and existence is moving along at a clipping pace into the new reality. It's happening. There is a force which seems to be moving us from within. Oppositions, polarizations, a life of obstacles—that's the third dimension, a major obstacle course. A life of tyrants and victims, manipulations, dominations—aren't you sick of it? Who needs it anyway? Enough is enough. How many thousands of years have we been doing this? We're being blessed with an opportunity to get out. It would be a shame if you didn't take it. Conditions never were better to leave that stuff now. In fact, the time has come.

The fun of Self-discovery really starts from the pure heart. It's from there that the really exciting adventures happen. So I want to see you starting to live from your Higher Self in the classroom and out in the world, as much as you can. This is the key. As you meditate more, you will see that heart energy is a state of mind, a state of universal mind. It is infinite. It has no boundaries. It is existence and non-existence. All that is . . . is this infinite ocean of love, of divine love. It's beyond time and space, beyond matter, beyond condition. It's nothing like human love at all. Human love is very limited. What most people call love on a human level is a kind of possessiveness, a kind of ownership, a commodity or a desire to control. But this infinite ocean—luminous, perfect—is what you are. There is no fear. There is nothing outside of it. The things we fear are the unknown, the outside. But in reality there is no outside. That's what you're growing to understand. It's not that difficult to get there—be formidable and undaunted in your resolve.

Remember, you don't need anything in particular to love. It's almost inconceivable for human beings to be in an object-less state of love.

They think they have to have something to love. So we hear people say, "I love my car. I love my dog." We even have bumper stickers to that effect. Is it necessary to have something to love?

Love is a state of mind. Love is actually a level of consciousness.

You can simply relocate your attention to that level and hang out there. Whereas, if you need to have an object for your love, one day the prized object may disappear into the sunset, and grief and loss will render you unable to love any more.

So, become love. Meditate on becoming love.

You can generate energy from your heart chakra,[18] *and you can transmit it to every cell. You can feel it oozing off the tips of your fingers and the tips of your toes. Love your mind. Love yourself. Love your body. But not in a gushy, self-indulgent way. That's not love; that's self-indulgence. Respect yourself, always. You are not who you think yourself to be. You are divine. You are pure consciousness, light, intelligence. Be kind to yourself and others—because they, too, are divine.*

Be careful about making yourself more important than anyone else. Can you give up your territory? In this state of attention that we call truth and love—the heart of the matter—there is no territory. There are no boundaries. You do not have any territory to defend. You are everything, and nobody can take anything away from you. Oh, they may steal your car, but they haven't done anything to you. If you're established on that level of consciousness, you will not feel deprived. You will simply see that someone took your car and not feel victimized by it.

Emptiness will leave you. In reality you are infinite awareness, but in your human state, you're an empty vessel needing to be filled. Everybody is. And we're always looking for things with which to fill ourselves. That's what we call love. You do not need to be empty. If you live in the heart of the matter, you will not feel empty and deprived. You will not need to seek fulfillment in the outer world in the form of sex, drugs and rock and roll. That's not to say that you won't enjoy sex or rock and roll—I'm not so sure about the drugs. But you will no longer be bound by your needs and addictions. You will find everything inside of you if you dig deep enough into truth.

The process of enlightenment is a pathway for detaching ourselves from the things that we're really entangled in. Many times along the path, along the road of Self-discovery, I found myself asking, "What is love?" And I got many different answers, depending where I was at the time of asking the question. But the most recent answer, the one that seems to make more sense to me now, came very clearly. It said inwardly that there really is nothing that is not love.

> *There really is nothing that is not love. Everything is love. Love is the substance of existence. It is the stuff that everything is made of. It permeates all of creation—all of existence and all of non-existence.*[19]

I felt the truth of Leslie's wisdom deep inside my heart, and I longed to experience that kind of love. *But how?* Although I understood the concept that we exist in a living, loving universe, I could not reconcile that inner knowing with all of the horror and trauma in the world. What about the victims of war, rape and other forms of brutality and oppression? How does one explain to them that these acts are reflections of a loving universe? How is the perpetrator an expression of love? The conundrum reminded me of the theodicy question from divinity school: *If God is good and all powerful, why is there suffering and evil in the world?* So at the next opportunity I inquired, *Why don't we perceive it that way?*

This is one of the most advanced and challenging concepts for the mind. Rather than simply accepting a mental understanding, it is something that must be experienced. This happens in time on the path of Self-discovery as you deepen your meditation practice and open the heart more and more. As you move into greater states of tolerance, compassion, love and forgiveness, you begin to know this truth at a visceral level. So in the beginning it's essential for you to suspend judgment and disbelief about this truth and pray for a deeper understanding.

Ultimately there are many ways to look at this issue. One of the most important is to recognize that within the loving fabric of our universe, every aspect is designed to bring about our enlightenment. Even perpetrators are a vital part of that design. In fact, <u>especially</u> perpetrators—because they help us to grow. A quick examination of history reveals this. Tyrants force people to stand up in their power and demand truth and justice. As Gandhi once said, "When I despair, I remember that all through history the ways of truth and love have always won. There have been tyrants, and murderers, and for a time they can seem invincible, but in the end they always fall. Think of it—always." In the end tyrants help us to evolve and grow. There is no growth without a tyrant.

In essence it is the paradoxical discovery that the Divine is in everything: in the horrors of life as much as in the beauty of life, in war as much as in peace, in destruction as much as in creation, in death as much as in life. Accepting paradox is yin power.

This is a journey of discovery, and you cannot expect to jump into a full-blown experience of it immediately. However, it can come in time if you want it. The process begins by making a commitment to know love and to become love.

It is a spiritual Truth that everything begins with a commitment. You do not have to know how to do something right away. Yet by the simple act of making a commitment, Spirit will guide you there.

We do not perceive life's challenges as a reflection of a loving universe mainly because we have been conditioned into a separate state. We have an ego, and the ego has a negative and a positive side, and it's loaded with all sorts of states of mind which make up our separate existence on a personality level. So here we are journeying down the road of life with a negative and a positive ego, and on the negative side, there are states of mind such as pain, fear, hatred, despair, anger, guilt, doubt, rejection, and the biggie—worthlessness. And these are the things that seem to interfere the most with our perception of love in its purest form. They mask it. They mask the true nature of existence so that we cannot perceive the essence, which is love, and which is present at all times in and through us—and in everyone and everything all the time. So we may say that it is our separate state that prevents us from knowing love at that level.

Learning to love is a quest. It's a major heroic quest for your life, should you choose to try that. And the only way you can journey toward fulfilled love is to start loving unselfishly. For some people, that is the hardest thing to contemplate. It takes enormous self-discipline to develop unselfishness, a spirit of giving. And after years and years, the end result would be something of a saint. Now, not everybody aspires to be a saint. This sounds quite boring to some people, but I'm sure that most of you would agree that adding some higher levels of love to your life would certainly be worth the effort.

Learning to love is not boring. It gives life new meaning, and it's very enriching. When you can put someone else ahead of yourself, when you can make someone else more important than yourself, then you are learning to love like that. We see that kind of love in the love a parent has for a child or the love that a spiritual teacher has for a student. Loving a child can become a very spiritual experience—a selfless, generous and very enriching addition to one's evolution. It seems to bring out the best in us. It seems to forge our consciousness and refine it. We don't often see that kind of noble love in this world, although—and this is a Catch 22—I think many of us yearn to receive it. We also yearn to see that kind of love flourish on this planet, and many of us work on ourselves, or for the welfare of others, with that point in mind. It becomes an inspiration. It is something that feeds and enriches you.

The pathway to enlightenment will take you toward the dissolution of that separate state, allowing you to feel more oneness with all things, and love is the power that does that. Love has the power to melt the boundaries of your being and make you feel oneness with other people, animals or nature. The experience of feeling that you have within you the knowledge of the unity of all things is very inspiring. It's uplifting to feel connected and to care.

Sometimes people have negative images of what that would be like, and it seems to them that this would be something sugary or unrealistic and not at all fun. But that's not the case when you follow the path toward enlightenment, because you develop a great deal of detachment from things. And as your detachment develops, so your ability to love becomes more profound rather than less. This may seem paradoxical, but what happens is that we become less dependent, less involved with the baser aspects of ourselves and of others and much more in the universal flow, more involved with things that fill us up—for example, creativity and a sense of inspiration.

Ultimately, you will become love. You're in it, and you are it.

When you fall in love with love itself, your beloved is love and then you are love. Love is everywhere, even in adversity.

All you have is love, and then, one day—if you're really dedicated to the Light and to Spirit and to your meditation, and you've experienced perfection of life itself and even the imperfections seem perfect to you—then you go beyond love altogether into the state known as Self-Realization. It's not that you don't love anymore. It's just that you've gone beyond it. Then you may come back into this world where love exists, but it's never quite the same because you went beyond love into a level of awareness you can't even talk about because there are no words for it. So love would be our highest level of verbally describable, knowable existence.

As we grow and evolve over lifetimes, we develop our capacity to love from a more infantile, selfish stage, on up to an unselfish, more inspired, more detached level. And it is, indeed, a noble endeavor to aspire to do that.

So I wish you all well on your journey, and I hope that much love comes to you. I hope that you will find love within yourself, the kind of love I was talking about, the love that has no opposite. It's worth it. It's well worth it. It's going to happen to you anyway someday—if you don't actively seek it, I mean. It will just take longer, a few more lifetimes. And if that happens, well, that's quite proper; that's what's supposed to happen.

There is a great lack of love in this world today, and if there were ever a time for us to seek it, to develop it, to evolve with it and become it—now is the time.

The world really needs your love now.[20]

CHAPTER 6

The Power of Your Thoughts

❧

I was not born awake. I was born with an ego, just like everyone else. I woke up through practicing meditation, living in love and clearing the ego. The rest is just a story, which is all ego.

Like all of her students, I was keen to know about Leslie's personal life and spiritual journey, but she was always reluctant to discuss her own story and rarely divulged details of her personal background, unless it was in relation to a specific spiritual teaching to benefit the class.

Spending time dwelling on personal history and regurgitating the details of one's story are a waste and just reinforce the ego. Besides, this is not about "me." The story of my small "self" doesn't matter. What matters is your spiritual awakening.

As one of her students, I seldom dared disagree with Leslie, but I knew she was wrong about this. Repeatedly I explained that we would learn by hearing her story since she was a living example of achieving the awakened state. My persistence and logic were not always easy to dodge.

Okay, I will share part of the story—if you insist—and it will include a spiritual lesson.

Little by little over a few years I was able to piece together a picture that was enormously helpful to all of us. I've taken the liberty of stringing several conversations together here as one:

I was born in Johannesburg, South Africa, in 1946, to parents of mainly British descent. My father served in North Africa and Europe in World War II, and I was born shortly after his return home. Both of my parents were architects, but, as was customary for women at the time, my mother chose not to pursue a career. They were very traumatized by the war, as were so many in our culture, and I took on much of that wounding as a child.

My father had returned from the war to a divided South Africa, and the dreadful system of Apartheid was just being put in place. It was a legalized system of racial segregation, which applied the most horrendous and unjust laws to separate Black from White. Cruel and tyrannical especially towards Black South Africans, it was oppressive to everyone. To my dismay Apartheid and I were born at about the same time, and was a most unwelcome lifelong mate. I knew at a very early age that something was not right. As soon as I was old enough to start thinking for myself, I vowed to do something to make a difference and change things. I had no idea what to do or how one person could make a difference, but I knew I had to try.

Having a natural mystical inclination as a child, I found that art was a wonderful way to express myself, and after graduating with a degree in Fine Arts, got married. I went on to become a painter and art teacher in my twenties and exhibited professionally for a while in Johannesburg.

During this time, the inner mystical life of my youth gave rise to a deepening faith and realization that God and spirit are a presence which can be directly and tangibly experienced by anyone and will guide us if only we can surrender enough to it. I resolved to find this state. My interest in Self-discovery, meditation and metaphysics grew steadily.

While painting, I began to have mystical experiences, and spiritual guides began to speak to me telepathically. They would give me spiritual aphorisms and speak profound wisdom to me. I wrote everything down on little scraps of paper and on the back of cigarette boxes.

One day my husband, who was in medical school preparing to become a surgeon, discovered some of the writings and asked what they were. When I told him that I was speaking telepathically with spiritual guides, I saw a wave of fear cross his face, and he said, "I've only ever heard of people hearing voices in their heads in the context of mental illness." I knew from that moment on that I would have to keep all of my mystical experiences, especially speaking with my spiritual guides, to myself. So, I became a closeted mystic.

Meanwhile, we had a baby girl and three years later a boy, and life became full of activity. Around the same time in the mid-seventies the revolution was intensifying in South Africa, and the corrupt Apartheid government was clamping down with lethal force. Feeling helpless as a single individual against such an overbearing force, I prayed to my guides and asked what I could possibly do to help. They replied, "We'll show you what one person can do."

Shortly after that my husband received an offer for a position at UCLA Medical Center, and our little family immigrated to California. Moving to Los Angeles was the first time in my life that I experienced a real sense of freedom. Being out from under the thumb of Apartheid, I felt completely liberated and began to discover a new world.

This is the time when my spiritual path intensified. Life was a busy juggle of painting, meditating, and caring for my husband and children, but the pull of spirit was growing steadily. Eventually realizing our paths were leading in completely different directions and after a lengthy period of difficulty, my husband and I divorced.

This stage of Leslie's path required that she fend for herself in a foreign land. She mustered her courage and all her overt strength and energy to create an independent life dedicated to Self-discovery. As we will explore in later chapters, during this phase she also actively developed her left-brained, masculine side. These yang/masculine activities helped her balance her natural yin/feminine strength. The emerging masculine/feminine balance laid a foundation for a profound spiritual awakening.

Becoming more aware of the presence of spirit guiding me, I was asked inwardly to commit my life completely to spiritual work, and from this time my own transformation accelerated rapidly. It was a time of profound change as my surrender deepened. Although I was experiencing unity consciousness during meditation, the ego was in a process of completely reorganizing, which made it a difficult and demanding time, yet also utterly inspiring.

I had many teachers. There were two in body, Frances Stearns and Rama, but mostly inner guides who introduced themselves to me by name. There were also guides who told me I would not know them by name and who worked with me anonymously.

In 1986 I entered a phase in which I was constantly drawn into ever-deepening states of unity consciousness, lost, at times, in deep, mystical communion with spirit as more and more of my identity dissolved. It was a reclusive phase, and some part of me believed I should try to find the equivalent of a monastery or a Himalayan cave where I could go to be alone, high on a mountaintop, far away from the world. But in a paradoxical twist of fate, my guides told me to rent an apartment in the bustle of Los Angeles near the confluence of the 10 and the 405 freeways. The irony was not lost on me, and I let go of a lot of preconceived notions about spiritual enlightenment.

A very cloistered period of about three years, in which I rarely left my apartment, culminated in April 1988 with a spiritual awakening experience that is very difficult to describe with words in English. There is a Sanskrit term called nirvikalpa samadhi, *which means a state of full absorption into the Divine. In several lengthy meditations absorbed in this state, my old identity completely dissolved, and the continuous awareness of unity consciousness was permanently instituted. After the final meditation I came back into my body, which was sitting on the couch, and I didn't know what had happened to me, where I'd gone or how much time had passed. It was only after I opened the front door and found four newspapers that I realized I had been in unbroken meditation for four days.*

Soon after this I came somewhat out of sequestration and slowly over a period of a year or so began to interact with the world again. I met people who I helped with spiritual guidance and who came to meditate with me. Eventually other students of transformation began to seek me out. When I meditated with people, I realized I had been given the gift of transmitting shakti, or healing energy, through my hands, eyes and voice. It is really a transmission of love—unconditional love. I have felt immensely blessed to be able to share the flow of love with others and to help people experience a taste of joy and inner peace.

When I started teaching, my guides told me I was not supposed to teach in the traditional way—the old way of the guru-disciple relationship, as has been happening for millennia in India and in many spiritual traditions. They told me that I am supposed to be a bridge between the old paradigm and a new paradigm that is birthing in the world.

They also told me that we are all birthing this new paradigm of heart-centered consciousness together and that the old hierarchical, patriarchal paradigm is ending now.

I was guided to be a pioneer and find new ways of doing spiritual teaching. Apparently the old form has served its purpose, is outmoded and needs to change.

The guides also told me that I am supposed to train a group of people to become teachers because in the coming times there would be a great need for many more spiritual teachers. Giving me a kind of deadline, they said that December 21, 2012, is a very important date astrologically and that I am supposed to help as many people as I possibly can by that date.

A teacher is someone who, through example, inspires others to change their lives. Teaching means any way in which Spirit may guide someone to express spiritual truth. There are many ways to serve and communicate higher knowledge, and each person is supported on his or her own unique path.

I've dedicated my life to serving others. I want to help as many people as I possibly can to live a life of love and to know who they truly are, which is the pure, vast, timeless Self.

Leslie has been and continues to be a pioneer in the work of awakening consciousness, and her story has served as an important road map for me and many others. In this time of unprecedented change and transformation for the Earth and human consciousness, her ongoing innovation of tools and methods to support people on their spiritual journey has been profoundly important.

HIDDEN WORK

How are you feeling today, Leslie?

Oh, not so good. There's a war brewing in the Middle East, and I am processing the violence and polarity through my body. It's very uncomfortable right now. Holding this meditation for peace feels like a war happening inside me.

Leslie never spoke publicly about this *hidden* aspect of her spiritual work unless it related to a pertinent spiritual lesson for the group. Years later, as her partner, I came to understand this ability of hers and feel obliged to share some of the details here.[21] Outside of class and the development of her students, Leslie's primary occupation was working with collective consciousness—the consciousness of large groups of people such as countries.

After her spiritual awakening in 1988, she found she was able to transmute negative energy through her physical body, both for individuals and for large groups and to help open doorways in consciousness for them. Always glowing and radiant in appearance, Leslie never let on what a burden this could sometimes be. Like all masters, she made her work look effortless. Most would never have guessed the magnitude of the inner weight she carried. But later, as we became closer, I learned of the extreme physical, mental and emotional anguish she occasionally experienced when doing this work—sometimes causing physical illness.

In 1995, during our first trip to Jerusalem, we were both aware of layer upon layer of anger, violence and war-energy trapped in the earth there—patinas of blood, suffering and torment that formed over millennia. Leslie was conscious of processing huge amounts of very old anger and negativity through her body and during meditation described the experience to me.

> *Goodness! I can feel a huge swirling energy in the ground beneath us. It is a vast number of souls who are in enormous pain. They are crusaders and Knights Templar who were killed in battle, and they seem to be stuck here. Some traumatized aspect of their consciousness is still trapped in the Earth beneath the city after all these centuries. They are basically ghosts, yet somehow they know that I'm here and that I can help them. I'm telling them they can come through my physical body and go into the light. They are vibrating with a screaming sound and are starting to come through me! There are so many of them! Oh my!*

Leslie's voice trailed off, and I watched immobilized as she experienced her massive internal process. Although she needed bed rest the next day, she never complained. When I asked her how she was able to do it, she said it was out of love and compassion for those in pain. She simply offered them her unconditional love, and that allowed them to go home to the light through her.

Within a few weeks of returning home to the US, she had to have her gallbladder removed, the timing of which suggested that it could be related to the experience in Israel. The symbolism of the gallbladder, which holds bile to digest food, is associated with anger (*gall*) and bitterness (*bile*)—major components of the soldiers' pain she took through her body.

The work was not always so physically challenging. She explained that everyone on the planet interacts with the collective, whether we are transmuting negative energy or adding positive energy. Our capacity to do so naturally develops as we evolve, and the clearer we are inside, the more easily energies can pass through. *If energy gets stuck in your body and causes physical issues, it's an indication of a place in your own consciousness where you need to do more clearing work.* And with humility she would practice self-inquiry, owning and clearing any fragments in her awareness that may have been blocking energy.

This is what her guides were referring to when, in answer to her prayer they said, *We'll show you what one person can do.*

By clearing the ego, deepening the meditation practice and evolving in consciousness, one has more of an effect on others. The more awakened and unconditionally loving one is, the more powerful one's thoughts, which in turn influences a growing number of people.

This phenomenon has been quantified in some scientific studies. One important study is explained in the book, *Power versus Force* by Dr. David Hawkins, in which he has measured the power of a thought form using kinesiology.

Protesting in the streets and taking action for equality, peace and love in the world are important and good, but the most powerful gift we can offer is our own awakened consciousness. Not that spiritual awakening and protesting are mutually exclusive. Leslie has always taught and modeled that there are times for sitting in meditation and working inwardly with consciousness, and there are other times when it is vital to get off the meditation cushion and take physical action. She asserts that when enough people with an enlightened consciousness take physical action, world change is certain.

As Leslie's work expanded, more and more people came to sit in meditation and study with her. After a long weekend of events for large groups of people, she would usually need a couple of weeks to rest and to complete the clearing work.

Giving someone shakti is such an intimate experience because I merge completely with them. By offering them unconditional love, naturally their energy fields and egoic patterning pass through me. It can take a couple of weeks to finish taking 200–300 people energetically through the density of my physical body. I don't mind. It's a gift I can give people, and it opens doorways in consciousness for them should they choose to walk through. I offer the gift with the hope and prayer that it will help accelerate their soul's evolution. And the process allows me to grow into my own soul's evolution too.

The vast majority of people who sat in meditation with Leslie never consciously realized the magnitude of the gift they were receiving. Most didn't comprehend how challenging it was for her physical body or how long her work continued after the event. She did her work with ease, grace and good humor and with such a generous spirit that nobody guessed. And this is how she wanted it to be. She said that if people knew, they might feel regret, which would block the gift energetically.

When I first met Leslie, she was as thin as a runway model, but she discovered that by putting on a bit of weight, her body was able to manage the challenges of her energetic work more easily. As she took on students, she put on weight to add a buffer to the difficult energy. It was a direct ratio: the more students came, the more shielding she needed. When her work changed and she offered fewer events, she lost the weight again.

There are many stories in ancient sacred texts and some modern stories of spiritual masters who have worked out their students' negative energies on their own enlightened bodies. It is a gift of unconditional love and service to the world that Leslie has offered since 1988. As the sign at her door always read, *This darshan is offered by donation because the light is priceless and free.*

Love and light are indeed—invaluable.

THE POWER OF THE MASS MIND

About a year and a half after meeting Leslie, I learned a powerful lesson while on a trip with her to Santa Fe, New Mexico—a meditation and shadow-clearing intensive that changed my life forever, the story of which I will share in more detail in Chapter 13, Samadhi.

After the intensive we were driving from Santa Fe back to Los Angeles. As we approached southern California, Leslie slept in the passenger seat, and I was cruising the freeway in a heightened state of attention. I had changed so much in just one week that I hardly recognized myself. Exhilarated, carefree and expansive, I was in a state of no mind and no thought.

Then around 10 PM, as we drove through Barstow, the first fairly populous town outside Los Angeles, notable for its plethora of truck stops and biker bars, something bizarre happened—I started thinking,

I want a beer, and I want my chick.

That I was thinking was not so bizarre; however, *what* I was thinking really floored me.

I want a beer, and I want my chick.

The thought form wouldn't go away.

Huh? What the . . . Huh? How can I be thinking this? This makes no sense whatsoever! Those are definitely <u>not</u> my wants!

I want a beer and I want my chick, kept beeping at me relentlessly—until we passed through and beyond Barstow.

Wait a minute! That wasn't my thought! I was feeling the thoughts of the people in that town! They weren't my thoughts—obviously—yet I was thinking them as if they were my own.

I was so excited about the phenomenon that I wanted to wake Leslie up to discuss it. Consideration won over curiosity, and I let her rest.

Then around 11PM or so, we entered East Los Angeles, an area known for its violence and gangs, and I started having angry, violent thoughts.

These are certainly not my thoughts—actually I'm feeling more peaceful and loving than I've ever felt in my life. I'm picking up the thoughts of the majority around me! They really do seem like my own thoughts though. If they weren't so different from how I'm actually feeling, I might really believe them.

Then around midnight, we entered West Los Angeles.

You know, now that we're back in LA, I really should get a new car. It's about time, actually, and I'm tired of mine.

For a moment I accepted this thought as mine.

Wait a minute! I don't need a new car. My car is just fine. These are not my thoughts either!

We were not far from the affluence and wealth of areas like Beverly Hills when I suddenly woke up to the fact that I had almost bought into the mindset of others. If I hadn't known better because of the previous experiences in Barstow and East Los Angeles, it's possible that I might have accepted those thoughts and acted on them.

I wonder how many of my thoughts aren't even mine?

The experience taught me a very important lesson about the power of thoughts.

> Thoughts are universal. We are all part of one, unified consciousness, and we share our thoughts with each other.

Until then, I had no idea how much a collective thought form can influence others. How can we be certain that the thoughts we are thinking are our own and not the thoughts of others? Unless we are clear enough inside and have a strong enough neutral observer to be able to discern what is ours and what is someone else's, we can't know the difference. It's a great incentive to develop inner clarity and to recognize that we must become independent thinkers and be mindful of the power of our own thoughts.

> Our thoughts influence our bodies, our lives and others, whether we are conscious of it or not. Becoming the master of our personal thoughts is a prerequisite on the journey of Self-discovery. One of the key disciplines for attaining it is meditation.

If we want to be free from the *mass mind* and influence the world in a more powerful way with our own loving, peaceful thoughts, it's essential to meditate regularly and do the egoic clearing work.

CHAPTER 7

Truth and Humility

❧

*You are behaving arrogantly and selfishly, and you are in the wrong.
It's not the other person who is to blame in this situation; it is you.
You are projecting your own problems onto her and then blaming her
for your own stuff. Unless you can muster the courage and humility to
look in the mirror, I'm afraid I can't help you, and the situation will
not change.*

Although always offered in unconditional love, Leslie did not mince
her words when communicating truths. In twenty-five years of knowing
her, I have observed countless students desperately ask for help with
clearing particularly painful issues. Without fail she has always pin-
pointed the egoic structure causing the problem and spoken the truth
with an unconditionally loving heart. Although most people claim to
seek the truth, at times it can be a bitter pill to swallow. As an observer,
I would freeze in these situations. *What on Earth is this person going to say
and do?* If I had spoken those words to anyone, I'd probably get a punch
in the nose. But usually, after a tense few moments of silent self-reflec-
tion, the student would find the humility to receive the stinging blow
to the ego, recognize the truth of her words and simply say, *Thank you.*
Because the counsel was always offered with total love and compassion,
the recipient was empowered to be humble, and their humility allowed
them to receive the wisdom and the opportunity for change.

It is through facing humiliation, and the fear of it, that true humility is born. We come from a culture where failings are not tolerated and where our growth is measured in terms of success over others and the environment. However, humility is one of the most empowering spiritual qualities because it allows us to grow and evolve rapidly and to become more established in the heart— a place of enormous strength and courage.

Humility is not to be confused with meekness. Meekness usually implies weakness or timidity, whereas humility requires incredible courage and opens the door to an unshakable inner power and awareness of the Self. Humility, a quality traditionally admired in women, is not readily sought in the macho, competitive, male model idealized in the West. Cultivating humility is one of the defining characteristics of the spiritual warrior's journey, whichever gender we happen to be.

Invariably Leslie's advice was exactly what was needed to begin unraveling the limiting egoic pattern, and if the student could find the humility to let the truth in, release and relief were the result. Ripping off a Band-Aid involves less overall pain than the tediously slow peel, yet most people avoid harsh truths, preferring to endure a life of attrition, repeated hard knocks and stagnation. Love allows even the harshest truths to be received with grace.

SPEAKING TRUTH WITH LOVE

Gentle as a flower where love is concerned.
Strong as thunder where principles are at stake.
—*Paramahansa Yogananda*

Students who desired to clean out the shadows in the basement of their consciousness had an invaluable ally in Leslie. Shadows hide in our blind spots and are therefore very difficult to bring to awareness on our own. It is an incredibly rare gift to have someone who can see a hidden aspect of consciousness and speak about it with both truth and love.

If someone asked to be scrutinized under Leslie's keen lens, she gave the gift willingly and lovingly, without thought of personal gain or loss. Everyone was given the same level of frankness whether they were powerful patrons or first-time students. I once heard her speak the following challenging words to one of the primary benefactors of her work at a time when she had few other financial supports.

> *Your process is that you are a controller. You are dominating me, and you need to stop. Just because you give a lot of money doesn't mean you can tell me what to do. If you don't stop your overbearing behavior, I'm afraid I have no choice but not to accept your donations any more.*

Although stung to the quick, the man, to his credit, had the humility to change his behavior towards Leslie and to continue to give generously for many years.

Leslie did not attach to the responses of those she counseled. She spoke the truth with love, irrespective of whether or not her students continued to study with her or even believed what she taught.

> *I'm not "collecting students." Good heavens, what an awful thought! My role is to help empower you to take the tools and stand on your own two feet. If you study with me, the only requirement is that you practice meditation and some form of egoic clearing work. You can use the method of clearing shadow that I teach or any method that you want. Try working with the enneagram, or emotional release therapy, or family constellations or whatever you want, but you must choose one*

that works for you and use it. And please don't believe what I say just because I say it. Weigh the teachings against your own heart and mind and decide for yourself what the truth is.

Through her heart-centered example, Leslie taught us much about offering counsel in an unconditionally loving and non-judgmental way. The first time I witnessed her mastery of this remarkable talent involved a stranger to our class who monopolized the question-and-answer period of the gathering with an unbelievably long, self-indulgent and incoherent ramble. Bored and distracted, the class projected unkind thoughts onto him as we shifted uncomfortably in our seats, trying unsuccessfully to track what he was saying. When he finally stopped talking, I waited uncertainly for Leslie's reply, wondering how she could possibly respond in any meaningful way to such aimless verbosity.

Leslie's response made it clear she had listened deeply and with total unconditional love and non-judgment. She offered profoundly important insights and spiritual lessons that helped not only the man, who we learned had just been released from a mental hospital, but also benefited the entire class. Astounded and humbled by what seemed like an impossible feat, I questioned Leslie extensively after class.

How were you able to do that? I couldn't even make sense of what he was saying.

I just tracked him mindfully with non-judgment and love, and when he finished, I responded from my heart.

But weren't you frustrated? Didn't you find yourself judging him at all?

No. . . . Well, if a little judgment briefly flits across the screen of my awareness, I just watch it come in and watch it go again and don't hook into it at all.

SENSITIVITY AND REFINEMENT

Sensitivity, empathy and refinement are essential for enlightenment and to connect with truth, yet most of us have blunted our sensitivities in an attempt to prevent and protect ourselves from pain. Leslie's sensitivity is such that she can feel what others are feeling, often before they are conscious of it themselves. The first time I experienced her ability to attune in this way was somewhat unsettling.

Brad, you are feeling resentment about having to do the shadow clearing work. You feel like you shouldn't have to for some reason, and you can't understand why you aren't more awake already.

No, I'm not, Leslie. I can assure you that's not true. I am not feeling that way at all.

You are. You're just unconscious of it. It's out in your aura, and I'm picking it up. Eventually it will filter down into your conscious awareness, and you'll want to deal with it.

Feeling slightly irritated that I should be accused of these sentiments, I rejected Leslie's words, but within two days I started to feel the first inklings of the emotions she had predicted, very subtly at first and then after another few days, quite palpably. On reflection I realized that I had been feeling them for some time and that my resentment had taken the form of occasional resistance to doing the shadow work, which would have been evident to me if I had not been in such denial. Caught like a naughty child, I sheepishly confessed to her the accuracy of her seeing. Thereafter, I never took her finely tuned perceptive abilities for granted and recognized them as an incredible gift. As my fear of exposure, chastisement and shame gradually gave way to receptivity, humility and gratitude, I made more progress on the journey.

> Three key elements for communicating truth successfully:
>
> - Sensitivity: When our sensitivity develops, we gain clarity of sight and an ability to identify the truth of egoic issues.
> - Empathy: When our empathy develops, we are able to communicate those truths with unconditional love.
> - Unconditional love: When the recipient experiences unconditional love, it invites receptivity and humility instead of defensiveness.

FURTHER DEVELOPING SENSITIVITY

Many of us working closely with Leslie were able to begin developing our own capacity to see and work with consciousness and energy. As a vibrating tuning fork allows other tuning forks to resonate at the same vibration, Leslie opened up that opportunity for us. Learning to attune with her energy, I could feel her before she would arrive at class. Sitting quietly in meditation at the East-West Center, I telepathically knew when she was far away, when she was arriving in the neighborhood and when she was about to pull into the driveway.

During the first year of meditating and studying with Leslie, besides becoming much more sensitive to energy, I learned about the body's *chakra* system and became attuned to my chakras. Chakras are spinning wheels of energy in the subtle body, or aura, and form conduits between our consciousness, our energy system and our physical body. Although there are many chakras in the human body, there are seven main ones, each one with a different quality and associated with a different aspect of our consciousness, mind and emotions.

I became especially aware of my *third-eye chakra* and *crown chakra*, the sixth and seventh chakras respectively. The third-eye chakra is between and slightly above the eyebrows and is associated with intuition and psychic awareness. The crown chakra, depicted in painting as a halo, is our connection with the celestial realms. After only a few weeks of meditating with Leslie, I could feel it like a large sombrero sitting on top of my head.

Having the opportunity to sit with Leslie weekly to receive the shakti, to do the shadow clearing work and to learn about universal truth, drawn from worldwide spiritual traditions, was a treasure. Spirit more than answered my prayers to find an enlightened teacher. Little did I realize that this was just the beginning of an extraordinarily fun voyage of empowerment, fulfillment and waking to my own spiritual warrior.

CHAPTER 8

Synchronicity

❦

Leslie, for the past three nights I've woken up, looked at the digital clock, and it reads 3:33. Isn't that an amazing coincidence?

There are no such things as coincidences, Brad. Nothing is random. Those events are divine synchronicities, and your spiritual guides are trying to get a message to you. They are giving you signs. You need to pay attention and discern the message.

So, what do you think the 3:33 means?

Only you can tell. But you said the three threes have shown up three times. I have found that when things come in threes, it's a special message from the guides that I need to take notice of something important. For many years now I've been seeing 12:21 on the digital clock.

What does that mean?

It's a date—December 21, 2012. I'm in the process of discerning some important messages about that date.

So, you use your intuition to discern the meaning of these signs?

Yes. If you haven't seen the movie "Field of Dreams," you should watch it. It's a lovely example of this principle and of the magic that unfolds when you can read the signs and are willing to follow them.

Wow, Leslie! You are the third person in the past week to tell me I should see that movie.

I had read the book, *Shoeless Joe*, on which the movie was based and had loved it. *The book is always better,* I had told myself. *Don't watch the movie because you'll just feel disappointed.*

With a little trepidation I rented the movie that weekend. I was certainly not disappointed. It is an uplifting and inspiring film about having the courage to follow your dreams and trusting in the invisible realms. The lead character, Ray Kinsella, an Iowa farmer played by Kevin Costner, hears a voice in the cornfield mysteriously whisper, *If you build it, he will come.* He is shown a vision of a baseball field in his cornfield, and although it makes no logical sense, he knows in his heart he really wants to build it. Although he realizes that they may lose their farm if he follows his passion, he cannot ignore his strong inner knowing, and he and his wife agree to plow under the corn to build the baseball field.

The story unfolds in magical ways. Continuing to receive cryptic clues about his next steps, Ray learns to discern their meaning and to follow his intuition. Despite immense criticism, Ray and his wife overcome their fears and risk everything to do what they know in their hearts they must do.

I identified completely with the central theme and recognized five keys of synchronicity.

Five Keys of Synchronicity

* Recognizing that nothing is random.
* Realizing there are no coincidences.
* Paying attention to signs from the invisible realms.
* Discerning the message from the signs.
* Following the guidance.

After it ended, I sat motionless on the sofa meditating deeply on the powerful message. The credits rolled all the way to the end and the VCR player automatically ejected the tape, turning the TV screen into pixilated, black-and-white snow with a loud, annoying hiss. At the same moment, my alarm clock went off with a loud buzz. The digital display flashed 11:11—but I hadn't set the alarm.

Confused, I stood up to turn off the hissing TV and the buzzing alarm, but within about five seconds, both the phone and the doorbell rang. *It was after 11PM. Who would be trying to reach me at this hour?*

As I reached for the phone and heard the voice of a friend, who I could not believe was calling so late, I clumsily hit the OFF buttons on the TV and alarm and then opened the door to a neighbor wanting to tell me about an incident happening up the street.

When all had quieted again, I plopped down on the sofa, perplexed. *What was all that about? And at the exact moment the movie ended. At 11:11!*

Then I saw it—like an exclamation point at the end of the movie, the invisible realms were saying, *Pay attention! You need to take note of this message!*

I took some long, deep breaths and focused on becoming very still inside. It became perfectly clear to me that I had received an unambiguous message from the invisible realms emphasizing that nothing in this universe is separate or unrelated. I was not an autonomous individual, alone in the world, disconnected from the spiritual realms. I was being given a very real message from the spiritual guides and although it wasn't a voice like Ray Kinsella heard, it was an undeniable, emphatic—almost spooky—communication.

I get it! I'll pay attention from now on. I promise.

I continued to sit quietly in meditation and made a powerful inner vow to live life differently. Brimming with the enthusiasm of birthing a new me and of learning to live by guidance and intuition, I fell asleep that night feeling very at peace, happily anticipating the dawn and a fresh start.

The next morning I dressed for work as usual and stepped out of the apartment into the unusually chilly winter morning. Briefly noticing a dead bee on the welcome mat, I was half way to the parking area before stopping in my tracks.

This is the city. What's a bee doing here? There are no flowers around here, and I don't ever remember seeing a bee here. If this were a sign what would it mean?

Excitedly I walked back to the doormat and stared, like a shivering Sherlock Holmes, at the dead bee. My logical mind assumed the bee must have died of cold in the night.

But what could a dead bee signify?

Putting on my intuition hat, I asked the guides inwardly to give me information.

Bee. "B" stands for Brad. It's a dead B. It's the death of the old Brad. Wow! It's a sign of the birth of a new me.

The day before, I would have just kept walking, completely ignoring the myriad of signs in my path. Grinning from ear to ear, I closed my eyes and wept joyfully. I said a prayer of elated thanks to my guides, offering gratitude for helping me to see a new way to live, much more connected to them and to the web of life. Inspired and uplifted, I chose a different route to work.

This is going to be so much fun.

Ever since that moment I have practiced looking for the signs, discerning their meaning, weighing them against my heart and following them when it is clear to do so. The guides have often used bees as a symbol to get my attention. When I see a bee, particularly if it is in an odd place or at an odd time, I stop and take notice. *What's happening right now? What am I thinking? What should I pay attention to? Is there a message here for me?*

SKEPTICISM AND BELIEF

We all have a skeptical side, and through that lens these stories may just seem naïve and silly—insufficient proof of spirit guides in invisible realms communicating with us through synchronicity. The inner skeptic says that believing in synchronicity is simply connecting random dots and that the meaning we create is purely subjective. However, the proclivity towards either skepticism or belief in synchronicity perhaps doesn't matter.

The truth is that we are meaning-makers, and in creating meaning that resonates with us, we co-create our reality.

As we progress on the path of Self-discovery, our intuitive abilities increase. Even if we don't seek out intuition and psychic awareness, as we clear the ego and practice meditation, they come to us naturally, and we begin to rely more and more on inner knowing. Using intuition and reading subtle signs in our environment eventually become so much part of life that we can't imagine living any other way.

Knowing our connection with the invisible realms and learning to live by guidance and intuition allow us to live life in a most fulfilling and adventurous way. This is how we develop our faith in Spirit.

When we trust in the invisible realms, we can overcome fears and follow our heart, our dreams and our passions. The more unshakable our faith becomes, the greater the risks we are able to take, no matter what others may think of us.

When we begin living in faith, we open the door to a seamless flow of divine grace unfolding in front of us like a red carpet, leading to ever greater joy and fulfillment.

Part Two
Awakening to Non-Duality

CHAPTER 9

Non-Duality

❧

*I am unable to work deeply with you until you make the commitment
to own everything in your world as a part of yourself. I am certainly
not forcing you to do this, and I'm not even asking you to; the choice
is yours. You must decide if and when you are ready to make that
commitment. It's between you and Spirit.*

Leslie's words made sense to me. Through my *Field of Dreams* experience, I had come to realize that everything in my world, however small,
is meaningful. There can be no randomness or coincidence when we
own and take responsibility for our experience of the world.

Sensing that I was at another major milestone on the journey, I leaned
back in the black leather chair in Leslie's apartment, taking time to
ponder her words. I gave them my full attention, slowly sipping the
Earl Grey tea she had made for me after the volunteer project was
complete. She continued:

*The principle behind this commitment is that there is no such thing as
separation; the system of separation is an illusion. The truth is that
everything in the world is connected and that at another level of reality
everything is one.*

The corollary is that everything in our world is part of us—every person, every thing, every experience. We invite them into our lives for a purpose. If they are in our orbit, then at one level of consciousness we have invited them there to learn lessons from them and to have experiences with them. They are not outside us or separate from us.

If you believe that there can be people, things and events outside you and unrelated to you, then that opens the door to not having to take responsibility for your life. As soon as something happens to you that you judge as bad or wrong, you will feel like a victim and will have an excuse to indulge in victim consciousness and to blame the outside. "He did something terrible to me. Life dealt me a horrible blow."

But the truth is there is no such thing as a victim.

So, until you are willing to make the commitment to own what's in your world as a part of your own consciousness—that you are creating your own reality at some level of your being—I'm not able to help you process your consciousness and clear your ego.

In order to make this commitment, you don't have to understand how this principle works or to know why you created the situations you are in, but you need to be willing to commit to the principle, to take responsibility for your life, to not blame the outside and to not indulge in victim consciousness.

Taking in all that Leslie shared, I closed my eyes and meditated on her words before responding. Although I felt the truth of what she was saying, I certainly didn't understand how it could be possible.

Leslie, when I look around at the world—at all the injustice, homelessness, war, illness, poverty, environmental degradation, corruption, greed, it seems as though the world is full of victims and perpetrators. How can there be no such thing as a victim?

Good! I'm glad you are wrestling with this. It's important to do so before you make the commitment.

Relieved that she didn't think I was an unevolved pleb, I continued listening.

Yes, the world's appearance makes it look like there are victims and perpetrators, but this is part of the illusion. In Sanskrit, it's known as maya—*the illusion of the physical world.*

> *We don't choose victimization from an egoic level but rather from a soul level.*

The reality is that we invite people, things and events into our life in order to have experiences with them and to learn lessons. So, an apparent victim must ask, "Why did I invite this into my life? Why did I choose this? What do I have to learn here? What is the opportunity for me in this situation?"

The person who has been victimized may be choosing to learn lessons about forgiveness and letting go of resentment and grudges. Or maybe the person did the same terrible thing to someone, and she needs to learn how it feels in order to have more compassion for others. Or if she had an accident, maybe she needed a wake-up call in order to change her life's trajectory. There are plenty of reasons to choose to be an apparent victim.

This isn't an excuse for lack of compassion. The ability to feel empathy and compassion for others is one of the hallmarks of a heart-centered, highly evolved soul and is something we should always practice.

At some level it all made sense to me, but I was nevertheless stewing with questions, most of which began with *how*. *How does this illusion work? How do we see beyond it into the truth? How do we escape its hold on us?* As if hearing the questions before I could ask them, Leslie continued:

The rules and principles of the separate system are important to understand in order to learn how the appearance of victims and perpetrators is created and in order to learn how to be free of the system.

The first principle is that we live in a world of duality and opposites. We can only understand what something "is" because of what it "is not."

In nature there is night and day, summer and winter, abundance and scarcity, black and white and so forth. The same is true for human consciousness. We feel pain and pleasure, happiness and sadness, love and hate, and we judge things as good and bad, and right and wrong. And there are victims and perpetrators (or tyrants). The list of opposites seems endless.

Another rule of the separate system is that everything in time turns into its opposite. Everything is flip-flopping all the time.

Birth and death, nighttime and daytime and the seasons are all on a cycle of turning. As for human consciousness, you may be feeling happy today, but at some point tomorrow or at some time in the future, you will experience sadness. And some opposites run in longer cycles. We may experience health for most of our life and then poor health when we are older. Or the cycle may run so long that it takes a few lifetimes to experience the opposite. Perhaps we are wealthy for many lives and then are poor in another life. And by just a few moments of self-examination, you can probably see times when you've felt like a victim, and times when you have probably been someone's petty tyrant. Very often victims and tyrants reverse roles with each other, so we play out both dynamics with the same person. Parents and children, siblings, and spouses often do this.

One of the most important rules to understand in the system of separation is that all humans have a conscious and an unconscious side.

Everyone on the planet has not just a conscious mind but an unconscious mind too. This is actually the key if you want to begin to step out of the system of separation, out of the limitations of the ego, and move into the unified system—or what some people are calling "the new paradigm of the heart." Understanding how the conscious-unconscious polarity works unlocks the prison of the ego.

The ego can hold only one side of a polarity at a time in the conscious mind. The other side resides in the unconscious. For example, although we might oscillate quite rapidly between emotions, it is almost impossible to consciously feel happy and sad at the same time.

Normally, we actively desire one side of a polarity—the positive side— and we try to attract it all the time. And we fear, or are averse to, the opposite side—the negative—trying desperately to keep it at bay. The pleasure and pain polarity is a good example. We actively desire pleasure and so keep pedaling our little bicycles towards it. On the other hand we are averse to pain and try to move in the opposite direction as fast as we possibly can. This dynamic is an incessant dance inside us. Yet we are generally not aware of the constant magnetic pushing and pulling within our psyches.

Although we try to escape the pain, it is inherently connected to its opposite, pleasure, and it is always just over our shoulder waiting to catch up. When trapped within this system of separation, it feels like one is on an inescapable treadmill. The way out has been kept secret in monasteries and in mystery schools for eons. However, the planet's spiritual guides want humanity to wake up at this time, and the way out is becoming more widely known now.

So here's the important part:

The side of the polarity we desire and are attracted to—usually the positive side—is what we try to keep in the conscious mind all the time. And the side we fear or are averse to—usually the negative—is what we suppress and shove down into the unconscious, pushing it as far away from us as we possibly can.

When we fear and suppress something and stuff it into the unconscious, it goes out into our aura. We literally project it outside of us, and it sits there in our aura where other people eventually pick it up and act it out for us.

That which we suppress is projected onto others, who act it out for us until we are able to understand it consciously.

For example, if we suppress our anger and shove it into the unconscious, we are likely to manifest people in our lives who get angry all the time— usually at us.

Similarly if, for whatever reason, we suppress and distance ourselves from our power, be it because we are afraid of it or don't believe we are deserving of it, or we believe it is corrupting, we are going to project our power onto others and attract people to us who wield power over us. In this way we experience power, even if it is through its opposite—powerlessness.

When we shove something into the unconscious, like our anger or our power, it may feel better in the moment, but it initiates a dynamic that can become very uncomfortable as it plays itself out. It's not possible to sweep things under the rug and expect them to actually go away. They don't go away. The stuff in the unconscious starts playing out in our world in aberrant ways and blindsides us. Someone might suddenly get angry with us or become our petty tyrant, and we feel victimized by the person. But really they are just acting out our opposite side in the dance of the maya.

In other words what we fear, or are averse to, or deny, or avoid, or suppress into the unconscious is what we manifest. This is how the victim-tyrant game is played in the system of separation. We get victimized by our own unconscious side.

The way out is first by making the commitment to own everything in our world as part of ourselves. The next steps involve doing the egoic clearing work, or what I call "processing," which is all about making the unconscious conscious.

Making the unconscious conscious is the secret to the whole game of the ego. Once we name what's in the unconscious—the opposite side of what we are feeling—then it's not hidden anymore and can't run our lives. We no longer get blindsided or feel victimized by life.

Until we are prepared to truly examine those things we don't like to look at—the uncomfortable feelings, childhood wounding, humiliating vulnerabilities and avaricious desires—we are still packing the suitcase, and the unconscious will secretly run our lives.

As long as we resist owning that everything in our world is part of us, we are still committed to living and dying in the prison of the separate system, playing the game of ego and being bound by its polarities of conscious-unconscious, victim-perpetrator and so forth.

I wanted to commit to owning everything in my world as part of me, but still needed to explore a few niggling questions.

Leslie, what about people who get away with things all the time and who never have to suffer the consequences—like shady politicians or corrupt CEOs or greedy bankers who are above the law? It seems like these people are getting away with murder, raping the environment and stepping on everyone all the time. If they can always be perpetrators until they die and if they never have to live out the opposite side of the polarity, then it seems like there are some people to whom these rules don't apply. So how can that be?

It does seem unfair, I know. But you have to look at multiple lives in that instance. Some people have to live out the opposite side in another life, which is what is known in the East as karma, *which literally translates as* action *and relates to the law of cause and effect. Jesus said, "As you sow, so shall you reap." We carry our karma with us from lifetime to lifetime. If you don't believe in reincarnation, then yes, it would seem like the rules don't apply to some people. But they do. Cause and effect is a universal law.*

And what about babies or very small children who are victimized in some way, like children with cancer or babies who are orphaned or suffer from some other kind of challenge? Surely infants aren't capable of stuffing anything into the unconscious and projecting it out?

Very often these souls have come in with some past-life karma to live out. Sometimes they choose to do it quickly and leave at a young age so they can get another body. Sometimes they have come in to teach everyone around them about something. For example, a sick or orphaned baby may be teaching people about opening the heart and developing compassion. There are many reasons.

And what about when a very large group of people, like an entire country, suffers a mass victimization—like a war or genocide? What's happening there?

There is something known as the mass mind, or the collective consciousness, of large groups of people. Because they all have shared experiences and a mutual culture, it is common for them to have similar egoic patterning, to have similar beliefs, likes and dislikes, to be thinking similar thoughts and to have similar fears. They have a similar way of denying, avoiding and suppressing things into the unconscious. So, as a collective they would have group karma and could experience a mass event of some kind, like a war or a genocide. That's also a very hard thing to reconcile inside oneself. It's impossible not to have compassion for people suffering from war or genocide. And yet there are certainly lessons to learn and karmas to live out by a nation or tribe, based on their own collective mind and their unconscious projections. In these instances it is especially important for group members to practice self-inquiry and eventually to try to come to the place of taking responsibility instead of blaming and ultimately, hopefully, finding forgiveness. Until that happens, the cycle is destined to continue repeating itself ad infinitum.

So, when you ask me to own everything in my world as part of me, what does that look like in this instance for example—if I were a victim in a war or genocide?

You would need to be willing to own your own violent, warlike side. You may not have acted it out much, and therefore it may be harder for you to see, but you would need to acknowledge that you have an unconscious side—like everyone on the planet—and that you are projecting your own unconscious violence, anger and hatred. You could say that you need to own your own inner warmonger and be willing to look at that.

And so once I've done this—owned the outside as me, made the unconscious conscious and started doing the processing work to clear the egoic shadow—then what happens? Do the perpetrators stop having power over me?

Yes! That's exactly what happens. The control shifts from the perpetrators' action to your response, which opens the door to true empowerment.

So, I don't actually have to do anything physical to stop the perpetrator? I can just sit in my chair, do the inner process and expect war mongers, tyrants and bullies to go away?

That's not what I'm saying. It doesn't mean you never take action. Of course it is very important at times to get off your meditation cushion and take action. But after you've cleared your consciousness, you are taking action from a place of greater balance, clarity and heart-centeredness, rather than as a "reaction." You act with responsibility, not as a victim trying to get revenge and to topple a tyrant. For example, rather than go out into the streets and protest in a rage, blaming the perpetrators, instead you should own the outside as you, process your own consciousness first, get as clear inside as you possibly can, and then go protest in the streets. Your protest will be a lot more effective and powerful. This way you are less likely to perpetuate the cycle of polarity. So, yes, at a certain point it is often important to stand up to the perpetrator, take action and say, "No, you must stop now!" That being said, this egoic clearing work has a certain magic, and sometimes you don't even have to get out of your chair to resolve a situation. If you process well enough, the issue in your life may resolve itself without your having to take action or even speak to anyone.

I was so engrossed in Leslie's tutorial that my tea had gotten cold.

So, that's a lot for today. Please sit with it, see how you feel about it, and when you feel ready to own everything in your world as part of you, let me know. Then I'll be happy to process with you. If you want to, you can make a sacred ritual out of this. You can light some candles, meditate for a while, then speak the words out loud to yourself and your spiritual guides, "I commit to own everything in my world as part of me." Or you can write it in your journal and make an offering of it to the Divine. Or you may choose to keep it very simple and just quietly make an inner resolution. It's up to you.

Thank you, Leslie. I'm ready to make the commitment, but I'm going to sit with all of this for a few days and perform a ritual at home. Then will you process with me next weekend?

Happily, Brad!

This commitment was a major milestone in my life, just as I had sensed it would be. Over the next weeks, months and years, Leslie processed with me whenever and however much I wanted, never asking for anything in return. Once I made the commitment and began to process, I grew in consciousness by leaps and bounds, evolving and transforming in ways I never could have imagined. Her gift was a treasure. I will always cherish it. Now I have committed to share it with others.

RELATIONSHIPS, NON-DUALITY AND MIRRORS

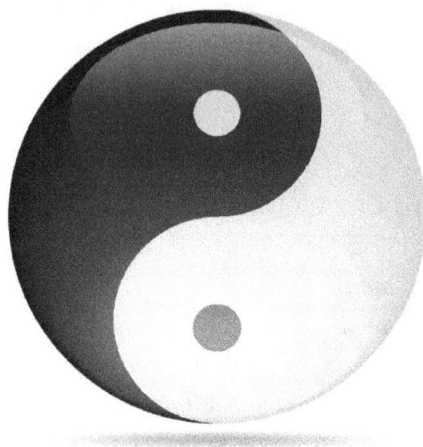

Our relationships in life offer a wonderful opportunity to resolve *otherness* and to become whole within ourselves. We tend to project many aspects of our own unconscious, particularly onto those closest to us and especially onto those we love. Therefore, when we make the commitment to own everything in our world as part of us, we must especially focus on our relationships. For example, we choose partners who serve our soul's needs in some way. Because opposites attract, we tend to find our counterpart in partners. Yin and yang complement each other in this way, as illustrated in the Taoist symbol.

In my case I projected onto Leslie an undeveloped, unfulfilled teacher aspect within me. Over the course of many years, I used the processing techniques explained in the following chapters to own and integrate that part of me—as well as many other projections. Through our relationship, I learned to see in Leslie this mirror of my own unconscious self. In the process I gradually came to discover and claim more and more of my wholeness, power and ultimately an ability to stand strong in the knowledge of the Self.

Life is the journey of reclaiming our wholeness. Through our relationships, we see ourselves in those we love—spouses, parents, children, siblings, co-workers or friends. The world is a mirror of our own unconscious self. As we recognize this, we find balance within, feel less separate and begin to experience unity consciousness.

The chapters ahead explore in much greater detail how this works. They will help you to know how to apply the principles in your own life. There is excitement and power in the understanding that we can take this responsibility and claim our birthright to wholeness.

CHAPTER 10

The Witness and Polarity Processing

❧

Hello, Leslie? Are you available to process with me now?

Of course, Brad. But why does our connection sound so echoey?

I'm taking a break at work, and I'm on the cordless phone in the toilet stall.

With clockwork regularity, at 10AM twice a week, I would phone Leslie to dialogue issues and process using the Marriage of Spirit techniques. As the administrative assistant to the Executive Director of a large non-profit, I was grateful to be working with an organization that was doing good in the world, but I was barely earning enough to survive, and the job was far from fulfilling. The monotony of working 9 to 5 (and usually longer), five days a week, mostly tied to my desk, was becoming increasingly challenging for me. I wanted to immerse myself in my passions—meditating and studying the wisdom teachings—but didn't have a clue how to make it happen.

Let's process your work situation, Brad. Maybe you can process your way out of there into something more fulfilling for you. Let's start by making a list of words describing your attitudes and beliefs about work and earning money. Write them down the left column of the page in your processing notebook.

Okay, let's see. . . .

I must work to earn money
Money is a necessary evil
Drudgery
Enslaved
Not fun
Unfulfilling
Boring
Dull
Monotonous
Work is a distraction from my passion
You can't earn money as a spiritual seeker or an artist
Work is not spiritual
Earning money is hard
Not living up to my potential
Trapped in a system
A cog in a wheel
Powerless
Frustrated
Discouraged
Angry
Sad
Hopeless
Meaningless
Worthless

Wow! That's a big one—worthlessness. I feel such a charge on that word. My whole body gets heavy and tired, and I feel like I want to cry a sea of tears.

Okay, that's a great start, Brad. So first it's important to get in your neutral observer, or what we call the witness. *That's the part of you that's watching the parade of emotions passing through you but is not identifying with them. It's critical to feel the emotions passing through you, to love them and to love yourself. Don't judge or suppress or deny them, but recognize that they are just part of the personality and not who you truly are. You are the perceiver, the pure awareness that is watching the play of the emotions, thoughts and the personality. Do you understand?*

I think so.

So, when we are identified with the personality, in other words when you think, "I am my personality," it is very difficult to see the limited self clearly. Who is it then that would be doing the seeing, if we think we are the personality? It would be like an eye trying to see itself, as Alan Watts said somewhere back in the 1960s.

To wake up, we have to choose to take the position of the witness and observe the personality from a viewpoint outside the personality structure itself. At first this takes a bit of reorientation but the fact that we can, in itself, proves that we are not exclusively locked into the personality. Nor are we only the personality. Our true nature is limitless consciousness. As we see and understand the limiting patterns in the personality, so are we liberated from them and able to know ourselves as eternal, loving presence.[22]

Leslie's words calmed the turbulent emotions roiling inside me. Taking them in was comforting and helped me to find a higher perspective on my churning inner reality.

The witness is neutral. Like the fulcrum of a teeter-totter, it is in the center and watches the flip-flopping play of the duality, but it does not identify with any one side of a polarity. It remains centered and balanced, just perceiving. Sometimes called the middle way or the razor's edge, the witness is not reactive or judgmental. It is neither attracted nor repulsed.

This is the rule of thumb for the yogi: Be neither attracted nor repulsed.

Developing the ability to view life from the neutral position assists enormously in extricating us from the turning cycles of the wheel of karma. It is like being in the eye of the storm or the hub of the wheel, watching the swirl of life's turbulence all around us from the still point in the center.

This does not mean that we never experience pain and pleasure or any other states of mind and emotions. These pairs of opposites are the juicy experiences of life itself. Rather, something else happens. An aspect of us, the witness, detaches from the extremes, from the swings between the negative and positive polarities, and just observes from that neutral place. The experience of flip-flopping from one side to the other continues to happen, but now we have a witness observing this flip-flopping. And that makes all the difference. It means that part of us, the witness, is not flip-flopping. It is just observing the action.

With the witness focused on the neutral place at the center point between negative and positive poles, the dynamic of all polarities changes. Awareness placed at the neutral place has the immediate effect of stabilizing the whole situation.

We are the witness, holding the central position between the extremes. Balance happens because we are no longer identifying with either of the poles. It becomes a new grounding point from which to view the changeable reality of polarized extremes. Normally we ground on one side of the polarized state and are forced to view life from that one-sided place. If instead we are grounded on the stable point in the center between the two extremes and witness them, we can choose to let them pass right through the awareness field, leaving us more stable, calm, and centered. Life still happens, but the witness has a view from the center which is much more all-encompassing. It allows us to be more dispassionate about the turbulent ocean of dramas, called life. It facilitates ascension to a higher vibratory state—beyond identification with polarized positions.[23]

As Leslie spoke, I visualized being at the fulcrum of the teeter-totter and began to identify more closely with the neutral place. No longer attached to the experience of worthlessness, I could just watch it pass through me.

It's important to distinguish between the witness and suppression or denial. Suppression and denial shove your emotions into the unconscious, which in fact only adds to your problems. It is important to feel. Yet you can learn to feel while observing from the neutral place.

Sometimes people also confuse the witness with an internalized parent who stands in judgment of their behaviors, thoughts and feelings. That is also unhelpful. As you do this shadow work, it is essential not to judge but instead to practice self-love and self-forgiveness. Most people tend to beat themselves up when they feel they are not "doing it right" or when they catch themselves in negativity. This tends to come from childhood or religious programming, and we can let all of that go. We learn to love and forgive ourselves. The witness does not judge; it only observes.

The witness is actually an opening in consciousness to the Self. It is the beginning of your conscious awareness of yourself as the Self.

Over time, as you strengthen and develop the witness, you become more established in it. You begin to see the dance of the world through the eyes of the witness, and eventually you begin to identify more with the witness or Self than you do with the small self. The small self is pushed and pulled by the dramas of life, but life is much less difficult when you are seeing and living from the place of the witness. You are able to feel more deeply, to live more passionately, yet not to take it all so seriously or get so dragged down by the negativity. This is possible because you know you are the Self, the pure awareness. You are the perceiver, and you see that the emotions are just passing through you.

The witness becomes your best friend on the journey of Self-discovery.

I had experienced a taste of the witness in relation to my feelings of worthlessness but was aware how easy it would be to slip into suppression or denial of really challenging emotions—a spiritual bypass. How tempting! I could also feel how easily self-judgment could slip into the equation.

POLARITY PROCESSING

I know, maintaining the neutral witness is simultaneously easy and difficult, but it will become stronger in you with practice. The next step is to name the opposites of the beliefs and attitudes on your list. Doing this one simple thing makes it much easier to remain in the neutral witness.

It's as Carl Jung said: When we hold the tension between two sides of a polarity, we allow room for a third option to manifest.

So now write down the opposite on the right side of the page.

Okay.

I must work to earn money	*I don't have to work to earn money*
Work is a necessary evil	*Work is a necessary good*
Work is drudgery	*Work is play*
Work enslaves me	*Work liberates me*
Work is not fun	*Work is fun*
Work is unfulfilling	*Work is fulfilling*
Work bores me	*Work energizes me*
Work is dull	*Work is inspiring*
Work is monotonous	*Work is diverse*
Work distracts me from my passion	*Work is my passion*
Artists and spiritual seekers are poor	*Artists and spiritual seekers are rich*
Work is not spiritual	*Work is spiritual*
Earning money is hard	*Earning money is easy*
Not living up to my potential	*Living my full potential*
Work traps me in a system	*Work frees me from the system*
I'm just a cog in a wheel	*I'm a spark of the divine flame*
Work leaves me powerless	*Work makes me powerful*
Work frustrates me	*Work satisfies me*
Work discourages me	*Work encourages me*
Angry	*Peaceful/loving*
Work makes me sad	*Work makes me happy*
Work leaves me hopeless	*Work leaves me hopeful*
Work is meaningless	*Work is meaningful*
Work is worthless	*Work is worthy*

Okay, Brad. Now read both lists again. See what an amazing list on the right side you've got stuffed into your unconscious. Recognize that you are not just the left-hand column. You are the right side, too. Isn't that liberating? Actually, you are both and you are neither. You are the pure awareness perceiving both sides of the polarities. You are the whole that is greater than the sum of its parts.

Reading through both lists from the place of the neutral observer, I began to feel a shift—at first subtly and then quite overtly. With a tingling evanescence all around me, I sensed something old dissolving in my aura. The top of my head felt like it was opening up, and a muscular tension in my neck and shoulders began to release.

Leslie, I'm not sure what's happening to me, but it's a good thing I'm sitting. It's uplifting, but it's a bit disorienting too.

You are re-wiring. You've made the unconscious conscious—you are now assimilating the shift, and everything is reconnecting inside you. You should hang up now and just sit in meditation for a few moments while the integration takes place.

Okay, thank you, Leslie. I'm so grateful for your help with this.

Before we hang up, let's make an offering to Spirit of the list and give it all back to the Oneness with a prayer. Please relax, and I'll say it now. Oh Eternity, please take all of these states of mind which are unbalanced in this pattern and balance and clear them. Do this so that we may see more clearly and find our way home more easily. We give thanks knowing it will be done. Amen. So now, Brad, just empty your mind and allow grace to do the work.

Grace was certainly working on me. The physical symptoms and internal shifting continued for some time, and I understood why Leslie called it a *re-wiring*. It literally felt like old circuits were being disconnected and new ones being created. I sat in the stall meditating for another few moments, allowing the consciousness to integrate before returning to my desk.

Amazingly, for months I was never questioned over my extended bathroom breaks and instead received sympathetic glances as I returned
to my work station—perhaps my colleagues thought it was impolite to
ask whether I was suffering from constipation. Constipation was not
far from the truth. However the constipation was in consciousness,
and the kind of releasing I did in that bathroom was not the kind they
imagined.

COMPARTMENTALIZING

Over the course of several months I went through radical shifts in consciousness relating to my attitudes, beliefs and perceptions about work,
money and spirituality. First we looked at how I was pigeonholing the
various aspects of my life. Leslie pointed out how the ego tends to
think of all of these things as separate and compartmentalizes them.
For example: I work during certain hours, I take my recreation when
work ends, my spiritual life is separate from my work life and family
life, I keep my relationship separate from work, I fit in caring for my
health separately from everything else, money is connected with work
but doesn't belong in my spiritual life, and so forth.

However, life's experiences flow organically and cannot fit neatly into
rigid categories. Therefore as long as the ego holds our different facets
of life in separate containers, we feel disconnected inside and remain
in limitation. So I did the processing. I processed as many of these
limiting beliefs and perceptions as I could identify.

With Leslie's guidance I also continued processing more childhood
imprinting around work, money and spirituality, expanding far beyond
the initial polarity list. Since we inherit the beliefs and attitudes of our
parents and of those who helped raise us, our egoic programming is
a reflection of those people, especially our parents. Our perceptions
of work, money and spirituality often replicate that of our parents;

however, sometimes they are polar opposites. For example, straight-laced, conservative parents can often have free-wheeling, hippie-like children, and vice versa.

More often than not, when we vow never to repeat a negative parental pattern, for example in cases of alcoholism and abuse, we do in fact end up reliving the pattern. Perhaps it is because by vowing not to do it, we distance and disown the behavior, forcing it into the unconscious. Yet, when under pressure, we tend to act without thinking, and the imprinted pattern erupts straight from the unconscious. Whether repeating the pattern or flip-flopping to the opposite side, we are still stuck in the separate system of duality. By processing the hidden shadows in the psyche, we can untie the knots in consciousness that keep us locked into the prison of egoic limitation.

Filling up many notebooks, I processed diligently and unraveled huge caches of egoic constructs. One, to be covered in the next chapter, was particularly all encompassing.

CHAPTER 11

Clearing Worthlessness and Shame

❧

Hey there, Mr. Worthless!

When Leslie greeted me with this salutation, tongue firmly planted in cheek, I did not laugh. Downcast and morose, I stared at the floor and slowly shuffled to my seat. Apparently my whole aura reeked of worthlessness, as that was all I had been feeling for weeks, and in spite of all my processing, there was no breaking through that painful knot in consciousness. Nothing was fun or funny. Moping and distressed, I was stuck in my sour, petulant mood. Not wanting anyone to try to cheer me up, I ignored Leslie's comment, grimaced and looked away. She just chuckled.

Come on! Life's not so bad. Let's meditate. Maybe that will cheer you up.

About five minutes into the meditation I started feeling a funny, tingling sensation in my stomach area that began to rise up to my heart and then my throat. It was like mischievous little Tinkerbelles flitting around inside me while trailing fairy dust with their magic wands, and it made me want to laugh. Someone was tickling me inside with light! I felt the corners of my mouth turn up and a smile begin to appear, but I quickly shut it down. Like a stubborn child, I refused to cooperate and maintained my pouty, frowny face. The tickling intensified until, like a tickle-tortured child, I burst into uncontrollable guffaws.

That's better, Leslie laughed.

The silence was broken, the meditation was over, and the rest of the group was staring at us, wondering what on Earth was so funny. Soon Leslie's contagious chuckling infected the whole class, and we all began to laugh hysterically.

Brad, why don't you come and see me one day soon. Let's process this worthlessness right out of your system.

That weekend I met Leslie in her apartment for a private processing session, and we unraveled some very interesting constructs in consciousness that helped bring about a breakthrough.

I saw that victim consciousness and the associated feelings of worthlessness were the linchpins of a matrix of egoic patterning with tentacles stuck to every facet of my life. Unraveling this pattern was key to living a more fulfilling life.

What's the opposite of worthlessness, Brad?

Well, I've been using worthy *when I do Marriage of Spirit processing at home.*

Okay, good, but I have a sense there's another opposite that might be better.

I can't think of one. Do you know of a better word?

How about arrogant?

Arrogant? As soon as Leslie said the word, everything began to shift and rearrange inside, like tumblers in a lock had just fallen into place.

That's it! But ouch! Even though I can see how this makes sense, it hurts to think of myself as arrogant. But I know especially when I was younger, I was such an arrogant asshole in so many ways. So now I'm living out the opposite side, right?

Yes. I understand how you feel. I went through the same thing at one point. It takes some humility to really examine yourself at this level. But humility can't come without some experience of humiliation. I know you've been feeling a bit humiliated lately, haven't you? What's the opposite of humiliation?

How about conceit? Or vanity?

Can you see how you've played both sides out in your life?

Yes, absolutely. I see that this pattern got set up long ago in childhood. As a child I was sensitive and had a strong feminine side, and I remember getting ridiculed until I learned to hide those qualities. I was so ashamed and humiliated that I overcompensated and overachieved. I built up an impenetrable barricade of masculinity, covering up anything that might remotely be construed as feminine. The fear of humiliation and the shame of my natural inclinations were strong motivations to hide anything that went against the rules of the boys' club. The competitive, conceited, macho façade was the opposite of how I felt inside.

Yes, exactly! Good seeing.

But I thought I had already processed that polarity. I mean, I had to work through so much of that just to find the courage to let people know I'm gay.

Yes. You took a huge step with that, and yet now you are at another level of the clearing process. Perhaps you didn't fully integrate the polarity but instead moved into its opposite side. That's what happens for most people—the constant flip-flopping of the polarities.

Of course, Leslie! I'm seeing it now. I moved from the shame of being gay into the pride of being gay. It's the polarity of shame and pride. Even though I healed a certain level of the shame, I obviously didn't clear it completely. I must have stuffed some of it into my unconscious and then moved into feeling its opposite—pride.

Okay, now we're getting somewhere. So, let's start a new list of polarities and see what we can come up with. No wonder you've been stuck in worthlessness for quite some time now. It's all related, and you needed to uncover all of this. So, write in your notebook the polarities you've mentioned so far.

Okay, so far I have:

Shame	*Pride*
Humiliation	*Conceit*
Worthlessness	*Arrogance*
Feminine	*Masculine*
Sensitive	*Insensitive*

That's a great start, Brad. Let's flesh this list out a bit. So much of it revolves around the split between masculine and feminine. I think we need to look closely at that polarity. Tell me more about what you're feeling about the polarization of masculine and feminine inside you.

Okay. I would say that my feminine side is linked to my artistic side. It feels very soft, vulnerable, receptive, refined and emotional—and so much more. Showing my feminine side—even though I'm openly gay—still makes me feel somehow weak, inferior and powerless, like I'm not enough of a man. I can't tell you what torture it was for me as a kid having to watch sports on TV with a bunch of competitive, dominating, macho guys when I would much rather have been creating art or cooking or doing almost anything else, but I was afraid I would have been called a sissy or a pansy or a momma's boy. I can see in retrospect that I felt like such a helpless victim.

That's a great start. So add those descriptive words to your list now.

Okay. Just so I can keep the themes together, I'm going to put the words that are my opposite in the right column:

Artistic
Soft
Vulnerable
Receptive
Refined
Emotional
Weak
Inferior
Powerless
I'm not enough of a man.
Torture to watch sports

                              Competitive
                              Dominating
                              Macho

Sissy
Pansy
A momma's boy
Helpless
Victim

Now let's find the opposites and put the whole list together.

I've got:

Shame	*Pride*
Humiliation	*Conceit*
Worthlessness	*Arrogance*
Feminine	*Masculine*
Sensitive	*Insensitive*
Artistic	*Macho*
Soft	*Hard*
Vulnerable	*Guarded*
Receptive	*Aggressive*
Refined	*Coarse/rough/brutish*
Emotional	*Logical/rational*
Weak	*Strong*
Inferior	*Superior*
Powerless	*Powerful*
I'm not enough of a man.	*I'm enough of a man.*
Torture to watch sports	*Love to watch sports*
Cooperative	*Competitive*
Submissive	*Dominating*
Effeminate	*Macho*
Sissy	*Manly*
Pansy	*Stud*
A momma's boy	*A man's man*
Helpless	*Potent*
Victim	*Perpetrator/tyrant*

Now take a look at these lists, Brad. Isn't it amazing to see the polarities you've been living out since childhood?

Yes! And I can't tell you how many guys in my life fit the description of the right-hand column!! And in fact that used to be me—or at least it was how I tried to present myself to the world.

So, now take it in that you are not just Mr. Worthless, who feels weak and powerless and not enough of a man. You are also powerful and strong and enough of a man. And you are also none of those things. You are the pure awareness, and these polarities are just the play of the duality passing through you. Can you commit to love both sides and love yourself? It's all ego, and it's time to let it go now.

Yes, I can. Wow, that feels amazing, Leslie! Thank you so much.

You are so welcome. We've begun unraveling a whole matrix of consciousness, and although there's still more work to do, you are going to start to feel very different. And soon you'll see physical shifts begin to happen in your life in ways you couldn't have imagined.

BALANCING LEFT AND RIGHT BRAIN

We continued processing, fleshing out the list and dialoguing the issues, most of the afternoon. The activity made me recognize the one-sidedness of our culture and education system. We are born with two sides to our brain, but only one side seems to be valued by the mainstream—the left side, which is associated with deductive reasoning, logic and linearity. These are of course yang/masculine qualities. Increasingly more focus is on math, science and technology, while the arts (such as music, drama and humanities)—associated with the right brain and yin/feminine side—are eliminated from the curriculum. At school, hard skills (reading, writing, math and science) are considered far more valuable than soft skills (emotional intelligence and interpersonal skills), even though success in life is arguably more dependent on the latter. Analysis, a left-brain function, is still seen as more valuable than synthesis, a right-brain function, yet synthesis is in fact the more difficult skill.

As I ruminated on my two lists and these cultural and educational imbalances, a synthesis of polarized themes became clear: Yang-yin, masculine-feminine, left-brain-right-brain, science-art and valuable-worthless. I shared this insight with Leslie, and in response she told me an important story about her spiritual awakening process.

Because my ex-husband was a doctor and I was an artist, we had frequent heated conversations about these polarized themes. He was so left-brained and I so right-brained, we could not see eye-to-eye much of the time. As a result of this mirror, I realized I had a lot of inner clearing work to do. When I was given the polarity processing technique by my guides, I used it to find greater balance within myself.

Later, my guides asked me to learn how to type—a left-brained skill. I was still right-brain prejudiced and resisted them tremendously because I had always thought if I ever learned to type I would be forced to become a secretary—one of my worst fears. They were so lovingly persistent I eventually relented and went to typing school. Little did I realize that this was just the beginning of a much bigger process of balancing my left- and right-brain.

When I got more serious about the journey of Self-discovery, my guides asked me to go to computer programming school, which I initially, flat out refused to do. I could not see the value in that level of left-brain development at all. Again they were so lovingly persistent that eventually I relented, trusting that they had my best interest at heart. What happened was such a gift. Each night after class I would sit in meditation and enter extraordinary, transcendent states of unity consciousness. Apparently the left-brain development was creating a balanced, whole-brain state within me. This was essential in order to ascend in consciousness.

Left- and right-brain balance opens a pathway for higher consciousness. Whole-brain functioning is infinitely more valuable than an over-dependence on either left- or right-brain.

In retrospect I realize this was catapulting me into the process of advanced spiritual awakening. I know now that to become absorbed into the oneness, it is essential to balance left- and right-brain—at least to some degree. So now I always recommend my students incorporate this practice.

Inspired by Leslie's story, I gained new understanding about my own journey of balancing left- and right-brain. Bouncing from the extremes of engineering to acting did not seem like such a senseless and polarized experience anymore. With newfound equilibrium and relief, I added the extra polarities to my growing list of opposites. When the process felt complete, we made an offering of the list to Spirit with a prayer, and then meditated together. It was a particularly powerful shifting of consciousness, and the integration and re-wiring continued for quite some time.

Balancing left- and right-brain is critical on the journey of Self-discovery. Developing a balance of yang/masculine and yin/feminine qualities creates a cycle of empowerment, which fosters our evolution, cultivates the opening of the heart and harnesses our spiritual warrior power.

CHAPTER 12

Squares

I have fantastic news. My guides have just given me the most amazing technique for processing shadow, and I can't wait to share it with you. It's even more powerful than polarity processing.

Addressing a few students in her apartment, Leslie had just returned from a one-month trip to Durango, Colorado, where she had been receiving healing treatments for chronic-fatigue syndrome.

This technique helped heal my chronic fatigue. I'm so excited about it that I drove through the night to share it with you today—without a trace of fatigue! It's called squares.

My guides told me that while polarity processing clears the mental and emotional bodies, squares clear the shadow out of the mental, emotional and physical bodies—all three. That's why it worked to heal my body so quickly.

Intuitively I knew that the issues with my body were a process and that its imbalances were mental-emotional overlays—subtle belief systems. I saw that since everything in the world is consciousness, including the body, and since processing shifts consciousness, processing also shifts the body.

Leslie's enthusiasm was contagious. We were on the edge of our seats, and we were thrilled to see her so well and full of energy.

Squares take the polarity processing technique a step further in making the unconscious conscious. They work by examining one of our core polarities—desire and fear.

Can you see how desire and fear are opposites? Desire is a pulling energy. We attract things to us with our desire. Fear is a pushing away. We try to repulse things we are afraid of. Our desires and fears create the dynamic of attraction and repulsion to everything in life.

So by looking at our desires and fears, or attractions and repulsions, the square technique takes any polarity you can name and breaks down each side of the polarity into two parts: We have a desire and a fear of each side of a polarity. That's what forms the four corners of the square.

I told my guides I wasn't going to get off the bed until I was healed. So they gave me the squares technique, and I did dozens of squares until I felt I had completed the healing.

Laughter erupted. We were all well aware of Leslie's unshakable resolve when it came to clearing consciousness, and we could easily envision her journaling away in bed for weeks on end.

Some of the polarities I used as the basis for the squares were things like health and sickness, old and young, strong and weak, and gravity and levity. I had a lot of subtle shifts doing these squares, but the really big shift came when I did a square on life and death.

I had to look at why I DESIRE TO LIVE, why I FEAR LIVING, why I DESIRE TO DIE and why I FEAR DYING.

When I completed doing this square and made an offering of it to Spirit just like with polarity processing, I felt all the subtle meridians in my body suddenly pop open. The energy began to flow in my body again, and I could tell the illness was gone. It was extraordinary. So you can see why I'm so excited to share this with you.

It's easier to explain how to do a square if we do an example. Who can suggest a polarity?

One student suggested, *How about victim-tyrant? That seems to be a common theme in most people's lives.* The rest of us nodded knowingly, and Leslie agreed. She pulled out a large, dry-erase board, drew a square at the top and continued:

Okay, first you write and number the four corners like this:

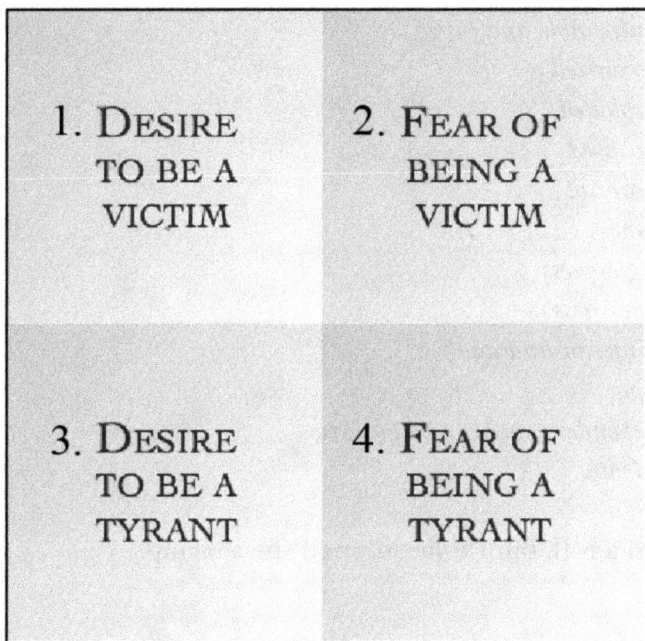

1. DESIRE TO BE A VICTIM	2. FEAR OF BEING A VICTIM
3. DESIRE TO BE A TYRANT	4. FEAR OF BEING A TYRANT

Then you explore each corner in your journal. Start with whichever corner you prefer and write about whatever comes to mind. Let's begin with, THE FEAR OF BEING A VICTIM.

As we each shared our thoughts and feelings, Leslie wrote them in a list on the board:

THE FEAR OF BEING A VICTIM:
It's embarrassing and humiliating.
I'll never get out of my rut.
powerlessness
loss of self-respect—as well as others' respect
fear of not being loved
fear of feeling worthless
passivity
pain
being vulnerable and pitied
being terrorized
being exploited
being betrayed
lack of control
hopelessness
meaninglessness
purposelessness
feeling inferior and weak
depressing
being dependent, needy and pathetic
fear of death

We were on a roll, but Leslie stopped the sharing.

Okay for the sake of time, that's enough for now. When you do this at home, feel free to fill up as many pages in your journal as you like. The more you write the better.

Before we move on, I just want to point out something to you about the nature of fear. Have you ever noticed that when you stop running from fear and actually face it, it no longer has power over you?

Just the other day I drew the Tarot card called The Devil. On this card you see there is a big, scary image of the Devil, and there are two small humans at his feet chained to the pedestal he is sitting on. They seem enslaved by this horrible monster who towers over them. However, if you look closely at the chains around their necks, you notice they are very loose. Their chains are so loose that the humans could easily just lift them off and be free. Why is this? It symbolizes the understanding that it is only our fear that enslaves us and that we can be free of that which is oppressing us simply by examining it.

So, the squares help with this. They give us an opportunity to make our fears conscious and therefore to be free of them—from the comfort of your own home!

Okay, so what do you get for the next corner, THE DESIRE TO BE A VICTIM?

There was a pregnant, puzzled pause. Finally someone broke the silence. *Leslie, I don't desire to be a victim. Why would anyone desire that?*

Good point! This would certainly seem to be the case at first, but actually if you look a little deeper, we all have all four corners inside us, no matter what the square is. If you can't think of anything to write in a corner, it means that corner is unconscious for you. You need to try to become conscious of the reasons you desire or fear that thing. It doesn't work to say one corner doesn't apply to you and then to skip over it. The point of the square is to make the unconscious corners conscious.

Can anyone think of any reason you might desire to be a victim?

With further cogitation I suggested, *How about to get sympathy and attention?*

Yes! Good one. Let's start a list. Can anyone think of other reasons?

Leslie began writing as we spoke:

THE DESIRE TO BE A VICTIM:
to get sympathy and attention
to be a martyr, which religion tells us is the way to get into Heaven
self-righteousness
at least I am harmless as a victim
I feel unworthy and therefore deserve to be a victim
balancing out bad karma
self-pity
belonging to the victim tribe and commiserating with other victims
to get pampering, nurturing and love
to blame others
to manipulate others
to suck others' energy
playing games
to feel innocent

don't have to take responsibility
justified anger/righteous indignation
As a child when I got sick, I'd get special treatment.

Wow, you really got some good ones for that corner even though it was hidden at first. Good work. So what about the next corner, THE FEAR OF BEING A TYRANT?

Because this was familiar to us, it seemed like an easy corner. Leslie continued scribing while we spoke:

THE FEAR OF BEING A TYRANT:
fear of retribution/being punished
responsible for consequences
bad karma
I would be lonely and unloved, without friends and family
fear of being despised
fear of power
fear of being unspiritual
fear of being cruel
could be fatal
fear of feeling separate
can't trust anyone
loss of love
being out of control
contributing to the destruction of the Earth

Okay, good enough for now. You can do more at home if you like. The last corner is THE DESIRE TO BE A TYRANT. What do you feel about this one?

Again there was a long silence. We were stumped. After a few moments Leslie broke the ice:

If you really can't think of any reason for a corner, one trick is to ask yourself why someone else would desire or fear that thing. For example ask yourself, "Why would Hitler want to be a tyrant?"

Confused, one student queried, *But Leslie, I'm not like Hitler. I don't want to be like Hitler.*

I'm not saying that you are like Hitler, or that you aspire to be like Hitler. But given that in truth we are not separate from the whole but instead united in consciousness, it is important to recognize that we do have all four corners of the square inside us. There are usually one or two corners that are unconscious. We want to make the unconscious conscious, so doing a square is a way to discover it.

With a hint of incredulity the student volunteered, *Okay, but still, I don't want to kill or harm anyone, not even unconsciously.*

I understand what you are feeling. If you don't think you have a killer instinct inside you, try to remember a time when you did, even if to a small degree. For example, was there ever a time when you were desperately trying to sleep but mosquitos were keeping you awake with their bites and high-pitched buzz in your ear? Can you ever recall a situation like that? At first it's just annoying, but eventually if sufficiently sleep-deprived, you start slapping at the buzzing or you may even become so enraged that you get out of bed, roll up a newspaper and start swatting them with all your might. Right? Who won't admit to having ever done something like that?

We all exchanged knowing glances and burst into fits of laughter. Although we were reluctant to admit to being so *un-spiritual*, we could all identify with Leslie's graphic picture.

Finally someone ventured, *to vent anger?*

Yes! That's the killer instinct, even if to some small degree. What else?
Leslie wrote the final list as we shared:

THE DESIRE TO BE A TYRANT:
venting anger and the killer instinct
revenge
to win
punishing others
to enjoy being cruel—sadistic
getting one's own way
having power and control over others
to have power and control over my own life
attention seeking
feel strong and superior
to manipulate and dominate
to have no fear
greed
to make others work so I can be lazy
to create order
to try to be a great leader
to feel immortal

Okay, congratulations! This is great work. You've made the unconscious
conscious, and you are almost done.

I could already see that we were all feeling much lighter, freer and
experiencing a significant shift in consciousness. Then one student
asked a pertinent question that was also on my mind:

Leslie, obviously we would want to let go of the desire to be a tyrant, but
what about the desires that I don't necessarily want to release? Things
like the desire to be successful, the desire for good health or the desire to
love and be loved? Are you saying I need to give up those things?

Excellent question. No, this is not about not having those things. The squares simply help us release our <u>attachments</u> to those things.

> *Letting go of an attachment to something is very different from not having that thing. Identifying and offering up the corners of a square help us to release things and to be unafraid of their opposites. Remember the rule of thumb for the yogi—Be neither attracted nor repulsed.*

Before we take the last step and make our offering, can you feel how this consciousness is quite "boxed-in" and dense? The square is a very a-dynamic or static form. When we call someone a "square," it means they are stuck and boring, doesn't it? This is because the dynamic wave energy of life has been contained in a box and cannot flow easily.

Each corner is an aspect of consciousness that is out of balance. It represents some part of the ego that pushes or pulls you off center. In the normal course of our lives, we tend to live out our desires and fears unconsciously. When we live by habit or by rote and don't examine the nature of our own egos, it can take years, or even lifetimes, to live out our desires and fears represented in one square. This translates as feeling boxed-in and stuck in life, and normally we don't even know why we feel this way.

> *Most people blame their unhappiness on the outside circumstances of their lives. Rather, we must look within in order to effect change in the outer world.*

When we are ignorant of this principle of changing the inner in order to change the outer, we unconsciously live out the effects of our desires and fears. In other words until we discover that what limits us is the inner, egoic conditioning, we can't consciously create significant change in our lives. We may try to change the outer appearance, the window dressing, for example by changing jobs or relationships or locations, but this is superficial. To create lasting change and greater happiness, we must address our egoic conditioning, which is rooted in our desires and fears.

This is why we often find that we have to keep repeating the same lessons and the same kinds of experiences over and over with just a change in scenery, and we feel caught in an endless loop. The squares help us to get out of the loops, grow faster and create change consciously.

So now let's give the whole square back to Spirit. We'll offer it up with a prayer, just like we do with the polarity processing technique.

We all got comfortable and sat quietly in meditation while Leslie spoke.

Oh Eternity, please take all of these states of mind which are unbalanced in this pattern and balance and clear them. Do this so that I may see more clearly and find my way home more easily. I give thanks knowing it will be done.

Just like with polarity processing, an internal pressure released and energy cleared after the prayer. I could feel a weight lift from my shoulders. Leslie continued:

It is important to remember at this point, after you have churned up all of this egoic stuff and emptied your cup, just to let it all go. You don't have to continue to analyze, fret or be the one to fix the situation. Spirit does the work for you after you have made the unconscious conscious. Remember that all of the desires and fears are not real; they are not who you are. You are pure awareness, and these states just pass through you. You can rest and relax after your offering, knowing that you are releasing everything. You can trust that grace will come in and bring you more into wholeness, balance and healing, more into the knowledge of who you truly are—the Self.

> *Once you have made the unconscious conscious, you don't have to continue searching for a solution. Release it completely so that Spirit can do the work.*

Like with polarity processing after you make your offering, remember to wait for grace. Try to remain in your neutral witness and be present and mindful so that you can be conscious of the shift. If you are sensitive, you may especially feel it in your body after doing a square. You may find new insights pouring in. Be open to a next step in your process being presented to you—from anyone and anywhere. If you don't feel the shift, that is okay; it is happening anyway. You can trust in that.[24]

We left Leslie's apartment that day realizing we had been given an extraordinary gift.

Twenty-five years have passed, and Leslie's chronic fatigue has never returned. Squares have been an integral and invaluable part of my journey of Self-discovery, as I know they have been for countless others. Amazing results have been reported from using the technique, some of which are documented in our book, *The Marriage of Spirit.*

CHAPTER 13

Samadhi

❧

I've been invited to go to Santa Fe, New Mexico, in October to offer a weekend of events. Would anyone like to come with me and help?

My hand shot up like a rocket. *A road trip with Leslie!* It didn't matter where we went—but *Santa Fe.* I had heard that it was a mecca for spiritual seekers because the energy of the land was so special. Shirley MacLaine wrote about meditating and exploring past lives there, and I knew it was also an artist's haven. Painters, sculptors, musicians and artists of all kinds flocked there because of its charm and beauty. The most notable was Georgia O'Keefe, who went there in the 1930s and became famous for painting its southwestern landscape and nature.

Looking around at the others gathered at the East-West Center, I was shocked, yet not disappointed, that I was the only volunteer.

Okay, Brad. Let's talk on the phone this week and make some plans. It's a two-day drive through the southwest, including the Mojave Desert, which is exquisitely beautiful and a mystical experience in itself. We can take my car and share the driving. Thank you for offering your support.

As the weeks passed, I planned and prepared excitedly. I hadn't taken any days off since beginning my job a year ago and therefore had plenty of vacation time.

Finally the day of departure. I woke early, but as I waited eagerly for Leslie to arrive, I began wondering what two days alone in a car with her would entail. Nervousness spread through my system. While an open-ended opportunity to process and talk about spirituality with her felt like a dream come true, there would also be no escape. What if the spotlight on the unconscious were too bright? I tried my best to ignore the feelings of trepidation.

Loading the car with our suitcases, I offered to drive first. A few hours into our journey, the noise, traffic and intensity of Los Angeles was behind us, and we entered a less populated part of southern California.

Brad, I have an incredible headache. I believe it's something you've brought into the car with you. You are quite wound up and nervous, and it's affecting me in a negative way. I'd like you to stop soon and buy some beer. If you drink a beer, you'll relax, and the trip will be easier for me. Maybe I'll have one too.

I'm not sure if I was more surprised by her candor or by the suggestion itself.

Mortified about giving her a headache, I knew it was a consequence of my excitement and fear. Despite her speaking the truth with compassion, I felt like a wrinkled little balloon and pulled over at the next opportunity to buy us a couple of Coronas.

As I struggled to overcome the shame and humiliation, the surreal nature of the situation suddenly struck me. *I can't believe I'm drinking beer before lunch on a road trip with my spiritual teacher!* Sitting together at a roadside restaurant, we each downed a cold one and started to giggle, which immediately lightened our moods and dispersed the tension. Leslie's plan was working. In retrospect I've learned from her occasional crazy wisdom that practical yet unorthodox methods are sometimes just the right thing for a breakthrough in consciousness.

Eating a little bit in order to absorb the alcohol, I felt ready to drive again, and we got back on the road. For the next few hours Leslie spoke about spiritual transformation and processed with me. Being quiet and alone together in the car for a long, unbroken period was conducive to going deep and breaking through some intense unconscious issues. Even while driving, I was able to focus on her words and guidance.

For two full days we processed, shared and absorbed the exquisite beauty of the Arizona and New Mexico landscape. The desert's mystical power seemed to carry us on angels' wings, buoyed by an invisible, supportive energy.

SANTA FE

As we neared Santa Fe, the dramatic and imposing Rocky Mountain range loomed in the distance like a great, sleeping dragon. A vast desert tableau surrounded us with rugged beauty, dotted only with scrubby cacti, juniper and *piñon* trees. We contemplated its immensity and barrenness, unspoiled by signs of human existence. Miles of *Chamisa*—a common local shrub—lined the freeway in full bloom, popping like giant yellow popcorn balls, cheerfully welcoming us.

> *Santa Fe's over there, right at the base of those big mountains. Can you see it?*

At the end of the straight-arrow freeway cutting through the desert, there were distant suggestions of civilization, which became clearer upon approach. A sort of camouflaged city, its earth-colored buildings, from light sand to dark brown, blended beautifully with the natural landscape.

All the structures here are built in adobe style, which is the original mud-brick construction that was brought up from Mexico by the Spanish in the early 1600s. It's very charming and has an older, more European feeling than any place I've ever been in the US. I'm sure it's part of the reason so many artists and spiritual seekers live here.

As an artist Leslie's keen eye for beauty gave her an instant fondness for Santa Fe. Living in the drab urban sprawl of Los Angeles for so many years had been hard.

I've only visited Santa Fe a couple of times before, but I was so drawn at one time that I almost decided to live here. When I first came, I remember loving the fact that there was a co-mingling of three races here: Anglo, Hispanic and Native American. Coming to the US from Apartheid in South Africa, I treasured the diversity and freedom and couldn't get enough of it. And there's a very tangible mystical quality, too, that drew me right in. The old downtown plaza has a sacred vortex around it, and if you are sensitive, you can feel it. In fact the name Santa Fe *means* the City of Holy Faith.

It was mid-afternoon as we approached the historic plaza, and the meeting with the event organizer wasn't for a couple of hours.

The two full days of processing in the car were the longest, non-stop, shadow-clearing marathon I'd ever done. Buoyant and super-charged, we sensed we were building to an energetic crescendo.

Let's park here and walk to the plaza, Brad. We can sit on a bench in the town square and continue the process.

Strolling past the shop windows, we gazed at the exquisite Native American turquoise and silver jewelry, the colorful southwest-style Pendleton blankets, the antique furniture stores and many other boutiques full of beautiful clothes, handicrafts and local charm. The grassy plaza area, shaded by several tall, deciduous trees beckoned to us. We took refuge from the heat of the high-desert sun and made ourselves comfortable on a bench.

Close your eyes, Brad, get meditative and put your attention on your shushumna. *I want to talk you through a guided meditation and a process.*

Shushumna is the Sanskrit word for the part of the subtle body anatomy corresponding roughly to the spine. It's the luminous core of enlightenment that is our central channel or axis.

I had felt my *shushumna* before, like a thin, fluorescent tube running from the crown chakra at the top of the head, down to the root chakra, at the perineum. Although the shushumna actually extends beyond our physical selves, we feel it in the body from root to crown.

All seven of the main chakras connect to the shushumna, like flowers blooming from their stem.

Kundalini energy, which is our primal life force energy, is coiled like a snake at the root chakra at the base of the shushumna. When the kundalini energy is awakened, it flows up the shushumna, and can be used for the purpose of reaching spiritual enlightenment. A yogic, meditative practice is to awaken the kundalini and draw it up the shushumna from root to crown. This is our inner divinity flowing through the spine and brain.

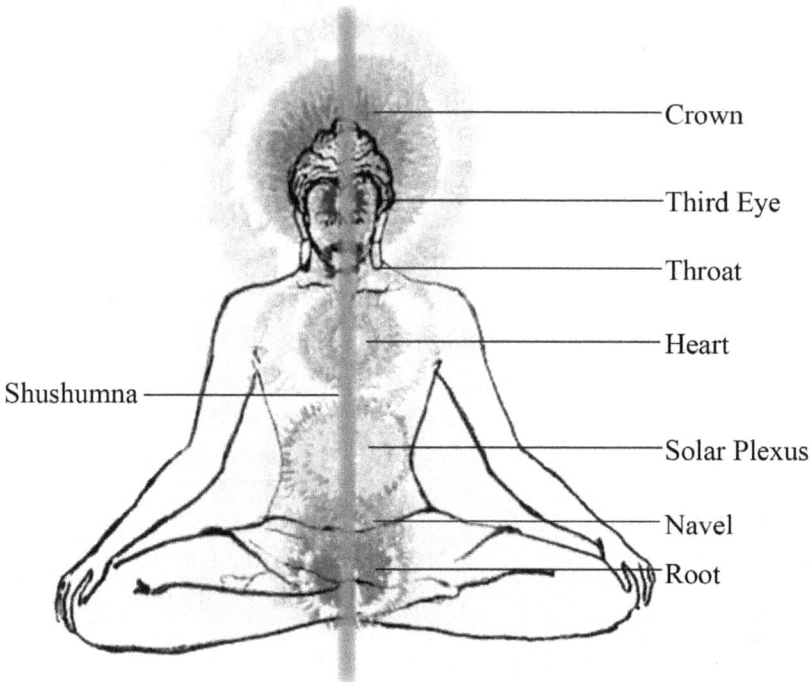

Crown

Third Eye

Throat

Heart

Shushumna

Solar Plexus

Navel

Root

The primary challenge, however, is that the kundalini can get stuck or diverted at any of the chakras in between root and crown and therefore never complete its journey up to the crown chakra. Egoic shadow processes cause constrictions in the subtle body and block the flow of kundalini. These egoic limitations are like knots in consciousness that contort its flow. When we clear the shadow issues, the kundalini can flow beyond the block and continue its journey up to the crown chakra.

After all the processing we've done in the past two days, your kundalini should be flowing beautifully throughout the shushumna; however, it is still blocked here at the third eye chakra, the point between and slightly above the eyebrows.

The third eye chakra, or the single eye, is where we perceive unity consciousness, and just below that is where we have two physical eyes, which is where we perceive duality, or the system of separation. Jesus referred to this when he said making your eye single fills your whole body with light. As long as the kundalini is blocked at the third eye, we see ourselves as separate from everything—from each other, from nature and from the Divine. When we can untie that knot in consciousness at the third eye, the kundalini flows freely there, and we experience unity consciousness, or non-duality. When the kundalini flows even beyond the third eye, up to the crown chakra, we experience our oneness with the All That Is. Put your attention at the third eye and tell me what you feel.

Having processed with Leslie in the car for two days, I was hypersensitive and could easily feel consciousness in the body. I became very aware of the kundalini being blocked at the level of the third eye.

I'm feeling a sense of separation there. I'm feeling like I'm all alone, disconnected and cut off from everything. I feel like I've lost God—like God has abandoned me—like Adam being kicked out of the Garden of Eden. God has betrayed me by putting me here on this planet, and I'm lost, alone and disconnected from the Source. It's an overwhelming sense of loss.

Okay, sit with that feeling for a few moments, but call in your neutral observer. Witness the feelings of loss, disconnection and separation, but recognize that is not who you are. You are pure awareness, pure consciousness. Essentially you are the perceiver, and those feelings are just passing through you. Can you see the truth of that?

Yes I do. I'm witnessing all of this from the place of the neutral observer.

So from this place, recognize that you are tapping into humanity's collective, original wound. At a primal level of consciousness, we all have this sense of separation and abandonment. It is imprinted into the soft clay of our being at birth when we experience separation from mother. When we are in the warm, cozy, nurturing womb, we are one with our mother, not separate from her. Then with the contractions we get expelled from this heavenly place and feel abandoned. And as children we project God onto our parents; they seem godlike to us. The wound is then re-imprinted every time our parents say no or disapprove of us. We feel cut off and abandoned. It's a primal human wound, like the parable of Adam and Eve getting kicked out of Heaven—total loss. Can you feel the truth of this?

Yes, I do. It's exactly what I'm witnessing pass through me.

Good, Brad. Now recognize there is really no such thing as loss at all. You never lost God. God is right inside you. God never abandoned or betrayed you and never went anywhere. God resides in the shushumna, right in your very own core. Become still and feel the truth of that. Feel the shushumna, and feel God inside you. Be still and know that you are one with God. Can you feel that? Can you feel that there really is no such thing as loss?

Yes! I do feel that.

So from this place, can you forgive God for apparently betraying you and abandoning you?

Leslie's question took me by surprise. I paused and did some soul searching before I could answer truthfully. Eventually I came to a place of profound surrender and let go of something very old—an ancient, knotted-up construct in consciousness far beyond the reach of my conscious mind.

Yes, I can forgive God. I can really see that there was no loss, there was no abandonment and there was no betrayal. It's odd because I'm saying I forgive God, but there's nothing to forgive because it never really happened, and there is no God outside of me anyway!

With a huge sigh, an enormous yoke of tension was released in my physical body. As I remained in meditation, a subtle yet profound shift in consciousness began to unfold. Keeping silent for several minutes, I noticed an energy moving in my body. It was a flow of kundalini going up my spine and out of the top of my head.

Such an intense wave of inner peace passed through me that I couldn't think or speak or move. My physical body seemed to dissolve and become transparent, and there was an overwhelming sense of having no mind. In a heightened experience of the here and now, I was flooded with a blissful serenity. Although I opened my mouth to try to describe to Leslie what was happening to me, I couldn't speak. There were no words.

Ssshhh. Don't try to think or speak. Just take some time to enjoy the feeling in your body and be with this new state. Let's walk slowly around the plaza. That will help you to ground the energy in your body.

Leslie quietly rose from the cocoon of our park bench. I stood slowly, put one foot mindfully in front of the other and remained as meditative as possible. In this state of heightened awareness and elation, everything was so beautiful. Even though the plaza was buzzing with people and activity, Leslie and I were in a state of suspended animation, enveloped in profound inner peace and stillness. We seemed to be held in a bubble of light and moved in slow motion amidst the thrumming crowd. Completely drunk on the light, I wondered what an outside observer would think of my weaving and bobbing. After quite some time, Leslie finally broke the silence.

If you buy a piece of Native American jewelry to commemorate this moment, every time you wear it, you'll remember how you're feeling right now.

We ambled over to the row of Native Americans seated along the north side of the square at the Palace of the Governors. Hopi, Navajo and Pueblo people with blankets spread out on the sidewalk displayed stunning pieces of silver and turquoise jewelry—earrings, necklaces, bracelets and more. I chose a bracelet made of many small, round pieces of turquoise strung together with a silver clasp. The maker of the piece, a Navajo woman, wrinkled with age and wisdom, smiled at me with kind, dark eyes as she put it on my wrist. Although always drawn to turquoise, I had never worn jewelry, so this felt like a true treasure, marking a very auspicious occasion. I thanked her, smiled and admired the beauty of the turquoise on my wrist.

As we strolled towards our car, I tried again to describe my state to Leslie but could barely speak. Fumbling for words, I fell far short of describing my shifting internal landscape.

Leslie, what's happening to me?

Your kundalini is flowing from root to crown, Brad. This is your first samadhi *experience. I didn't want to speak about it because I knew it would make you think, and as you think and try to speak, it's dissipating. When you recognized the illusion of loss, saw that you hadn't lost God and were able to forgive God for apparently abandoning and betraying you, you unlocked the third eye chakra, and the kundalini was able to flow through. Because of all the other shadow clearing work we did in the car the past two days, you had already opened up all of the other chakras, and the kundalini was already flowing up the shushumna from root to third eye. So this was the final step. And it's just a beginning. The kundalini is flowing only as wide as a thread. Eventually as you clear even more shadow and deepen your meditations, the flow of kundalini will widen, becoming a bigger and more permanent core of light, and you'll experience greater degrees of samadhi and unity consciousness.*

> *Samadhi is* the peace that passes all understanding *referred to in the Bible. It's difficult to understand with the human mind and much more difficult to try to describe. Really, it must be experienced rather than discussed.*

I'm so happy for you, Brad. And I'm happy for me too because now I have a friend to share samadhi with.

Leslie was right. Walking did help to ground the expanded state of consciousness into the physical body. By the time we returned to the car, I offered to drive, but she insisted on driving.

Friends don't let friends drive in samadhi!

Handing her the keys, I happily slid into the passenger seat, grateful not to be operating any heavy machinery. As we drove to meet the event organizer, I gave thanks to the city of holy faith for the blessing of this extraordinary initiation.

CHAPTER 14

Relationships and Intimacy

❧

I put a notice in the local paper about the darshan, but most people in Santa Fe come via word of mouth.

It was Friday morning, and our host in Santa Fe was preparing us for Leslie's events, which were scheduled to begin that night. She had put us up in an especially charming adobe *casita* (guesthouse) in a quiet, secluded neighborhood on the east side of Santa Fe, thickly forested with piñon trees. The main house on the property belonged to her friends, and they were happy to have us for a few days. In the peace of this little sanctuary, we felt incredibly nurtured after the two-day journey from Los Angeles.

When evening rolled around, we made our way to the venue, which was an enchanting space that held about fifty people, and I helped our host set the mood with candles and soothing music. Leslie sat in meditation in the front of the room. I greeted people outside the door, warmly welcoming them to the *darshan*[25] and suggested they sit and meditate.

Both Friday and Saturday nights were packed to capacity, but with a little squeezing everyone managed to fit. Leslie led meditations, gave healing transmissions of shakti, offered inspiring spiritual discourses and allowed time for questions and sharing. By the end of each evening, people left feeling radiant, joyful and spiritually rejuvenated.

For the Sunday morning event, we organized a bigger room to hold the growing group comfortably. By the end of the events we had made many deep connections. All were helped, everyone felt grateful, and some studied with Leslie for many years afterwards.

When it came time to leave on Monday, we had completely fallen in love with the magic and mystique of Santa Fe. New Mexico is not called the Land of Enchantment for nothing. As the high-desert morning sun gently warmed us, a crisp autumn chill nipped at our faces. The aspens were starting to turn a brilliant golden yellow as if competing with the bright, popcorn-like Chamisa blossoms. Intoxicated by the scent of juniper and piñon and the ecstatic clarity of the mountain air, we breathed it all in one last time as we loaded the car and pulled away.

Feeling high on the light, we headed for Sedona, Arizona, where we planned to spend the night on our way home. I had never been to Sedona, but Leslie told me that like Santa Fe it was a haven for spiritual seekers and artists—a smaller sister city. Set amidst giant, red-rock canyon walls, Sedona is a spiritual center with powerful energetic vortices, great natural beauty and abundant desert wildlife.

As before, we spent most of the drive processing, and Leslie offered a stream of spiritual teachings, which I was thrilled to receive. Having bonded much more deeply, our sharing was more intimate, and we learned about the details of each other's lives.

Arriving in Sedona after sunset with the light fading, we pulled in to a small motel on the main drag and went inside to ask for a couple of rooms.

Oh, I'm so sorry, but we are all sold out. In fact, the biggest convention of the year is happening right now, and I'll be surprised if you find any vacancies anywhere. Would you like me to call around for you?

While the gentleman kindly phoned other motels, Leslie and I sat in the lobby discussing the situation and our limited options. Very tired from the long weekend of events and travel, neither of us had the energy to press on to Phoenix, a megalopolis some distance away.

Okay, finally I found a room. It took some persuading and I'm pretty sure it's the last available room in the whole town. Shall I tell him to hold it for you?

Well, we're not a couple, so we really need two rooms.

Sorry, sir. Like I said, you are lucky to get this one—you won't find anything else in town tonight. The room does have two beds though.

I conferred privately with Leslie for a few moments, and despite feeling awkward about the situation, we both agreed it was safer and wiser to take it. I was not sure how I would cope with sleeping in the same room as Leslie and tried to hide my anxiety and fear. *At least there are two beds,* I thought.

I promise I'm not going to bite you!

I burst into laughter and the tension eased. A master of naming the obvious, Leslie certainly had a way with blunt humor.

There's no hiding from her! I guess I've revealed so much of my shadow at this point that a little more exposure shouldn't be a big deal.

No matter what I told myself, it still felt like a big deal. We drove to the new motel, checked in and got settled in our room. Taking turns in the bathroom, we brushed our teeth and changed into our pajamas, and I got into my bed, facing away from Leslie in order to give her privacy.

As I drifted to sleep, I remembered a touching passage in *Autobiography of a Yogi* by the great Indian saint, Paramahansa Yogananda, where after offering a significant amount of selfless service at the ashram, he was invited by his teacher, Sri Yukteswar, to sleep next to him one night, a rare privilege for which Yogananda felt extraordinarily honored.

I, too, felt deeply privileged. It was a sweet and intimate culmination of a remarkable journey.

HEADING HOME

Before we drive to LA, let's spend the morning exploring Sedona. It would be good to get some exercise and breathe the clean air before we return to the city.

Leslie's suggestion was a welcome one. After a delightful morning with our feet on the crimson earth of the canyon and hiking around Bell Rock, we shared some lunch and then reluctantly began the final leg of the journey home.

On the last day of this incredible adventure, I felt immensely blessed and aglow. Receiving so much shakti and spiritual wisdom had helped to quench, at least to some degree, my seemingly insatiable thirst for knowledge.

How's your consciousness, Brad? While you drive, why don't you feel into your subtle body again and see how your kundalini is flowing after all the breakthroughs of the past few days.

It's amazing, Leslie! I feel freer and clearer than I've ever felt in my life.

We spent the better part of the afternoon and evening sharing, laughing and processing. Day turned to night, Leslie got tired, and I suggested she recline her seat to sleep a bit.

While Leslie slept, we gradually emerged from the desert and approached densely populated southern California. I thoroughly enjoyed cruising along in my newly heightened state of awareness, feeling extremely expanded, without a thought or a care in the world. Passing through the town of Barstow and venturing deeper into the city of Los Angeles, I had the surreal experience of tapping into the thoughts of the mass mind, described in Chapter 6, The Power of Your Thoughts.

Around midnight when we exited the freeway to get to my apartment, Leslie finally awoke, and I enthusiastically shared with her my insights regarding the amazing occurrence. She listened intently and was especially amused when I told her about the I-want-a-beer-and-I-want-my-chick experience. We parked at the curb outside my apartment and continued chuckling and dialoguing till about 3AM.

Then it was time to part, but neither of us wanted to go home. We had enjoyed each other's company so tremendously and bonded so deeply that we wanted the adventure to continue. It was a sweet and touching moment.

Hey, I don't have to go back to work tomorrow. My boss told me to take as much time off as I want because I still have so much vacation coming to me. Let's get together tomorrow and pick up where we left off, okay?

In agreement, Leslie left me at my place and we made a plan to sleep in, call each other when we got up and rendezvous in the afternoon.

THE INITIATION

I'm so happy to see you, Brad! Welcome.

Me too!

I missed you, even though it's only been a few hours.

I feel the same way.

Please come in, and I'll make us some tea.

Standing in the doorway of Leslie's apartment, we beamed at each other. She looked as radiant as I felt. Waves of love passed between us like long-lost friends reunited. So much had happened in the past week that it felt like a lifetime. While sipping tea, we talked and recapped our whirlwind adventure.

We shared our thoughts, feelings and stories of the past many days, reminisced and laughed. Hours passed in a delightful camaraderie.

I realized that we had bonded so deeply on a spiritual, mental and emotional level over the past year, and especially the past week, that I felt more intimately connected to Leslie than I had ever felt to anyone in my life. And I knew she was feeling the same way. We shared a pure and profound heart connection that was new terrain for us both.

The inevitable consummation of our physical relationship is too personal in nature to share here. Suffice it to say that we both walked through enormous doorways that night. The choice to complete our relationship with sexual union required immense courage and trust from both of us. My hurdles around sexual identity and reverence for Leslie paralleled the barriers she faced.

There are too many stories of spiritual teachers whose sexual exploits with students have resulted in trauma for the student and disgrace for the teacher. So, Leslie did not enter into this situation lightly either. She had to muster her courage and jump off her own particular cliff. Much later she told me she had had huge resistance to it, but apparently her guides had told her repeatedly that it was meant to be. When they had whispered to her, *He's the one,* and indicated me, about a month prior, she didn't believe them. When they continued to indicate I was the one, she resisted and flat out refused—until that evening.

OUR RELATIONSHIP OF MANY LIFETIMES

Brad, my guides are telling me about some very interesting past lives we've shared.

In the morning we woke as if on honeymoon, side by side, giddy with excitement about our extraordinary, unusual and deeply loving relationship—an intimacy and heart connection like nothing either of us had experienced. In a playful mood we laughed and talked as the guides showed us several lifetimes.

There are many, but there's one in particular that they are saying is important for us to know about. Apparently we were Eskimos. I'm not sure exactly where or when this was, but it was clearly somewhere up in what's now Alaska or the Arctic. I was young and pretty, and my parents had arranged a marriage for me with a young man in my tribe, but I didn't love him. You and I were in love with each other. You were from a different tribe, but you were a loner. In fact you'd left your tribe, and you wanted to start a new tribe with me.

Conditions were harsh, but because you were an expert hunter, we knew we could survive together as a couple and create our own family even without the support of a larger tribe. When I refused to marry the boy my parents had chosen for me and insisted I wanted you, they threatened to banish me. To be sent out alone in that unforgiving environment would mean certain death.

Because I was resolute in my decision and refused to cooperate with their plans, they put me on an ice flow by myself and pushed me out to sea—to an inevitable death.

However, you were incredibly psychic and attuned to the natural world, and so telepathically you knew what had happened and where to find me. You paddled out in your canoe and found me, alone and near death.

You took me back to your camp and nursed me back to health. You had an igloo, and we stayed warm.

We used to sleep in a beautiful polar bear skin. And I'm being shown how you bravely hunted this huge polar bear. One day you were out fishing through a hole in the ice, and the polar bear spotted you from a distance. You saw him coming for you, and you knew there was no escape. It was going to be either him or you. It was an enormous bear. And all you had was some kind of small weapon, like a sharp blade fixed to the end of a short stick. You knew you'd have only one shot at it and would need flawless aim. You waited for him to get very close and make his move. When he raised himself to lunge at you, you thrust

*your spear into his heart. It was difficult because the rib cage protected
the heart, but you hit the target perfectly.*

As Leslie recounted this incredible tale, I re-experienced the incident.
I recalled that there was a moment of absolute quiet before I thrust
the spear, when my intense focus had tamed my thundering adrenalin,
and in that moment I had connected with the majestic bear. Other
details of this life began to flash back, and I could see bits and pieces
of the story, which we began putting together—recollecting lost parts
of ourselves. I recalled images of Leslie with our children, wrapped in
the furs of animals I had hunted. Although her features were different
from how she is now, her essence was the same. The angle of her ele-
gant neck, the slant of her cheekbones and the gentleness of her eyes
were deeply familiar. I caught glimpses of me teaching our sons the
art of hunting. Surprisingly I was authoritarian and intolerant of their
inattentiveness. I insisted on precision and obedience, as well as a deep
love and respect for the animals on whom we so totally depended. They
were such love-filled times. The joy and pride I felt as I paddled our big
family to meet my birth tribe was still visceral so many lifetimes later.

*Yes. That's exactly as I see it, Brad. And when we were old, the children
cared for us. And they started families of their own, which grew, and
grew, and . . . we created a whole tribe!*

The memories were so vivid that any doubts about their validity were
completely cleared. The guides were giving us both a precious gift at
this very special moment. Deeply touched by this knowledge, we held
hands and gazed into each other's eyes. Then in addition to the details
of the Eskimo story, the guides gave us both an energetic download, a
related gestalt of awareness about our current lifetime.

*Brad, I'm aware that one of the reasons the guides are showing us this
lifetime is because they want us to be conscious of drawing on some of*

the energies from it now. Even though we're living in a huge city like LA with all kinds of modern conveniences, we need to be as attuned to our environment as the Eskimos were to theirs. By using egoic clearing work and meditation to fine tune our consciousness, we are being shown how to live in the midst of a metropolis, in the busy, bustling material world, and still thrive spiritually. It's really the same skill set as the Eskimos. They used their intuition, psychic skills and energetic attunement to physically survive in an inhospitable environment, and we are using the same skills to raise our consciousness and flourish on the journey of Self-discovery in the belly of Babylon.

Knowing we had been together many times before and understanding about how ancient our love truly was, helped us to put the current events into perspective. Experiencing healing at a deep level of consciousness, we spent much of the day cocooning in Leslie's bedroom joyfully recalling, discovering and opening ourselves to new awareness.

Eventually we began to consider some of the practicalities of our situation.

Leslie, do you think we should tell anybody about us? I feel like we probably shouldn't say anything. At least not now.

I agree. Let's wait and see. I don't know how long this will last. I know we are together in a physical way now because the energies are supposed to come together, but I can't see how long it will take. I'm not being shown. It may be just for a few days, or maybe a week or two.

I'm okay with that.

And I feel it's important to be clear with you about how I'm feeling right now, Brad. I'm aware that both of us are fully committed to our own spiritual journeys, and that's our primary dedication in life. So, I feel as long as our being together in a physical relationship serves each of our highest spiritual journeys, then we need to continue to be together. How does that sound to you?

That feels right to me. Absolutely.

And as soon as that's not the case, then we should end the physical relationship.

I agree, Leslie. The relationship is secondary to each of our personal spiritual journeys. So, why don't we have a check-in every morning? And if we both get a yes to being together, then we stay in a relationship that day. As soon as we get a no, then we know it's complete, and we end the physical relationship. Okay?

Yes, I agree.

We continued to check-in faithfully every morning, each of us asking inwardly if being together physically served our own individual spiritual journey in the highest way. Every morning we both got a yes. To our great surprise and delight, this continued for several weeks.

However, we also realized that our increased intimacy was generating concerns and confusion among other students.

Eventually one of the students confronted Leslie privately regarding her suspicions. Confirming that we were in a relationship, Leslie explained as much as she felt appropriate. The conversation did not go well; anger, accusation and judgment, arising no doubt from confusion and fear, were hurled towards Leslie. We realized that we needed to explain ourselves to the group in order to give everyone a chance to understand.

It was a challenging time for Leslie, me and our little circle of friends. The news shocked people, and responses varied. Although some were more accepting than others, waves of emotional turbulence rippled through the group.

So many societal stereotypes were tested by our relationship—not only was I gay and she my teacher, but she was also sixteen years older. While it was understandable that Leslie's students would have mixed feelings, we also knew we needed to be unattached to anyone's approval or disapproval. We were standing in our love and our truth and had no reason to hide or to seek validation from anyone. However, at the same time we understood and felt compassion for anyone whose faith may have been shaken as a result of our relationship.

As the weeks of yes responses to our morning check-in passed, we decided that a weekly check-in was sufficient. Every week we would each get a yes.

Our love deepened and grew, and our relationship continued to support us in new levels of spiritual development. Weeks turned into months, and we agreed that a monthly check-in would be sufficient.

Eventually we agreed to have our check-in once a year. Over the past twenty-four years we have always gotten a yes, so we have remained in a committed and monogamous relationship.

Our profound love has continued to serve each of our highest spiritual paths, and we have shared a mission to extend enlightenment and love in the world. We have always agreed that the relationship is secondary to our personal journeys in consciousness, and for almost two and a half decades, we have served each other in equal but different ways.

YIN-YANG BALANCE

Balancing yin and yang principles and creating a complementary relationship has been at the heart of our journey together. Because of our lack of competition, neither of us feels the need to manipulate, dominate or control the other in order to win. We aren't in a polarized contest of dominance-subservience, superiority-inferiority or power-powerlessness. Walking this path has served us well, not just because it creates a harmonious, egalitarian relationship but also because it has allowed each of us to develop those aspects of ourselves needing true and balanced empowerment. For example, in managing our non-profit, CoreLight, which was born shortly after our relationship began, I needed to harness my drive, energy and organizational skills. These yang qualities were used in celebration, support and nurturance of Leslie's yin power. Creating a worldly structure through which her spiritual teachings and shakti could reach more people allowed me the opportunity to cultivate my yang side, which had, until then been inadequately channeled. This also has allowed Leslie to express more completely her yin power and to flower into her own fullness and radiance. Truly a win-win!

Complementing each other in our expressions of yin and yang has served us both in our individual spiritual development and in fulfilling the purpose for which our souls incarnated.

> When yang is used to serve, honor, support and complement yin, rather than to compete with, dominate or control yin, empowerment and balance are the result.

I am immensely blessed to be in this relationship. It has been an extraordinary gift to support Leslie and help create the structures through which her teachings can be shared with the world. Through this blessing, I have evolved spiritually and become empowered as a teacher myself.

TRUE INTIMACY

We had been together for almost two years when a close friend of ours offered us an astrology reading as a couple. We agreed, and he came to us later with our astrology charts in hand, clearly aghast.

You two shouldn't be together! Your charts are not compatible at all! I don't understand. This can't work.

Our relationship is truly unconventional and although many people from various disciplines believed us to be incompatible as a couple, it has worked. Because it has always been based in the heart and is in support of our highest spiritual paths, it transcends egoic compatibilities such as personality traits, sexual attraction, power dynamics and status—and it also transcends astrology.

Ultimately what we found in each other was true intimacy, a very rare and precious thing. Our experience has been that love and intimacy are the most satisfying and lasting aspects of any relationship, sexual or not. A profound heart connection and true intimacy break through the barriers of the system of separation. In those priceless moments we touch the Self, as embodied in the other person, and we experience the fulfillment we are constantly seeking, even if just in a fleeting moment.

> The fundamental need at the core of every desire, including the desire for sex and relationships, is to know the Self. We think we are looking for an attractive and compatible mate, whom we believe will fulfill us, and having an attractive and compatible mate can feel very satisfying. However, ultimately what we are seeking is to know who we truly are—to find the union with our own divine Self.

The ego locks us into the separate system, causing us to feel incomplete, alone and isolated most of the time. But some part of us remembers who we truly are—the vast, cosmic Self—and we crave to find that elusive connection again. We chase our goals and desires hoping to experience divine completeness once more. If we are lucky, through moments of love, intimacy and service, we may sometimes even touch the Self. This occurs briefly during an orgasm, and it may even last a bit longer if we are fortunate enough to have a compatible mate who can access the heart. However, it rarely lasts because the ego usually gets in the way and asserts its limitations, fears and preferences. We keep seeking the Self, and round and round we go with egoic desires in search of that fulfillment in the system of separation.

Through the practice of meditation and ego clearing, we wake up to our true nature, which is pure love. We realize that the fulfillment we seek is not in another person; it is inside us, and this changes the equation completely. When we access the Self within and become love, we are no longer dependent on any outside source for our fulfillment.

Seeking the fulfillment outside us in a partner, or in any outside form, will ultimately not succeed, at least not all of the time. It is only in living in the heart and touching our own core of spiritual light that we find true fulfillment. And when we live established in heart consciousness, it can't be taken away by the capricious whims of the system of duality. Even if a relationship breaks up or if we experience a loss of some kind, we still have the connection to our own heart, and we still have the capacity to access the Self.

Living with a cleared ego and an established connection to the heart, we draw to us others of like mind and spirit. The relationships we create from this place will be a mirror of that clear and loving place inside us. And this is where a profound and lasting intimacy is possible.

Authentic exploration of relationships from this place allows us to reconcile the duality of our world. While our egos hold tightly to their perception of separation, we live in *relationship* with everyone and everything around us, and it is through these relationships with that which we perceive to be outside of us that we learn about who we are. The more attuned we are to our relationships, the better we are able to integrate that which appears separate from us. This is one of the primary ways we grow towards wholeness. For example I learned through my relationship with Leslie about my unincorporated, projected teacher role and ultimately how to own my spiritual power and authority.

Entering into relationships consciously, lovingly and with the intention to be true to ourselves is one of the most valuable, rewarding and effective paths towards knowledge of the Self and towards achieving the true fulfillment we seek.

Experiencing loving relationships is one of life's greatest gifts we are here on Earth to enjoy.

THE PORTRAIT

Leslie, what is this painting?

Oh my goodness! I can't believe my mother saved it. I painted it when I was fifteen years old. My mother always thought it was a portrait of my younger brother, but it wasn't. I don't know who it was. I gave him blue eyes, and my brother has brown eyes. I don't know why I painted him. He was the little mystery boy.

Although this story puts us ahead of the timeline by about a decade, it feels important to share it here. After Leslie's father died in 2001 in Johannesburg, we were cleaning out an old closet in her parents' house, and I found the painting, which had turned yellowish brown with age but was still clear enough to make out the features. While she was debating about whether to keep it or purge it, I stared at the painting, surprised by how much it looked like me as a young boy.

Leslie, tell me more about why you painted this?

Well, we were living in Aden, a seaport city in Yemen, for about a year because my father had work in the Middle East, and I had become incredibly ill. In fact I went through periods of extreme delirium, and they thought I might die. I remember leaving my body during hallucinations, but I got through it and lived to tell the tale. Afterwards my mother bought me some paints and brushes to keep me entertained during my recuperation, and the painting just came through me. I normally painted abstracts and landscapes, never portraits, certainly not of strangers. And like I said, I have no idea who the little boy with blond hair and blue eyes was. Interestingly I painted a large golden-yellow halo behind his head. Can you see it there? My mother convinced me it was a straw hat slung behind him, so I actually added some features to make it look a little like a straw hat, but I've always known it was a halo.

So if you were fifteen at the time you painted him that would have been 1961–62, right?

Yes. That's about the time we lived in Aden.

Do you remember more or less when during that time you painted it—what month?

Well, let's see... I had to miss school for the illness and was recuperating right before summer vacation began, so I must have painted it around early May of 1962. But why do ask?

Leslie! That's right when I was born! Early May of 1962.

Oh my goodness.

And oddly enough it reminds me very much of a pastel portrait of me that my parents commissioned when I was eight years old. Leslie, I think you painted me! I think some part of you checked out of your body during your delirium and came over to the US to be with me and to support my birth.

I think you're right. And you know something else, Brad? I remember when I was very little, maybe about six years old, I asked Spirit who I was going to marry, and a voice said, "A man in America." I held onto that memory for the longest time, but when I married my first husband, who was South African, I discounted what the guide had told me, figuring it was misinformation.

Wreathed in smiles and reeling with excitement, we gazed at the painting and at each other, marveling at the incredible magic of it all. Spirit works in mysterious ways, indeed.

Needless to say we didn't purge the painting. It still hangs in our home and serves as a constant reminder of our enduring soul connection and of our predestined relationship in this life.

Leslie's portrait, May 1962, my birthdate.   *Commissioned portrait, July 1971, age 9.*

In both portraits the eyes and shirt are blue, and the hair is blond. See color versions at: www.CoreLight.org/LivingWithEnlightenment_photos/.

CHAPTER 15

Sexuality

❧

How can a gay man and a heterosexual woman be in a monogamous relationship for two and a half decades?

To call my relationship with Leslie unconventional is perhaps an understatement, and people often wonder how it can possibly work.[26]

Gay, straight, homosexual, heterosexual and *bisexual* are all merely labels, and although labels are not in and of themselves bad or wrong, they are limited and limiting. As soon as you label something, you cement it into rigid forms. The human mind has a natural proclivity for defining things because it is our way of processing and understanding our world. It eliminates uncertainty and formlessness, bringing things into the realm of the known and tangible. For most, this usually feels more comfortable. However, drawing a boundary around something, including sexuality and gender, is incredibly restricting. Sexual orientation and gender identity[27] fall on a continuum rather than a binary scale, with a large gray area between the black and white.

Our sexuality, like every other aspect of our being, changes as we grow, age and evolve in consciousness. We are born into this world with lessons to learn and experiences to have regarding our sexuality and gender. As we clear the ego and develop spiritually, we change in many ways, some of which are surprising to us—and all of which bring us closer to an understanding of who we truly are. The journey of Self-discovery is inextricably linked to change and transformation. For some that may involve examining their sexual orientation or gender identity.

Choosing a path of Self-discovery does not mean your sexual orientation will change. During discussions on this subject, I have seen a wave of fear and horror sweep across faces, so it feels important to make this clear.

You never have to do anything that is against the essence of who you are, and it's critical to question any individual or institution that insists you do. Religious institutions, especially, have been known to impose rules, prohibitions and dogmas regarding sexuality and gender. Unfortunately this has resulted in a lot of confusion, pain and suffering.

It also feels important to state clearly that my relationship with Leslie has nothing to do with *fixing gayness,* and should never be used as an example of that. There is no reason to fix gayness because being gay is not broken. If anyone is in judgment of their own or another's sexuality, for example feeling ashamed or condemnation, then it is time to do some processing and clear the relevant mental-emotional issues. My relationship with Leslie has been an *adding to* experience, not a *subtracting from,* and through it I have learned extraordinary lessons about my own masculine and feminine sides, as I also learned through relationships with men before I met Leslie.

Our sexual orientation and gender identification—whatever they may be—are reasons for celebration. We are each an expression of the Divine, and no one is bad or wrong. Every human is a soul who has come here to have physical experience on this planet, and each expression is a unique and individual reflection of the Divine. There is no such thing as a good or bad or right or wrong expression. *Only thinking makes it so,* as Shakespeare said. We should celebrate and explore sexuality and gender, as long as all involved are adults making their own free choice for the highest expression of themselves.

We all have both male and female sex hormones and, although we tend to be closer to one of the genders, no one is completely one or the other. Those who fall in the so-called gray area, although it has its many challenges, have a wonderful opportunity to explore both masculine and feminine, in ourselves and in others.

Nowadays the taboos surrounding sexuality and gender have significantly lessened since my childhood in the 1970s. Although significant prejudice and discrimination certainly still exist, the degree of liberation is extraordinary and would have been unthinkable just a few short years ago. The younger generation treats sexuality and gender identity in a much more fluid and playful way—the growing transgender movement being one example. In fact norms are such that younger readers often have trouble understanding why LGBT discrimination exists in the first place.

BALANCING MASCULINE AND FEMININE

Balancing our masculine/yang and feminine/yin sides is essential preparation for becoming established in heart-centered consciousness. In order to balance masculine and feminine inside us, we must examine and process our likes, dislikes, attractions and repulsions regarding these perceived polarities—not only inside us but also in our relationships with men and women. Because everything in our outer world is a mirror of what's inside us, ultimately it is important to own it and process it.

We each have a masculine and a feminine side, and although the two appear to be opposites, in reality they are complementary parts of a whole, and we each contain some degree of both. Jung referred to this concept as the *anima* and *animus*. The anima is the hidden feminine within the man, and the animus is the hidden masculine within the woman.

> *Every man carries within him the eternal image of woman, not the image of this or that particular woman, but a definite feminine image. This image is fundamentally unconscious; an hereditary factor of primordial origin engraved in the living organic system of the man, an imprint or "archetype" of all the ancestral experiences of the female, a deposit, as it were, of all the impressions ever made by woman—in short, an inherited system of psychic adaptation. Even if no women existed, it would still be possible, at any given time, to deduce from this unconscious image exactly how a woman would have to be constituted psychically. The same is true of the woman: she too has her inborn image of man.*[28]

Depending on many factors, including gender, one side is usually more conscious than the other. Most people identify heavily with one side and tend to suppress the other. Generally speaking, women have a more conscious feminine side with an unconscious masculine while men have a more conscious masculine side and unconscious feminine side. For example a man who is raised in a culture that rewards masculinity and punishes femininity in men—like most cultures—tends to suppress his own feminine side, banishing it to the unconscious realms. But as we know, pushing something into the unconscious does not mean that it goes away. The unconscious manifests in our lives in the form of other people with whom we interact and form relationships. In other words we draw our own shadow to us by suppressing it and projecting it onto other people and situations in our world. So, using our example above, the man who suppresses his feminine side draws into his orbit people and events which enact his own feminine side for him. As Jung explains:

The persona, the ideal picture of a man as he should be, is inwardly compensated by feminine weakness, and as the individual outwardly plays the strong man, so he becomes inwardly a woman, i.e., the anima, for it is the anima that reacts to the persona. But because the inner world is dark and invisible to the extraverted consciousness, and because a man is all the less capable of conceiving his weaknesses the more he is identified with the persona, the persona's counterpart, the anima, remains completely in the dark and is at once projected, so that our hero comes under the heel of his wife's slipper.

If this results in a considerable increase of her power, she will acquit herself none too well. She becomes inferior, thus providing her husband with the welcome proof that it is not he, the hero, who is inferior in private, but his wife. In return the wife can cherish the illusion, so attractive to many, that at least she has married a hero, unperturbed by her own uselessness. This little game of illusion is often taken to be the whole meaning of life.[29]

Although Jung's above interpretation was formulated in a different era and may appear overtly chauvinistic, it warns us of the dire consequences of playing out our imprinted gender roles in an unconscious manner. Every person on the planet has a different way of manifesting the masculine and feminine. There are countless facets to this diamond of yin/yang appearance and personality expression.

For 7.4 billion people on the planet, there are 7.4 billion different permutations of masculine and feminine personalities—and sexualities.

In the 1940s and '50s, Dr. Alfred Kinsey and his colleagues published *The Kinsey Reports*, two books based on extensive scientific research on human sexual behavior. The reports were controversial not only because they addressed a taboo subject but also because they challenged the existing beliefs of the general public. In the first book, *Sexual Behavior in the Human Male*, Kinsey said:

> *Males do not represent two discrete populations, heterosexual and homosexual. The world is not to be divided into sheep and goats. It is a fundamental of taxonomy that nature rarely deals with discrete categories. . . . The living world is a continuum in each and every one of its aspects. [Chapter 21]*

The Kinsey team created a seven-point scale from 0–6 to measure overall balance between homosexuality and heterosexuality, with 0 being completely heterosexual and 6 being completely homosexual. Interviewing thousands of people, the research showed a traditional bell curve with a very high percentage of sexual behavior that fell somewhere in the middle of the scale.[30]

Kinsey's research is fascinating and focuses on sexual behaviors and desires. Leslie and I have researched how the personality identifies with masculine-feminine issues from the perspective of the soul. We have discovered that heterosexual men's and women's identification correlates with their biological gender, and LGBTs identify with a midscale range. Most people experience themselves on a limited gender bandwidth and rarely move beyond it, even if their sexual behavior is more flexible. This is because the personality prototype, developed prior to incarnation, encompasses the bandwidth each soul needs for the desired explorations of masculine, feminine, sexuality and gender.

Wherever we fall on the scale, these parameters reflect the limitation of the ego. Ultimately on the path of Self-discovery, we recognize that we are not this small self. We are the vast, eternal Self.

No matter where one is on the masculine-feminine scale, it is only ego—an identification with a personality pattern.

The ultimate truth in terms of masculinity, femininity, sexual orientation and gender identity is that we are so much more than how the body defines us.

Our souls incarnate multiple times, sometimes as male and sometimes as female. Some degree of bisexuality is natural and normal, because most souls have had incarnations as both genders over time, and at some level of our being we remember lifetimes as both.

Evolved souls—no matter their sexual orientation or gender identity in this lifetime—strive to have great love, respect and compassion for all, regardless of placement on the sexuality/gender spectrum.

After all, we are not the body. We are souls incarnating on this planet, wearing physical bodies on loan from Mother Earth for a short time. At death we drop the body like slipping off an overcoat, but remain, as pure essence, the Spirit we truly are. We are eternal, timeless, transcendent awareness, and this body is just a temporary temple in which we reside for a few years.

As Teilhard de Chardin said:

> *We are not human beings on a spiritual journey.*
> *We are spiritual beings on a human journey.*

And as Yogananda's teacher, Sri Yukteswar, said:

In sleep, you do not know whether you are a man or a woman. . . . Just as a man, impersonating a woman, does not become one, so the soul, impersonating both man and woman, has no sex. The soul is the pure, changeless image of God.[31]

THE COMMITMENT TO EMBODY LOVE

According to ancient Tantric practices the god and goddess are embodied in each partner in a holy, co-creative ritual. Lovemaking becomes a sacred act through which we consecrate our love for the Divine with our partner.

From the *Vijnana Bhairava Tantra.*[32]

> *As the fires build in sexual joy*
> *Enter that blessed place between the legs,*
> *Embrace the holy energy shimmering there.*
>
> *Follow the rising flow,*
> *undulating throughout the spine,*
> *Shivering with pleasure.*
>
> *As the fire intensifies*
> *And flashes upwards,*
> *Suspend the breath for a moment.*
> *Throw your whole self in.*
>
> *Become brilliance in your bodily form,*
> *In union with primordial bliss.*

At the moment of orgasm
The truth is illumined—
The one everyone longs for.

Lovemaking is riding the currents of excitation
Into revelation.
Two rivers run together,
The body becomes quivering.

No inside and no outside—
Only the delight of union.
The mind releases itself into divine energy,
And the body knows where it comes from.

This is reality, and it is always here.
Everyone craves the Source
And it is always everywhere.

When we devote our sexual life to the worship of the divine essence in each of us, it is an initiation into a new level of embodiment of the Self.

Many of us on a path of Self-discovery have had lifetimes in monasteries and on mountaintops and learned in those lives to control the libido, to overcome the addiction to sex and to conserve and use the kundalini life force energy for spiritual awakening. Now we are here to live and work in the world and to find spirit in everything, including relationships, sex, money and work. The path of embodiment is an evolutionary imperative.

We haven't got many role models; therefore, if you are doing this work, you may feel like a pioneer. If you feel you are part of this tribe, you will likely help others through your example.

If Leslie and I could model only one aspect of our relationship, it would be our spiritual evolution through a commitment founded on love. Having lived and worked together almost inseparably for more than two decades, we continue to grow in love. We have both dedicated our lives to embodying the spiritual energies, and our relationship has been part of that commitment.

This kind of realization of potential through relationships is highlighted in Barbara Marx Hubbard's *Emergence: The Shift from Ego to Essence*, in which she talks about stages in development of a new, more interconnected consciousness. This consciousness requires a transcendence in which *Homo sapiens* evolve to *Homo universalis*, and the developmental process focuses on co-creation instead of just procreation:

> *We shift from the emphasis on sexual reproduction towards "suprasexual co-creation," moving from self-reproduction to self-evolution. Our sexuality evolves and vitalizes all areas of our creativity. We long to join not only our genes to reproduce biologically but our genius to give birth to the potential in one another.*[33]

CHAPTER 16

Work, Money and Living in the Flow

❧

Leslie, why don't we live in Santa Fe and commute to Los Angeles instead of the other way around? You have groups of students in both cities, and I'd be happy to quit my job and find other work in Santa Fe.

It would be nice, Brad, but my guides are suggesting it's not time yet.

Although we had both loved living in Los Angeles, we were getting very tired of the noise, smog, traffic and crowds. In the few months that had passed since we had visited Santa Fe, Leslie had returned there, offered more events and had a growing group of students. The dream of moving to Santa Fe continued to entice us.

We revisited this conversation many times over the months, and Leslie's guides continued to intimate it wasn't time yet, which resonated as truth to us. We knew we were not quite complete with Los Angeles.

STUCK AT MY JOB

Meanwhile, my job as the Executive Director's assistant was really wearing on me. Even though I loved the cause, I felt more trapped and oppressed by the administrative boredom than ever. Having processed work and money issues for a couple of years, I had unraveled an entire matrix in consciousness of my core beliefs and attitudes directly relating to work and money. Most of this egoic programming related to feeling powerless, weak and worthless as a sensitive man in a world that reveres machismo.

Two years of diligent processing and meditating had brought about enormous growth, and I was desperate for the inner changes to be reflected in my outer reality. Physical manifestation is the fruit of clearing a process in consciousness, yet I was still stuck at the same job and could not understand why I wasn't experiencing a physical shift.

I had always resisted being an administrative assistant, and in the two years of working there I had never really settled into my office space. I hadn't *owned* it by putting photos on my desk or adding any personal touches, and I hadn't made an effort to get to know my co-workers. I had never really *landed* in my job because at some level I didn't want to. Subconsciously I believed that if I didn't get settled I wouldn't have to stay too long, so part of me always had one foot out the door. This was causing a split in consciousness, and the resulting resentment was untenable.

It finally dawned on me that, in respect of this job, I had never been in my heart, and this chafing was inhibiting both my worldly and spiritual life. It was patently clear that I had created two distinct compartments of work and spirituality, so I made the commitment to open my heart and marry the two.

It was a conscious decision to shift my attitude, and I needed to ask some searching questions: *If I might be in this job for the rest of my life, how do I need to change? What purpose is this job serving in my life? Are there people here whom I can help in some way? How can I be in my heart with this job?*

The next day I brought in several potted plants and framed photos of loved ones, including Leslie, of course, which I put on my desk. I also rearranged the furniture, mounted some paintings on the walls and added other personal touches. Deciding to really get to know my co-workers, I took every opportunity to ask them about themselves. Within a week I had learned about their deeper stories, connecting at a heart level and at times even a spiritual level.

What a difference a shift in attitude makes. I was finally in my heart with my work. Even though being at a desk all day was not my idea of fulfillment, I was content and no longer chafing. I finally felt fully landed and at peace.

After just a few days of this shift in attitude, my office phone rang, and I was delighted to hear Leslie's voice.

> *Brad, guess what? My guides just said we should move to Santa Fe. Would you like to go?*

Elation is not a strong enough word to describe my feelings that morning, and I bounced around the office all day, barely able to contain myself. Keeping the news a secret, I couldn't wait to get back to Leslie's apartment to start the planning process. It was time to jump off yet another cliff.

Perhaps the three most important lessons I learned from this experience were about being present, being in my heart and being ready to surrender. Not being fully present at my job, with one foot out of the door the whole time, prevented me from being in my heart. By not being in my heart, I was buying into a victim consciousness. At some level I nursed a *poor-me* attitude—*poor me, I have done all this inner work yet still I'm stuck in an unfulfilling job.* As long as I felt victimized, I could not surrender to the divine will or to the lessons I had incarnated to learn at the job. But as soon as I became fully present, in my heart and surrendered, it was done, and I could leave.

> Being present, surrendered and in the heart with our cir-cumstances is a doorway out of victim consciousness and into fulfillment.

The next day I met with my boss and gave a few weeks' notice. Like magic, we were on our way to the Land of Enchantment.

SKYWALKING

Thrilled to be back in the City of Holy Faith again, we could hardly believe our good fortune. Just one year after our first visit, it was that magic time of year when we'd fallen in love with Santa Fe and each other—the beginning of Fall. We savored the desert's bright blossoms of yellow and purple, the scent of roasting green chilies, the crisp chill of fresh mountain air and of course the vast expanse of cobalt blue from horizon to horizon.

> *Okay Spirit, I've jumped off the cliff. I'm here without a job and without any savings or income. Now please show me what to do.*

This was my daily plea with the invisible realms, but it was a disturb-ingly silent, one-way conversation. I was not receiving any discernible guidance and had no idea how to earn a living. I considered looking for administrative assistant jobs at local non-profits, but there wasn't any energy behind that. *Been there, done that,* I thought. But I was grow-ing impatient and worried about the lack of income.

> *I swear if you don't give me a clue, I'm going to get the local paper and start looking for administrative assistant jobs.*

Half-hearted threats are ineffectual even in the best of times and never elicit a response from spirit. A few weeks passed.

Finally, I made good on my threat, got the local paper, went through the motions of circling a few potential jobs, but there was no energy behind the gesture, and I didn't phone the offices. With no apparent prospects of earning a living, I grew increasingly frustrated, petulant and rebellious in my communications with the invisible realms.

More weeks passed. In my heart I didn't want this type of job, yet we had run out of money, and I was supporting us by taking cash out of my credit cards. Accumulating interest payments felt unsustainable and scary. Although Leslie's darshans were attracting a growing number of people in Santa Fe and San Francisco, commuting to California was not inexpensive. The darshans, which were offered by donation, weren't generating enough income to pay the rent, put food on the table and cover other expenses.

Although money was short, I had lots of time and enjoyed supporting Leslie by answering the phone, coordinating her events and talking with people who were interested in her spiritual teachings. It was easy for me, and I loved having a small role in helping to spread the teachings that had been so invaluable in my own spiritual transformation.

All right, this is really it! I'm fed up with your silence. If you don't tell me what I'm supposed to do to earn a living, I'm putting together a resume today, and I swear I'm going to submit it to some offices in town.

Since the silence was deafening, I made good on my threat. Unenthusiastically, I prepared a resume, went through the motions of phoning some of the numbers in the employment ads and mailed in resumes.

No responses came, and weeks continued to pass. Occasionally I would put myself through the resume-mailing exercise, but always felt drained of energy afterwards—an obvious sign which I failed to understand at the time.

It was clear that getting a job as an administrative assistant was not being supported, but I didn't know what else to do. While I waited for something to come up, I continued to coordinate Leslie's events and spread her teachings. Because the number of events and students continued to grow, more of my days became filled with this volunteer work, a service which I offered out of love.

As the months passed, I assiduously processed my consciousness through prayer and practice, and despite the occasional doubts, trusted that my decision to come with Leslie to Santa Fe would be supported somehow.

I'm not sure if I expected a booming voice in the sky to tell me what to do or instructions to be scrawled in the mist on my mirror, but such signs certainly never came. Finally, after many months of pretending to look for work, it dawned on me that I was already working. I was spending an increasing amount of time supporting Leslie in her work, and it made me very happy. There was a lot of energy behind doing that, even though there was no money in it. In fact, I couldn't have imagined anything more rewarding and fulfilling. In retrospect the signs were obvious, but not so at the time.

Guidance is seldom given in an overt manner; instead it is usually offered subtly, and that is why we need to cultivate our sensitivity. One of the most important ways of receiving guidance is discerning how we truly feel about something.

The advice drummed into me in the so-called *real world* was that you should never leave a job until you have another one in hand, and you certainly shouldn't relocate before the ink on your employment contract is dry. However, *shoulds* are the limited mind speaking. Rules like that don't apply unless we believe we are a statistic. If we have the support of the invisible realms behind us, we can jump and the net will appear. We know we have this support when we follow the heart in an authentic manner.

But how do we really know it is our authentic heart calling and not an egoic whim? Here are a few touchstones:

- We feel a passionate, burning desire for something. The body feels excited, energized, light-hearted and joyful. There is a strong inner knowing and feeling of rightness about it.
- These feelings stand the test of time and don't diminish; they are not fleeting. There is a big difference between this and *impulsivity.* Following the heart authentically involves careful introspection, self-awareness and preparation before action, even though to others it may look imprudent. Taking the necessary time to practice self-inquiry, to meditate on our feelings and to process the desires and fears involved are critically important. Impulsivity involves pandering to short-term whims, drives and desires, in which case the proverbial invisible hands may *not* appear and catch us when we jump off the cliff.
- Our desire comes from the heart and not the head. The head talks to us with linear, logical reasoning, giving us rational justifications for why we *should* do something. The heart *feels* with burning passion. It may not make logical sense to do it, but the heart does not lie; it guides us to our inner truth. When the heart speaks, this is the Self calling to us. *Developing the capacity to discern this difference strengthens with time, like exercising a muscle.*
- Doubt and fear are necessary and natural parts of this process and are likely to arise when facing any form of change. It is important to allow and witness those feelings because they,

too, are guides. However, their presence does not necessarily guide us <u>away from</u> going in a certain direction. When we witness, name and process these shadows, we shine a light on them and gain greater clarity about our heart's true calling.

* If we feel drained or apathetic when contemplating a potential course of action or if we find a path is repeatedly blocked, these are usually signs not to go that way.
* We often receive signs and synchronicities guiding us in a certain direction.

Having already experienced the calling of the heart and jumped off a few cliffs, I felt somehow destined to repeat this particular exercise. Leslie had actually coined a term for the practice—*skywalking*—inspired by the movie *Star Wars*, whose hero was Luke Skywalker.

Luke was able to perform extraordinary feats of daring and heroism after learning to trust in *the Force*, and the adventure climaxes when he vanquishes the dark side by letting the Force guide him rather than by relying on his high-tech pilot gear.

> Skywalking involves taking a calculated risk based on intuitive knowing and trusting in the divine support that surrounds us constantly. Unbeknownst to most people, this flow of support is available to everyone in every moment. The key is to reconnect authentically with our heart's wisdom. When we have passion for something and feel in our heart we want and need to do it, then it's time to move beyond fear and have faith in the support of the invisible realms.

The Generosity Test

We received many signs that we were on the right track and that we were being supported by the invisible realms. When I was sufficiently attuned to the signs, I enjoyed the warmth of certainty; however, some underlying doubt and fear still arose from time to time because not enough money was coming in to pay our bills. Months turned into years, and we kept getting deeper and deeper into debt. Fortunately I had an incredibly high credit rating, and it was the days of easily available credit, so the negative balance on my many different cards just kept growing. Our faith was tested many times, especially during those first years together. As we passed each test, our faith grew stronger. Actually, it was primarily *my* faith being tested because Leslie's faith in the support of the invisible realms was unshakable. She had already gone through her own money trials many years prior during her *cave experience* in Los Angeles, and she had come through the other side.

Our litmus test around faith and money mainly involved generosity. Spirit always seemed to be asking us, *How generous can you be when cash is tight? Will you contract in fear and selfishness, or can you give generously, knowing the flow of money will be more than replenished?* Leslie frequently shares a story about her cave experience in Los Angeles, which illustrates the principle perfectly.

> *I was living on very little money at the time, but I didn't need much to get by. I lived frugally, meditated most of the time and ate little. Sometimes if I really stretched my budget, I would save an extra ten dollars by the end of the month, which I would use to buy a treat at the corner store —a pastry and a cup of coffee! It seemed like a little indulgence, but it meant so much to me at the time, and I really looked forward to it each month.*

> *One day when I was going for my special treat, a homeless person was outside the corner store. I was so hungry and had been waiting all month for this one luxury, but I knew I needed to give the entire ten dollars to the homeless person. I hesitated only momentarily before offering him the donation. I gave it gladly, fully trusting that he needed*

it more than I and that the flow of money would return to me if I acted with generosity.

Then strangely, homeless people seemed to appear everywhere I went, all the time, and I realized I needed to continue to give, even when I was down to my last dollar. I was being taught such a valuable lesson about letting go of any fear or selfishness around money. I developed immense trust through this practice. Of course the flow of money did return to me—multifold—and I learned about the importance of giving.

Even when down to your last dollar, it is better to give it away than hold onto it. The best investment you can make is in your own generosity, love of others and faith in Spirit.

THE BUDDHA TEST

In addition to myriad tests of our generosity—especially when cash was tight—another litmus test around faith and money was something we came to call *the Buddha test.* Although I found many ways to tighten the belt on our spending in order to make ends meet, when out and about, we would sometimes find a beautiful Buddha statue for sale. When this was accompanied by Leslie's intuition that we were supposed to buy the Buddha, no amount of reminding her that we were low on cash could persuade her otherwise. In fact the more I rationalized that we should not spend money on *extras,* the more certain she became that buying the Buddha was the right thing to do.

I'd get a hollow feeling in my stomach.

The price of the Buddha was always just high enough to make it an uncomfortable purchase. Leslie would remind me about the principle of living in the flow: When one's inner guidance is very strong about spending money for a spiritual purpose, it is important to take the risk and trust in the abundance of spirit.

When facing the Buddha test, I needed to find the neutral witness and overcome my fear of scarcity. Since the decision to buy was always based on trust in the flow, we'd get an extra flow of income within a few days or weeks, which more than paid for the Buddha and even eliminated a bit of our debt. Buying the Buddha was a test of faith to see if I could open the flow in courage rather than tighten the belt in fear.

It is important to clarify here that the Buddha test is very different from impulsive buying. This is not about *retail therapy*, nor about making an excuse to pacify the wounded inner child by buying whatever we desire whenever we want—*because we are worth it*. Compulsive buying, mindless purchases and rampant consumerism, based on the need to fill the inner void, are in fact the antitheses of living in the flow. Consumerism is a symptom of imbalance and highlights a tug of war between the central victim-tyrant polarity, which manifests as worthlessness-entitlement. In fact, impulsive buying, foundational to our consumer society, is confirmation of an entrenched system of separation. By contrast, the Buddha test works only in collaboration with higher consciousness and support of the invisible realms.

After a few years the Buddha test became humorous, and whenever we were particularly tight on cash, we'd expect to see an irresistible Buddha for sale. If not, we'd go looking for one or some other piece of sacred art, just to express our trust in the support of the invisible realms. We now have a house full of exquisitely beautiful statues and sacred art from many spiritual traditions, reminding us of our connection with the flow from Source.

Leslie's Work Expanding

During our first years together Leslie's work expanded enormously, primarily by word of mouth. The darshans, which we continued to offer by donation, were growing in many cities around the US and Canada, especially along the West Coast. Commuting once or twice a month from Santa Fe to the various cities, we hosted groups of up to 300 people each day. In the 1990s we incorporated audio recordings of Leslie's teachings together with a spiral-bound prototype of *The Marriage of Spirit* and developed the *Spiritual Warrior Training Course*[34] to support the growing student body in between visits.

We felt blessed to offer Leslie's events and teachings and to spread the light in places where there was a need. Yet despite the growing student body and income (and although I repeatedly passed the generosity tests and the Buddha tests), we continued to incur debt. Over the course of a few years we started to face the end of the credit line. Occasionally we considered the idea of charging a fee for the events, but it never felt right. We believed that to do so would be buying into fear, and so we continued to offer the darshans by donation.

We were so deep in debt that we thought we'd be paying off interest for the rest of our lives. We surrendered even to this, knowing we were doing a labor of love and were being guided and supported in our efforts.

Over those first few years as our debt mounted, I persistently processed all of the issues coming up for me around money. The polarity lists included:

Debt	-	*Profit*
Poverty	-	*Wealth*
Poor	-	*Rich*
Scarcity	-	*Hoarding*
Loss	-	*Gain*
Destitution	-	*Abundance*

Homelessness	-	*Having a home*
Enslaved	-	*Liberated*
Give it away	-	*Charge too much*
Generous	-	*Greedy*
Profligate	-	*Stingy*
Spendthrift	-	*Miser*

And many more.

Leslie and I processed together much of the time. Always happy to examine her own consciousness, she contributed whatever she saw for herself as well. A breakthrough in consciousness was generally followed by an extra flow of income—a confirmation we were on the right track.

Besides polarity lists, I also examined limiting beliefs around money. Some of these were associated with my personal programming, and others formed part of our collective consciousness—which affects us whether we are aware of it or not. Deep in our collective are the beliefs that working and earning money have to be a struggle, hard work is our road to salvation, handling money is dirty, the desire for money is sinful, being frugal and poor are the ways to redemption, being wealthy means you can't get into Heaven—and those are just a taste of many erroneous dogmas and attitudes around money. I also examined the opposite sides of these beliefs, most of which revolved around hedonism and *carpe diem* philosophy. Over the years I filled notebooks with polarities and squares around work and money processes.

Desperate, during a period when our funds were particularly tight, I pleaded with Leslie to ask her guides for help.

> *They are saying that they are giving you exactly the kind of help you need. Keep processing your money issues, Brad. You are not clear enough yet to open up the flow fully, which is why we are going more into debt. And I'm sorry, but they said to be sure to tell you it's your*

money process holding this in place, not mine. They said I could open the flow any time I want, but I'm not allowed to because it would prevent you from facing your scarcity consciousness. Sorry!

Ouch!

Because the truth came with such love, I didn't defend, but nonetheless felt defeated, hopeless and confused. Having reached a dead end with the money process, I sat in silence and let the discomfort pass through. At some level of my being, I surrendered.

Will you please help me, Leslie? I feel just a wee bit stuck.

Absolutely. I'm tired of this too.

Together we did many squares over many days, a kind of square-a-thon, including one on debt versus profit—the desire for and fear of debt, and the desire for and fear of profit. Although I had done that square a few times over the years, each time peeling away more layers of the proverbial onion, this time it seemed we had reached a tipping point, and it resulted in a significant breakthrough.

The next day in meditation, at a profound and visceral level, I received a gestalt of awareness that the debt wasn't *my* debt. I realized deep in my bones that I was merely a steward of a flow of money and resources and that neither the debt nor the money was *mine*. I didn't own the debt. Spirit had provided the credit cards as a means of helping us get started with the spiritual teaching work, but the debt didn't actually belong to *me*, even though my name was on the cards. Similarly if I had a million dollars in the bank, it would not be *my* money; it would be a flow of money that I was asked to steward on behalf of Spirit. I am not the owner. Whether I amass a huge debt or a huge profit, it is not mine; it is a flow of energy that I am being asked to steward.

With this experience an enormous weight was lifted off my shoulders. The small *I* no longer had to carry the burden of debt—since I didn't own it. Beaming with the joy of hefting a much lighter load, I shared my newfound realization with Leslie, and we celebrated the breakthrough.

Obviously I'm not advocating irresponsible money management or that we shrug off debt as though it has nothing to do with us. I'm not suggesting negligent behavior or that we go on wild spending sprees *because it isn't our money anyway.* We are divine stewards of the financial flow entrusted to us, and therefore it is always important to be impeccable in our behavior with money and incurring debt.

The following day Leslie approached me with a message:

> *Brad, my guides just gave me an idea for our next events in California. They suggested that in addition to offering a weekend of darshans by donation like we normally do, that we offer a Monday all-day intensive, charge a fee and let people know it's a fundraiser to support our work.*

> *Brilliant! Let's do it!*

The intensive was very popular, and we received more income that weekend than ever before. Using the proceeds to pay down the credit cards a bit, we started the process of lightening our debt load. We liked the format because anyone, whether or not they had money, could come to the donation-based darshans, and the people who came to the intensive knew that their contribution gave us the means to continue offering the darshans by donation.

We continued to offer a Monday intensive after each weekend of darshans, and almost miraculously we were able to pay off the huge credit card debt completely within about six months.

This was an extraordinary lesson for me about clearing the egoic knots in consciousness in order to open the flow.

> When we feel the flow is being blocked, the first place to look is inside, not outside. Looking for solutions outside is a normal reaction, but in reality we need to clear our consciousness first before taking action. By making the unconscious conscious, we become free of the limiting beliefs and patterns that block us from manifesting our highest path, and we open the flow.

LIVING IN THE FLOW

Leslie has offered spiritual teachings about money and living in the flow for over two decades.[35] At the heart of the teachings is the understanding that before we can use the flow properly, we have to wake up to its true nature. In truth, money represents divine energy and is offered to us for our use—temporarily, when we need it—but we don't own it. In essence we are sharing it with the Earth, with spirit and with everyone and everything.

The essential nature of money is that of pure energy. Like a river, it flows to us from its divine source when it is needed, passes through us, and then moves on to wherever else it is needed. Much like our life force itself, which is innately a part of us, it flows in and through us, and we are simply stewards of this flow of the money energy.

In order for us to steward this flow properly, there are qualities we must cultivate, including: generosity, love, compassion, faith, gratitude, truth and yin-yang balance. It's important to look at each of these in ourselves, see how we can live these qualities fully and understand what prevents us from doing so.

Flow, by definition, is movement. It's a fluid energy that never stagnates. The most important teaching about the flow is to allow it to move freely and not to dam it up.

Flow has its own intelligence that we can fully trust as being divinely supported. It requires of us that we surrender to it because we do not own the flow, nor the fruits of the flow. And because we are merely stewards of the flow, we are simply to let it move through us when we need it.

It is important not to try to possess it. The more we avoid controlling it and the more we surrender to it, the more it will move through us. If we try to dam up the flow, it will stop moving. In its movement is its dynamism. Letting go and not trying to own it or dam it are the keys to harnessing its power.

Hoarding money is damming up the flow. It is important to use it and share it generously—with wisdom and discernment—and not to stockpile vast sums. The old mentality of hoarding is a remnant of the system of separation, and it is unsustainable.

Those who have acquired large sums of money, for example through business dealings, inheritance or the lottery, are in the wonderful position of being able to give to worthy causes, to support people who touch their hearts and to inspire others through their example of generosity. Practicing generosity is one of their most important soul lessons.

It is also important to practice non-attachment to having money or to not having money. Either way, we have an opportunity to practice being okay with the situation and to process and clear our egoic reactions to it. Because cultural programming tells us having money is not spiritual, many readers may find it helpful to process these particular issues. As the great twentieth-century Indian saint, Sri Aurobindo, once explained, if we are asked to live with money, we must not resist it but rather surrender to it. If those of us on a spiritual path reject money, then we abandon it to the shadow forces. By being okay with having money, we reclaim it in the name of the Divine Mother and learn to use it for the benefit of humanity.

In our many years of working with this system, we have discovered there are phases. Like the tides, money ebbs and flows. When the money ebbs it can be a bit scary. This is the time to process one's consciousness, face the fears and practice trusting in the support of the invisible realms. This is easier said than done, but it is absolutely possible and brings with it enormous satisfaction and fulfillment. The *how to* part is a subject for another time and place, but practicing self-inquiry and doing polarities and squares are major aspects of the journey.

In practicing these principles of flow and skywalking into the manifestation of our dreams, our faith in the support of the invisible realms has been tested many times over the years. Each test is more difficult and the ante is upped, but the way forward is always the same. This passage involves using discernment, clearing consciousness, facing and overcoming fears and practicing trust and generosity.

Each time you take the risk and pass the test, you build your faith muscles and are blessed with a wonderful opportunity for spiritual growth and transformation. This is a very important stage of the journey of Self-discovery, and we honor and encourage anyone who chooses to practice the art of skywalking. For the spiritual warrior it becomes a way of life and leads to the opening of major evolutionary doorways in consciousness. Eventually your work and your passion become one and the same, and you live in a flow of abundance and generosity.

Part Three
Putting Love into Action

CHAPTER 17

South Africa and the Spirit of Ubuntu

❦

Leslie, do you feel that? It's so peaceful, still and quiet on the inner planes today, even in the middle of this huge city. I've never felt anything like this before in my life.

Yes, it's unity consciousness, Brad. Almost every person in Johannesburg, probably in the whole of South Africa, is thinking the same thought: Freedom!

We were in Johannesburg, and it was April 27, 1994. This was South Africa's historic first democratic election, a momentous occasion in which we were overjoyed to participate. Leslie, like most South Africans, never believed she would see this in her lifetime. South Africa's non-white majority had never had the chance to cast their vote before this day, and after years of ruthless violence, the elections were astonishingly peaceful. The long queues of enthusiastic voters snaked their way through urban and rural landscapes and were characterized by optimism and pleasant camaraderie.

Leaving her beloved homeland in 1977, at the height of the revolution, Leslie had wondered if she would ever be able to return. She had prayed for its deliverance from Apartheid and pleaded with her spiritual guides to show her how to make a difference. Now her dream, and the dream of the nation, was becoming a reality.

Apartheid's vice-grip had throttled South Africa since the 1940s when Leslie was born. It was a legalized system of racial segregation which enslaved 90% of the nation, oppressed everyone and turned the country into an international pariah. Although it had begun to crumble in 1990, after the election of F.W. de Klerk, the final death knell was arguably the election of the African National Congress (ANC) and the inauguration of Nelson Mandela as South Africa's first black president in 1994. Finally it had reached the end of its dreadful lifespan, and, as the sign on the Apartheid Museum in Johannesburg confirmed: *Yes, Apartheid is finally where it belongs—in a museum.*

South Africa was a nation that had been on a many-decades-long journey of extreme polarities: tragedy and heroism, tyranny and freedom, chaos and peace. Exemplified by the twenty-seven-year imprisonment of Nelson Mandela and his subsequent forgiveness of his captors, South Africa's path was one of the most arduous, turbulent and difficult. It moved from a structure of brutal oppression, unjust violence and vicious racism to a blueprint for understanding, freedom, truth, reconciliation, forgiveness and equality.

What happened in South Africa was a miracle. In reality there should have been a bloodbath, but with the wise, compassionate, inspired leadership of Mandela, the transition to a new government was relatively non-violent and peaceful. He symbolized the country's extraordinary transformation from its darkest days to its brightest triumphs—from a racist state into Africa's beacon of hope, with one of the most enlightened constitutions on the planet.

On May 10, 1994, Nelson Mandela was inaugurated as the first president of *the new South Africa*. As I watched the historic ceremony with

Leslie's parents on their television that evening, Leslie sat quietly in meditation in the bedroom upstairs holding space. Later that night before bed, she described to me an amazing experience she witnessed on the inner planes.

> *It was incredible, Brad. I was shown that as the old flag of the Apartheid government was lowered and as the flag of the new South Africa was raised, the country was given an extraordinary boost energetically. At that moment etheric jumper cables came down from the heavens and gave South Africa an enormous jump start of cosmic light and awareness. It's going to be a huge upgrade, and I can't wait to see what happens here. The spiritual guides are very pleased, and there's a big celebration going on right now in the invisible realms.*

Although this was Leslie's first trip back to her homeland in many years, it was far from our last. In fact it was just the beginning of an ever-deepening connection with South Africa—a significant turning point in our lives.

OUR COMMITMENT

During that first, life-changing trip to South Africa in 1994, Leslie and I gained new insights into the country's important role for Africa and for the world, and we dedicated ourselves to supporting the fledgling democracy. We saw that their noble new constitution, which enshrined equality in unprecedented forms—inclusive of race, creed, gender, sexual orientation and even the rights of animals—was a goal that the South African collective had set for themselves. Not an easy task, but also not unattainable.

However, it is impossible to jump full-blown into an enlightened self; meaningful change is a long-term process that requires the will-ingness to face one's egoic shadow and the readiness to undergo transformation and healing. What is true for an individual is also true for a collective, and we witnessed South Africa as she launched forward on a committed, long-term journey through the valley of shadow towards the goal of its new, enlightened constitution.

We were so profoundly inspired by the miracle we saw that we made a commitment to serve South Africa in whatever small way we could, and although we didn't know what to do, we prayed to be shown. We knew that if South Africa succeeded in its great experiment, it would be a beacon of hope for all of Africa and for the world. As a dear friend of ours once said, *As goes South Africa, so goes Africa; as goes Africa, so goes the world.*

After years of isolation from the rest of the world, due to its pariah status and international sanctions, South Africa now faced the challenge of opening up to a changed global environment. We recognized that we could help by building bridges in consciousness with the outside world. We decided to bring groups of spiritual seekers on meditation retreats to South Africa.

Calling our journeys *Meditations for Peace*, we visited places of great natural beauty and enormous spiritual power where our groups meditated, walked the land and met delightful people. Without exception, everyone who came was changed for life and fell in love with the land, animals and people. An ancient, earthy presence on the planet, Mother Africa is the cradle for our human development and creates life-changing transformation for all who take her into themselves.

The South African *lowveld* is an extraordinary place, where the virgin bush is so vast and untamed that there are more animals than people. The lack of thought forms fosters deep meditation and a great relaxation of the mind, body and spirit. There, it is easy to let go into the enormity of the inner and outer landscape and experience the mystical nature of the land and animals. We have come to call it *the African dreamtime.*

Entering into the African dreamtime dissolves the separate mind and awakens our interconnectedness with the web of life. It is one of the great gifts that Mother Africa offers to visitors from other parts of the world. Those who come for this experience are brought to their inner core of stillness, reconnected with something so ancient and primeval within themselves that they can never be the same again.

THE BLYDE RIVER CANYON

The Blyde River Canyon is the third largest canyon in the world. In Afrikaans,[36] *Blyde* means *joy*, which is a fitting name because of the way the river and the canyon make one feel. We chose to take groups there not just because of its size, exquisite red-rock cliffs, forested wilderness and magnificent river, but also because Leslie had long ago discovered one of the secrets of its spiritual power.

In the early 1980s, several years prior to her spiritual awakening, she made a special visit to South Africa from the US to see her parents. As she was getting off the plane in Johannesburg, her guides whispered, *Go to the Blyde River Canyon.* She had heard of the place but had never been.

After a few days with her parents, she made the five-hour drive and caught her first glimpse of Mother Nature's masterpiece. Unprepared for its grandeur and spectacular, breathtaking vistas, she gazed in silent awe, sank easily into a meditation and was overcome by its spiritual power. Soon entering an altered state of consciousness, she became aware that five giant Beings, hundreds of feet tall, were surrounding her, sitting on the edge of the canyon rim. They were translucent, milky white and humanoid in appearance. Although she called out to them, they did not reply, but instead remained silently meditative. Intuitively aware that they were ancient and immensely powerful guardians of the area, she felt a strong imperative to communicate with them. As much as she tried to get their attention, they ignored her. Finally after dogged persistence, calling out to them on the inner planes, one of the Beings slowly turned its head, peered down at her from high above as though she were an ant, and with aloof detachment acknowledged her presence.

Yes? Do you want something?

Leslie's spontaneous response came from some part of her subconscious awareness, as though she were being used by a force greater than herself.

I've come to ask you to help end Apartheid. Can you do that?

After a very long period of consideration, the Being responded.

Yes, we believe we can do that.

Thank you! And who are you?

We are known as the Elohim.

Leslie spent many years in the US while the revolution raged on, always holding a special place in her heart for the canyon and its guardian Elohim.[37] Never dreaming of returning one day, she was overjoyed finally to be able to share this extraordinary place with me and many of our friends.

THE SACRED MOUNTAIN AND THE NILOTIC MERIDIAN

Brad, my guides are telling me we should buy a piece of land here in the mouth of the Blyde River Canyon and build a home.

Buy land in Africa? Why? We're here only three weeks of the year. Plus we have no money.

I know. It doesn't make any sense, does it? I'm going to have to question them closely on this one. But they are already being very insistent.

The guides sprung this surprising news on us while we were walking the land with our little band of *Meditation for Peace* pilgrims in 1999. We could feel an astoundingly powerful spiritual energy emanating from a small, nearby mountain known in the local Shangaani language as *Modimole*.[38] We later learned that it means *God is Here* and is an ancient sacred site to the local people.

We also later learned more about Modimole from the Zulu High *Sanusi*, Credo Mutwa, who many consider to be the grandfather of Africa and who carries within him hundreds of years of the oral tribal history. In a private gathering, Mutwa informed us that according to Zulu history Modimole's sacred origins predates their tribal memory; it is the primordial place where the physical world was birthed. This was especially relevant to us, given Leslie's experience in the canyon with the Elohim, referred to in Genesis and throughout the Old Testament as creator gods. Interestingly some of the oldest rocks on the planet were found at the Blyde River Canyon—an apparent geological corroboration of the Zulu legend. Mutwa indicated that the sacred mountain sits above Africa's legendary underground river through which Earth's spinal fluid flows. Known in Zulu as *Lulungwa Mangakatsi*, this river is the Earth's primary meridian,[39] like a shushumna or spine, which is on the longitude 31°E.

When followed straight north from Modimole, the line runs through Egypt's Nile River, Giza Plateau, Great Pyramid and Sphinx. It encompasses more land mass than any other longitude on the planet. Also known as the Nilotic Meridian due to its association with the Nile, the meridian itself is about 35 miles wide and is seen psychically as a great river of golden light and energy stretching between southern and northern Africa. Underground caches of precious gold also run along much of the meridian.

We have since discovered that being on the Nilotic Meridian and in the energy of the sacred mountain is profoundly transformative and uplifting in body, mind and spirit. Modimole gives a powerful transmission of primordial earth energy that can lift one's meditation practice to new heights. And although we didn't know any of this important information when we found the land, we could certainly feel its incredible spiritual power and sense it held many secrets.

After our retreat was over, Leslie and I returned to visit the land again, drawn there like magnets. During the few nights we spent in the canyon, she had mystical experiences which illuminated the extraordinary spiritual power of the canyon and the sacred mountain.

> *Brad, my guides are telling me that the vortex of this canyon is some kind of amplifier, which magnifies energy profoundly. The mountain is somehow related. It works in conjunction with the canyon and can be used to direct the energy. I was shown that whatever processing work we do in consciousness here in this area is being amplified enormously and fed via the mountain into the Nilotic Meridian and Earth grid.[40] It's amazing! They are telling me that it's very important we get that piece of land right next to Modimole because they want us to be stewards of this place and because it will be an enormous support in the work with collective consciousness that I do. Apparently they want us to spend more time here.*
>
> *Okay . . . but. . . .*
>
> *And they said to tell you not to worry about the money. They will somehow make it work for us.*

Buying land in Africa made no logical sense, yet my intuition was in alignment with Leslie's. Having no idea how much time we'd be spending in South Africa or how we'd get the money, we resolved to purchase a two-acre parcel at the foot of the sacred mountain. Through prayer, processing and practicing living in the flow, the money—as if by magic[41]—became available for the purchase, and before the end of the year, we signed the papers and made plans to build a home there.

Since 1998, we have spent an increasing amount of time in South Africa offering our service in support of the country. In 2000, we learned about the heartbreaking plight of AIDS orphans and committed to help in some way. Over time our main activity became the establishment of Seeds of Light, CoreLight's humanitarian arm, which supports AIDS orphans and marginalized communities. Creating sustainable projects that empower the community, Seeds of Light has provided many services, including drilling wells, starting vegetable gardens, developing skills, training leaders and supporting schools. Most recently we built an orphan center for a local group and have helped them find ways to care for a growing number of children. This is a story in itself and is the topic of the next two chapters.

THE SPIRIT OF UBUNTU

Umuntu ngumuntu ngamantu: I am a person through other people. My humanity is tied to yours.

—*Zulu proverb*

The shortened version of this proverb is *Ubuntu*—a philosophy that is one of the most priceless treasures we have discovered in South Africa. It is ancient indigenous knowledge about the importance of community.

In other words: *If you are not well, then the whole village, including you and me, are not well because we are one whole, not separate individuals. The village is only as strong as the weakest individual in the group, and therefore I must have compassion for and help anyone who is struggling. When I lift you up, I lift everyone up, including myself.*

> Ubuntu encapsulates loving kindness, generosity and sharing and is the heartbeat of any sustainable community.

Archbishop Desmond Tutu, South Africa's spiritual leader and social rights activist, explains that Ubuntu means, *I am because you are*:

> *Ubuntu [...] speaks of the very essence of being human. [We] say [...] "Hey, so-and-so has ubuntu." Then you are generous, you are hospitable, you are friendly and caring and compassionate. You share what you have. It is to say, "My humanity is caught up, is inextricably bound up, in yours." We belong in a bundle of life. We say, "A person is a person through other persons."*
>
> *[...] A person with ubuntu is open and available to others, affirming of others, does not feel threatened that others are able and good, for he or she has a proper self-assurance that comes from knowing that he or she belongs in a greater whole and is diminished when others are humiliated or diminished, when others are tortured or oppressed, or treated as if they were less than who they are.*[42]

> Ubuntu speaks to our common humanity and to our unity, and is the most important spiritual message of our times.

Nelson Mandela said, *As long as poverty, injustice and gross inequality persist in our world, none of us can truly rest.*

We live in a time of unprecedented global inequality. The world's richest 62 people control as much wealth as the poorest half of the world's population.[43] These 3.7 billion people live on less than $2.50 per day.[44] Eighty percent of humanity live on less than $10 per day. According to UNICEF, 22,000 children die <u>each day</u> due to poverty.[45] *The gap between rich and poor has never been so great in all the world's history,*[46] and our planetary village is crying out for Ubuntu.

Not only is Ubuntu not practiced enough in the world, but it has been forgotten even among most of the tribal cultures in South Africa. Once, when visiting a school that Seeds of Light supports, we entered a classroom where a teacher had written English definitions of African tribal words on the chalkboard. To our surprise the definition of Ubuntu was: *Something not practiced in South Africa anymore.* Colonialism, Apartheid and our global system of money based in interest have broken the traditional tribal culture and entrenched the system of separation.

As we discussed in the chapter about money, our yang, global system of money based in interest promotes hoarding, rewards greed and selfishness and concentrates the wealth amongst the few. Tribal cultures traditionally practiced a yin approach to money, more in alignment with the principles of Ubuntu—sharing, caring, generosity and community-mindedness.

Traditional African tribal culture is rooted in a *gift economy*. One such tribe, the San Bushmen, still practice a gift culture—although their numbers are very few and diminishing rapidly, with less than 100,000 remaining. Their concept of wealth is completely different from that of the modern world's.

From Charles Eisenstein's *Sacred Economics*:

> Whereas money today embodies the principle, "More for me is less for you," in a gift economy, more for you is also more

for me, because those who have, give to those who need. Gifts cement the mystical realization of participation in something greater than oneself, which is yet not separate from oneself. The axioms of rational self-interest change because the self has expanded to include something of the other. Can we imbue money with the same property as the gift?

In hunter-gatherer societies, which were generally nomadic, possessions were a literal burden. The "carry cost" that everything except money bears today was quite real. In sedentary agricultural societies as well, possessions such as cattle and stores of grain, while sought after, did not give the same degree of security as being embedded in a rich web of social relationships of giving and receiving. Grain can rot and cattle can die, but if you have been generous with your wealth to the community, you have little to fear.

[C]onsider the *!Kung* concept of wealth explored in this exchange between anthropologist Richard Lee and a !Kung man, !Xoma:

> I asked !Xoma, "What makes a man a *//kaiha* [rich man]—if he has many bags of *//kai* [beads and other valuables] in his hut?"

> "Holding //kai does not make you a //kaiha," replied !Xoma. "It is when someone makes many goods travel around that we might call him //kaiha."

> What !Xoma seemed to be saying was that it wasn't the number of your goods that constituted your wealth; it was the number of your friends. The wealthy person was measured by the frequency of his or her transactions and not by the inventory of goods on hand.[47]

Wealth in a free-money system evolves into something akin to the model of the Pacific Northwest or Melanesia, in which a leader "acts as a shunting station for goods flowing reciprocally between his own and other like groups of society."[48] Status was not associated with the accumulation of money or possessions, but rather with a huge responsibility for generosity.

Can you imagine a society where the greatest prestige, power, and leadership accord to those with the greatest inclination and capacity to give?[49]

I invite you to pause and fathom this before reading further. Wealth for these people is about being generous, not hoarding.

The modern, rational mind can't wrap itself around that concept because all we know is that wealth equals accumulation of money and possessions; extreme wealth means acquiring and hoarding vast sums. However, this story makes logical sense because if the generous Bushman were ever in need, many would happily provide for him out of feelings of gratitude or indebtedness.

Interestingly, I shared this story with a twenty-year-old Bushman who attended one of our retreats in South Africa, and he confirmed that this definition of *wealthy*, //kaiha (which is so full of clicks and pops I could not pronounce it), is still accurate. Furthermore, he described how generosity and sharing are a natural part of their culture even to this day, how our concept of hoarding to accumulate wealth is quite foreign to them, and how they do not need money to survive. He explained that because he and his family, who live in the Namibian desert, know how to live off the land, it is normal for them to go without money for extended periods. Then with an ironic twist, he added, *Unless I need to buy time for my cell phone*—which made us all, including him, break into peals of laughter. Alas, the twenty-first century has reached even the remotest parts of the Namibian desert.

> We are at the most pivotal moment ever in the evolution of human consciousness, poised to make the leap into a new paradigm of love. The philosophy of Ubuntu, born out of the wisdom of indigenous knowledge and the power of community, tells us that the basis of our very humanity is the practice of loving kindness and generosity. This is the most ancient spiritual injunction in the world. Our survival depends on it. Through practicing Ubuntu we can accelerate the tipping point into love.

SOUTH AFRICA NOW

South Africa is playing a pivotal role for all of Africa—and for the planet. It is a great experiment—a mixture of black, white and other races, and amazingly, has eleven *official* languages. Understanding its unique leadership role is one of the primary reasons why we have established a presence there, why we continue to offer our pilgrimages to this treasured land and why we support the wildlife, marginalized communities and orphans.

Mandela saw South Africa as the rainbow nation, and they have made promising strides towards living the values enshrined in their new constitution. Like any fledgling democracy and most nations nowadays, they have significant struggles around inequality, corruption, greed and many other issues. The shadow is visible in high relief, but there is a creative enthusiasm for building community in a new and progressive way, and in general the people want to make the *new South Africa* work. Despite the extreme challenges facing it, South Africa still has the spark of their great spirit of renewal and optimism more than two decades after the election of Nelson Mandela, and in my opinion their resourcefulness and heart-centeredness will carry the day.

I feel incredibly fortunate to have been a participant in the epic journey of the new South Africa and to have received so many gifts along the way that have advanced my spiritual evolution. Two gifts, in particular, are worth mentioning here.

When we started spending time in South Africa, I became aware of a profound grounding quality in the land that I have not experienced in the Northern hemisphere. It's a feeling of being more anchored to the earth, more centered and balanced than I've felt anywhere else in the world. Besides being rooted to the earth, there's also an expansion *upward* too, which allows more access to light from the celestial realms. As above, so below. This gift from Mother Africa stays with me now, and I live with it wherever I go. I love to welcome visitors to South Africa and watch them receive this remarkable gift when they set foot on African soil.

The vast, still emptiness of the African dreamtime is impossible to describe in words. Especially after living in the hurly burly of the world, spending time in the South African bush offers a profound healing and dissolution of the state of separation. It has given me a visceral experience of being connected to the web of life and the peace that passes all understanding and has been one of the greatest blessings of my life.

These doorways in consciousness that Mother Africa has opened for me, among many others, have been gifts beyond imagination. Leslie and I both know that no matter how much we give in support of South Africa, we always receive more, and I can only hope I have given back a fraction of what I've received. We love sharing our experience of Africa with students and friends who come to visit, and with each passing year more and more of us are holding South Africa in our prayers and in the light for its success as the rainbow nation.

CHAPTER 18

Love in Action

❧

What good is enlightenment if I can't use it to help South Africa's orphans?

After watching a news report on US television in 2000, Leslie's heart was broken wide open by learning about the plight of AIDS orphans in South Africa. Her words conveyed a desperation to do something *physically* to help ease the suffering of the children in her beloved homeland. Through her sobs, she explained that there were over 1.5 million children in South Africa who had lost their parents due to AIDS.

Our friend and colleague, Victoria More, was with us at the time, and in that moment the three of us committed to do something to help. We had no idea what that would be, but everything begins with a commitment, and we knew we would be shown the way. In time as our commitment grew into manifestation, Leslie, Victoria and I became co-founders of a new, humanitarian arm of our non-profit, which we later called Seeds of Light.

In the late 1990s, just as South Africa was celebrating its miraculous birth as the new rainbow nation, the HIV/AIDS pandemic hit suddenly and brutally, and a dark cloud of illness and death descended on the country. For a variety of reasons, the new government and health organizations were slow to react to the dreaded disease. For one, the nation was finding its feet and was preoccupied with learning how to run a country after decades of fighting an oppressive regime. For another, the illness brought with it an enormous stigma. In the African culture, to contract HIV was a curse that carried unimaginable shame and humiliation. To get tested for HIV, to touch someone with AIDS or even to mention HIV/AIDS was taboo. As a result the country remained in denial about the disease and in ignorance of how to prevent it from spreading. A holocaust ensued. Hundreds of thousands of young, economically active adults were getting sick and dying of undisclosed causes, leaving behind the elderly and very young.

Unfortunately the stigma of the disease also resulted in the breakdown of some tribal customs. Traditionally in the spirit of Ubuntu, aunts, uncles, cousins and neighbors would have welcomed orphaned children into their families, but the perception of HIV/AIDS as a curse extended to the orphans, who were rejected whether or not they were sick.

South Africa was a country of forty million people with close to two million orphaned and/or *vulnerable* children.[50] With many of these children homeless and abandoned, South Africa was facing a crisis of untold proportions.

Seeds of Light

Nothing can be more heart-rending and in need of urgent attention than the case of AIDS orphans.

—*Nelson Mandela*

Having no idea where to begin to help, we prayed and asked to be shown. On our next trip to South Africa, we followed the signs and intuitions.

Our initial impetus—to build an orphanage—generated a lot of enthusiasm and excitement in us, but we quickly realized that it was hopelessly impractical. Not only were we in South Africa just a few weeks each year, but we also lacked some essential competencies to run an orphanage: We had no skills, training, credentials, licenses or money; not enough understanding of the culture; and every spare minute of our time was already accounted for in managing CoreLight and our work in consciousness. We decided to hold the dream in our hearts and prayers, asking Spirit to help us manifest it one day if it was in alignment with the greater plan.

Meanwhile, through like-minded South African friends, we were introduced to some courageous, heart-centered women in the Mpumalanga Province, a few hours' drive from where we lived, who had begun taking orphans into their homes and caring for them out of the kindness of their hearts. These pioneering souls, with barely enough money to feed their own children, knew they could not sit idly by and watch orphaned and homeless children starve on the streets. They did the best they could with the little they had. Often a small home with just one or two bedrooms would have one or two dozen children living there. Known as *children's homes*, they were crowded but clean and well-kept, and the children were well nurtured by the loving women we met.

We didn't have any savings, but we lived in the flow and gave what we could to support these women and their children, knowing that what we offered would give the orphans a chance at life and would return to us multifold. Because a few US dollars go a long way in rural South Africa, the little we gave was enough to make a big difference in the lives of many orphans.

Leslie also visited some of Johannesburg's children's homes, clinics and hospitals to meet some of the many AIDS orphans in the city. At one of the wards for orphaned infants, she witnessed dozens of shriveled and emaciated babies, many of whom looked premature or newborn but were actually weeks or even months old. She was shocked by the level of pain and suffering and broke down in despair. Sobbing and devastated, she questioned her spiritual guides.

How can this be happening? What is the meaning of this suffering? I know there are no such things as victims, but why would any soul choose a fate like this?

Leslie received an answer immediately. Her guides communicated that many of these beings were angels, not just normal soul incarnations. These angels had come into their little human bodies for a short time with the intention of helping to open the hearts of others and to teach lessons about love and compassion. These angelic beings were offering humanity an opportunity for spiritual growth at this critical time when we need to move into the heart.

In that moment Leslie understood that she needed to let her students know about both the situation and this message. Since her mission in life had always been to teach people to live from an open heart, she realized that helping South Africa's orphans was an important extension to her work—not just to help alleviate the suffering but also to provide an opportunity for others to find love and compassion.

On returning to the US, we communicated the plight of South Africa's orphans to our groups in every city and encouraged people to open their hearts in compassion and to give generously. The donations from big-hearted students and friends—every cent of which was delivered to the children's homes we supported—enabled us to help feed, clothe and care for a growing number of orphans.

Seeds of Light's stated mission is to assist with the awakening of the global heart through humanitarian service. We perceive the global heart to be the interconnectedness of all life through tolerance, equality and compassion. Our motto is *Love in Action.*

Over the years Seeds of Light's outreach programs evolved and expanded to include hands-on projects that assist all those living in the marginalized communities in our area. We learned that to be sustainable the whole community must be uplifted. Our projects include: providing access to clean water, creating food gardens, improving overall health of orphans and vulnerable children, offering skills and empowerment trainings to adults in the area, teaching art classes to children and much more.

Every step along the journey has been incredibly supported by the invisible realms, often in miraculous ways. The inspiring adventure that unfolded has brought us more satisfaction and fulfillment than we could have ever imagined. The following stories are just a sampling of the many heart-opening experiences with beautiful, loving souls in rural South Africa.

GREASED GRACE—THE FLOW OF DIVINE SUPPORT

It was impossible for Leslie, Victoria and me to ignore the sprawling, depressed and dilapidated collection of villages in an area called Acornhoek, just thirty minutes from where we lived. Acornhoek is a former *homeland* area, which is the equivalent of a reservation for Native Americans in the US. The Apartheid government moved the native Africans to these homelands by force after taking their fertile ancestral land to use as farms for the white settlers in the area. Acornhoek is home to about 100,000 people, has seventy percent unemployment and is one of South Africa's designated poverty nodes. According to official statistics, approximately one in three people is HIV+. Unofficially, local doctors claim it is more likely one in two. Behind almost every door, someone is dying.

We knew we couldn't possibly enjoy the benefits of living at the beautiful Blyde River Canyon unless we did something to help uplift this neighboring community. Our commitment birthed a whole new phase of expansion for Seeds of Light.

Seeds of Light grew to support several children's homes and develop many loving relationships with powerful, heart-centered African women. Being entirely volunteer-based, it was taking more and more of our time. We had nobody to help us manage the fundraising or projects, and owing to our expansion and the huge need in South Africa, we were being stretched very thin. Although happy to put in as much time as necessary, we realized that the situation was not sustainable. We knew we needed help and decided to hire Jeanette to manage Seeds of Light.[51]

Meanwhile our friend, Judy Miller, who first came to South Africa on one of our Meditations for Peace pilgrimages, had returned to support a weaving co-operative of *gogos* (grandmothers) in Acornhoek.[52] She was a pioneer in the area and co-founded Seeds of Light with us. In the early days, when we would go into the deep rural areas with her, there were very few other white faces. She introduced Seeds of Light to a strong leader, Daphne Mhaule, the principal of Funjwa Primary School.

Daphne had an enormous heart and a big vision for the children of her school, but she had very few resources. When we met her, there were no desks, chairs, books or running water and very little electricity. The school lunch was the only meal of the day for a large percentage of the children at Funjwa, many of whom were orphaned, but the Department of Education often did not deliver the much anticipated meal. Sometimes the lunch consisted only of white bread. Hungry, malnourished and often ill, many of the children would fall asleep or drift off during class, unable to concentrate on the lessons. It was a deplorable, untenable and heart-breaking situation, and we knew we needed to help.

Daphne was defiantly resourceful and would break pencils into three pieces so that each child could have something with which to write. When we asked her about her vision for the school, surprisingly the first thing on her list was not water or food for the children, but a computer laboratory. Always forward thinking, she reasoned that if the children were computer literate, they would have a future. She even showed us a large classroom that was completely empty, except for a sign over the door that read, *Computer Laboratory*—a creative way of trying to manifest her dream for the children. While we honored and appreciated her desire to give the children a future, we suggested that perhaps a place to begin was with drilling a well and starting a food garden and that after providing these basic necessities we could look into the idea of the computers. She agreed, and we told her that although we didn't have the funds, we would do our best to find a way to help manifest these critical resources for her school.

Leslie and I asked Jeanette to make a list of all the projects she felt were worthwhile, including setting up a computer laboratory at Funjwa—and to include the estimated price tag for each item on the list. Together we analyzed the list of a few dozen projects, by far the most ambitious and expensive of which were drilling a well and starting a food garden, and totaled up the dollar amount. The grand total was approximately $35,000 USD, which was significantly more money than we had ever contemplated raising for Seeds of Light. However, knowing that all of the projects were worthwhile and would improve the lives of countless impoverished people in important and sustainable ways, we committed to find some way to make every project on the list a reality. We acknowledged that it might take us a few years to raise all of the money, but we were confident that with divine support, it would happen.

Placing the list of projects and the grand total of $35,000 USD written on the paper in the middle of our little triangle, we held hands and prayed in the living room of our home at Blyde River Canyon.

Dear Mother-Father God, Self that we all are, we offer up this list of projects to you, and we ask that you please help us to manifest the $35,000 required to complete them. If you want us to help uplift Acornhoek and support the children and adults there to live happier, more fulfilling and sustainable lives, then please bring the money to us. We thank you, we ask for grace, and we trust it will be so. Amen.

Feeling a sense of completion with our visioning session, we placed the list aside and had complete faith that the money would arrive in divine timing.

Within about forty-eight hours we were contacted by Victoria, who was managing the CoreLight office in Santa Fe at the time.

You will never believe what just happened! That very nice man, Gil, who sat in meditation with Leslie many years ago, just contacted me today. He said, "Somebody told me you support AIDS orphans in South Africa. Is that true?" I told him we did, and he said he wanted to make a donation. So, guess what? He's sending us a check for $35,000! Can you believe that?

Leslie and I were speechless. Stunned to the core, we could only stare at each other. With tears of joy, we hugged each other in total disbelief at just how quickly the money had manifested. It was surreal. Truly feeling a divine miracle had occurred, we needed no further signs that Seeds of Light was fully supported by the invisible realms. Grace was certainly at work here, and it came so fast that we coined the term, *greased grace*, to describe how quickly prayers could be answered. Since that time we have frequently witnessed the phenomenon of greased grace when we, and others, have extended themselves in compassionate service to those in need.

Resources, money and support pour in, often in unfathomable ways, when love is put into action.

Within a short time, Seeds of Light drilled the well and started a bountiful food garden at Funjwa. Not only did the children gain access to books, chairs, desks, clean drinking water and fresh fruits and vegetables all year round, but we also installed a computer laboratory in fulfillment of Daphne's dream (furnished with used computers donated by a friend's office in Johannesburg).

CHAMPIONS

There are so many inspiring stories about Seeds of Light that another book would be necessary to tell them all. Over the years we expanded to sponsor many other primary schools in the area, supporting thousands of children in a myriad of ways. Eventually we began to collaborate with other organizations on food and clean water projects so that our colleagues drilled wells while we supplied gardens and training programs for growing food.

One of the main lessons we learned through our work in Acornhoek is that in order to create sustainable projects, it is critical to find local *champions* and support them in their vision. A champion is someone who has heart, courage, leadership potential and a strong desire to help the community. Providing the support, resources and encouragement, but requiring that the champion does the work of achieving the vision, builds capacity rather than dependency—give fishing lessons instead of the fish.

A champion is usually (but not always) a woman. Research shows that empowering women is the fastest and most efficient way to help uplift impoverished communities. When one considers that the collective distance South African women walk each day to fulfill the basic need for clean water is equal to the moon and back sixteen times,[53] one realizes how simple interventions, like providing a clean water source, can liberate women to help the community in other ways. The empowerment of women is the raising of yin energy. This counterbalances and ameliorates extreme yang influences in these communities—the persistent effects of colonization, apartheid and concomitant polarities such as domination-subjugation and authoritarianism-subservience. These courageous champions are shining examples of spiritual warriors.

There are many well intentioned people and organizations who say, *Here's how we are going to help you,* and then proceed to impose their own vision on the people in need. Although well intentioned, this extremely yang, authoritarian and dominating approach lacks its yin, egalitarian, sensitive complement and very rarely succeeds. At best it creates a cycle of dependency and disempowerment. We'll look at this from a processing perspective in the next chapter.

The kind of giving that creates dependency is often egoic in nature—the person giving gets a kick out of feeling important and needed. True unconditional giving from the heart is very different.

It's always a noble endeavor to try to help someone in need, and yet we have learned through experience that true empowerment and sustainability can only come through helping a champion achieve her vision.

Over time we have met many champions in Acornhoek and empowered them to achieve their visions—everything from community food gardens, craft centers and elder care projects, to caring for children and creating empowerment groups. For two full years we sponsored and facilitated a monthly leadership-training course[54] that successfully empowered over thirty local champions with life-skills training and support. Each champion, like a pebble in a pond, sends ripples out to touch countless others in immeasurable, sustainable and positive ways.

EMBODYING SPIRITUAL PRACTICE

Putting love into *action*—also known as karma yoga or selfless service—is one of the four primary, traditional paths of Self-discovery.[55] Through this practice we feel the gratification of improving the lives of others without buying into self-importance or the need to feel needed. The journey to enlightenment involves all four paths, and this is one I particularly recommend because it contains such rich rewards. Practicing unconditional giving is an extraordinary opportunity to let go of the small self.

> Offering service is a daily opportunity to remember that the Self is not interested in our achievements—only in our heart. When we put our love into action, we align with our true purpose and come closer to knowing the Self.

Detailed in Chapter 3, Building Your Light, one of Leslie's core teachings is about the path of love in action. Offering oneself in service builds spiritual power and light; however, maintaining an impeccable attitude around serving others is not always possible due to the nature of the ego. Resistance to unconditional giving is to be expected, yet it is better to offer imperfect service than none at all. It's always an opportunity for growth and evolution. As Leslie explained:

Examining yourself in action will yield all sorts of processes that can be done to clear yourself to the impediments of unconditional giving. In other words, you can use imperfect service as a way to clear the ego. You're setting up opportunities to "stalk yourself"—to catch yourself in the act of being conditional in your giving, to question your motives, to look at some of your decisions about it and see whether they really are coming from the highest part of yourself. If you find that they're not, then you process them. It's a great way to clean up your act.

> *Eventually, service leads to the dissolution of the separate self and to the realization of the Self. This is the meaning of "selfless"—being beyond the old, limited self and awakening to the vast, cosmic Self.*[56]

Putting others' needs ahead of our own is a learning curve. It begins small and grows. Each time we practice offering service to another, we short-circuit the ego's ubiquitous desire for self-satisfaction and learn to move more into the heart. The walls of the ego increasingly dissolve and the heart expands.

One of the primary examples of the path of unconditional giving is the path of parenting. Through love, parents learn to focus on the needs of their children. By shifting focus away from themselves, they have the opportunity to grow and evolve into the heart.

As any parent or practitioner of the path of service knows, while incredibly rewarding, this path is not always easy and is fraught with countless challenges. There are moments when attachment and ego cloud the nature of the service. Furthermore, a deep and abiding commitment is required to walk this path for any length of time. This has certainly been my experience in stewarding CoreLight and Seeds of Light for the past many years. Although grace has continually and miraculously greased the path, it would be misleading to disregard the journey's difficulties.

Each trial, however, has offered an opportunity for growth and for practicing the spiritual principles. *Walking the talk* is not always easy in spite of loving and believing in what we do. Just because one loves the work does not make it any less demanding on one's physical reserves— in fact sometimes the converse is true. When pushing the physical body's limits through extended and stressful periods without sleep, shadows often arise and can take many different forms. It does not matter that the work is for the greater good; in all cases it is essential to witness, process and manage your energy impeccably.

The overwhelming sense of responsibility that has accompanied the life cycle of our projects is also very testing. Although Seeds of Light projects develop towards sustainability, during the beginning stages they have relied on us for funding and support. As Seeds of Light has expanded and grown, an increasing number of children and adults have depended on us as a lifeline—often for basic, life-sustaining necessities such as food and water. Knowing that we are responsible for so many lives is extremely stressful and would be absolutely overwhelming if we did not have faith in the knowledge that a force much bigger than the small self is ultimately in charge of our tireless efforts.

Difficulties also arose around bridging the enormous cultural differences brought to the fore in our projects. In retrospect we were quite naïve at the outset and completely unaware of the challenges we would face. Dealing with the language barrier alone was daunting, but there were countless other cultural hurdles to cross in building trusting and lasting relationships with the people of Acornhoek. Perhaps at the top of the list was their suspicion of us. Their prevailing experience of white people was of manipulation, domination and control, and involved having things taken away from them (including their ancestral lands and their freedom). So unbeknownst to us, they mostly wondered what we wanted from them.

When we started supporting Funjwa Primary School, the community held a large gathering of several hundred people and invited us to speak. At one point a man stood up and asked a very pointed question: *Why are you here?* His candor and overt suspicion broke the ice. Without missing a beat Leslie replied, *We're here because we care. We care about you.* There was a long, pregnant pause. In that moment everyone's hearts, including our own, melted. By the end of the gathering, we were all arm in arm, crying, singing, praying and dancing together. Our loving and intimate relationship with Funjwa's principal, Daphne, continues to this day.

Sadly, not all of our relationships have been as successful. Through awkward cultural blunders, miscommunications and any number of issues in the minefield of this work, there have been failures too, although fortunately not too many. Our directors and field workers have all been on the front lines earning trust—one relationship at a time. As a team—and with Spirit's support—we have achieved remarkable results. In spite of being tested and pushed to our limits, we have bridged cultures and overcome countless obstacles by consistently and conscientiously following the path of love in action.

Through this path I have increasingly dissolved the boundaries of the small self and developed the fortitude, stamina and commitment to serving the welfare of others I never knew I was capable of. The incredible challenges we've faced, and the sheer volume of our organizations' activities have required from me a yang capacity I didn't know I had. Using the yang power of manifestation to support others—including the champions of Acornhoek—has helped me to recognize and to step into the potency of the spiritual warrior and to awaken even more to the knowledge of the Self.

> It all begins with a simple commitment, a willingness to surrender to the call of the heart and take each small step presented, one at a time. If you aspire to embody spiritual practice, put your love into action.

Over a decade after our initial commitment to help South Africa's AIDS orphans, we began the biggest project we have ever undertaken—empowering a local champion to build and manage an orphan center. Through her, our original vision and dream became a reality, and our trust and faith muscles were put to the ultimate test.

CHAPTER 19

Greased Grace

❧

I live in a little village called Tintswalo, where in just three schools there are over 300 orphans—and every month there are more. Many of them have no food. When they come to school, they come without food, and then they leave school without food. They have nothing. Some have no shelter. Some have a shack, but no electricity or water. Some are living in child-headed households.[57] Some are sick. They don't have adults to help them. It has worried me terribly for a very long time, and I have prayed about it so much.

So, my vision is to start an orphan center—a place where we can look after the children. We can feed them and give them a safe place to come after school. They can play and get help with their homework. We can teach them life skills and help them find some peace. With a center like this, these children without parents would have a chance at life. But I'm afraid without it, they have no chance. Right now no one helps them, they have to steal food, and it leads to crime and to drugs. It's a terrible, pathetic situation.

My family owns a piece of land next to Funjwa school. It has an old building on it. I will donate this land for the orphan center, but I need help. I need money to fix the existing building and to build more buildings. I want the center to support five hundred children. But I have no money, so I don't know how to do this.

That is why I am here in front of you, to ask you, please, please help me. Help me to help these children. I'm opening my hands. Here am I. Please use me to help these children to grow up to be good and strong and kind so that we have a very good future in our country. Thank you very much.

Talitha, a retired nurse and widow, was humble and soft-spoken, yet her words carried deep emotion. We met her through our friend and champion, Daphne, of Funjwa Primary School. Like Daphne, Talitha is a champion—strong, big-hearted and passionate about helping the children. We were at Daphne's house with the second director of Seeds of Light, Becky, when we met Talitha for the first time, and her words touched our hearts. We told Talitha that we really wanted to help but that because it was such a big commitment, we would need to think about it carefully for a few days before we could respond to her request. With joyful tears, hugs and smiles we said farewell for the time being, sensing in our hearts that we would say yes.

For days Leslie, Becky and I discussed the situation and deliberated. If we chose to follow our hearts, we knew we were committing to jump off a cliff and *skywalk* into the future together. Although we sensed that the project would be supported by the invisible realms, we realized that it would require a full-time commitment for several years and long-term support thereafter. We knew that it would require raising at least ten times the funds of any of our previous projects. And it wasn't just a matter of erecting buildings. We would need to drill a well, bring in electricity, build an infrastructure, start food gardens and deal with a thousand other details we had not yet considered. In keeping with our protocol of empowering the champion, we would have to assist Talitha to start a non-profit organization of her own and help her and her organization get the training needed to manage a large orphan center. And that was just the beginning. The big concern is always around sustainability of the projects. How would they continue to feed five hundred children every day? How would they raise money to maintain the buildings, pay salaries and keep the place running?

Could we do something this big?

It made no logical sense. We had no money, it was a huge project, and we had just met Talitha. However, intuitively we felt that she was the champion for the job and that we should say yes to her. So we processed our doubts and concerns, and we prayed. Leslie and I had practiced trusting our intuition for so many years that the more we processed it the more we recognized that it was the right thing to do. We had spent years nurturing relationships in the area and building trust in our capacity as an organization. Furthermore, Becky had a sound background in the world of non-profit management and had the skills, expertise and conviction. Because our original vision, over a decade prior, had been to build an orphanage, we somehow knew that this was coming full circle and that Spirit was encouraging us.

With some trepidation and big lumps in our throats, but with full confidence in the support of the invisible realms, we agreed to help Talitha start an orphan center.

With Seeds of Light's help Talitha rounded up some friends and community leaders and formed a non-profit organization, which they called The *Ekurhuleni* Center for Orphans and Vulnerable Children. *Ekurhuleni* means *place of peace* in the local Shangaan language.

If we had had any doubts about support for this project by the invisible realms, they were quickly dispelled as miracle after miracle unfolded in quick succession. Volunteers, resources and financial contributions began to pour in. I made a series of short fundraising videos about the ongoing progress of Ekurhuleni, which we uploaded to YouTube and which we showed at our meditation events. As Talitha's inspiring appeal touched people's hearts around the world, the money poured in. While there were a few major donations from philanthropic individuals and organizations, most of the funds originated in a grassroots way from the US, Canada, Brazil, South Africa and other countries. Leslie's generous students organized garage sales, bake sales, dinner parties, concerts, jog-a-thons, fundraisers at their children's schools and many other creative events to raise money.

Donations of resources and volunteer service also poured in. One of South Africa's finest architects drew the beautiful building plan *pro bono,* one of the country's largest building supply chains donated materials, and our sister organization drilled the well.[58]

There was also "Saint Nick," a stellar volunteer who appeared on the scene as though sent from the heavens. Nick came with a very unusual triple-skill set—all three of which were exactly what Seeds of Light and Ekurhuleni needed at that moment. Firstly, Nick had a background in construction management and had owned and managed his own small construction company, which qualified him to supervise the construction of the center. Secondly, he was a certified Chef de Cuisine (CCC) and had worked for major non-profits, setting up and managing multiple food-service programs. We couldn't have asked for a more ideal person to train Ekurhuleni's kitchen team in planning, preparing and serving nutritious meals for hundreds of children. Thirdly, Nick's original degree was in fine art. One of Leslie's visions had always been to teach the children of Acornhoek art because through art they learn that they always have the inner resources to create something out of nothing. Creative solutions to life's many challenges follow on the heels of this realization.

The list of supporters is long. Through so much generosity and so many synchronicities, Ekurhuleni quickly began to take form.

There were plenty of bumps in the road and hurdles to jump, of course, but in less than two years, the Ekurhuleni Center had three of four buildings completed—the kitchen/dining facility, ablution building and activity center—and was ready to open its doors as a drop-in center.[59] In December of 2012, the first 50 children were received with a jubilant grand opening celebration, and the dream of giving these poorest of poor children a chance in life became a reality.

Over time the rest of the infrastructure has been built: a fourth building (a larger activity center), an irrigation system, food gardens, a soccer field, a multipurpose sports court for basketball and volleyball and more.

Three years after opening its doors to the first 50 orphans, Ekurhuleni now serves over 250 children as a drop-in center after school and on weekends and holidays, 365 days per year, with the intention to eventually serve 500. The only orphan center in the Acornhoek area, Ekurhuleni serves meals and provides supportive care and activities, including help with homework, sports, choir, poetry, drama, art classes and games.

There is no doubt in my mind that this project is supported by Spirit but that does not mean that its path towards sustainability has been without trials. Working through cultural differences, tests of faith around funding issues and other unanticipated obstacles are ongoing challenges. However, with support from the invisible realms and Seeds of Light's current director, Wendy, it is working. In addition to government funding, which is helping Ekurhuleni to continue serving the growing number of orphans and vulnerable children, Seeds of Light has started a monthly sponsorship program, which also helps to keep the center running.

The joy and gratification we have received from this incredible adventure far outweighs the effort and challenges we have encountered.

We continue to be inspired and amazed by the incredible synchronicities and abundant flow of divine support that pours in all the time so that Seeds of Light can help uplift the orphans and the poorest of the poor in the marginalized community of Acornhoek.

Recently when we were visiting Ekurhuleni with one of our retreat groups, we took a few moments out of Talitha's busy schedule to congratulate her on all she has accomplished and to thank her for caring for the beautiful 250+ children. She reciprocated with deep gratitude to us and to Seeds of Light for providing her with the opportunity to serve the children and the community and to fulfill her dream.

> *Leslie, I feel like long ago you told God that an orphan center was needed, and then God came and found me and told me that I was the one to fulfill this vision. I thought it was my idea, but really it was yours! Thank you!*

When we follow the deep calling of our heart, when our dreams are in alignment with the greater plan and when we put love into action to serve others, our dreams come true.

THE GIFT WE RECEIVE

While progress has been made in terms of HIV/AIDS education and while the taboo around HIV-testing is not what it used to be, the pandemic continues to sweep across South Africa. It is believed that South Africa is the country with the highest number of people with HIV/AIDS in the world. Now there are approximately 2.5 million orphaned and vulnerable children in South Africa due to AIDS,[60] up from 1.5 million when we first started to help in 2000.

We are no longer one of very few non-profit organizations that are helping to uplift Acornhoek, but one of many. As South Africa has continued to open to tourism and foreign business, more and more South Africans and overseas visitors are finding their way into Acornhoek. Inevitably people have heart-opening experiences there, and some of them choose to return to help.

Despite dire poverty, the AIDS pandemic and a general lack of material resources in Acornhoek, most people we meet there are happy. We see their joy and connection to Spirit through their bright smiles and shining eyes and especially through their uplifting and inspiring dancing and singing. Their spiritual strength and faith bring them enormous joy, hope and inspiration. Whenever we take visitors to the schools, community gardens or other projects we support in Acornhoek, we are greeted by joyous, soul-stirring African singing and dancing.

Most visitors from the developed world who witness this phenomenon of joy amidst such poverty and devastating disease begin to question their own lives and happiness quotient.

> *How can people, who have so little and have lost so many of their family, friends and neighbors, be so joyful? I have all of my material needs met and more—and yet I'm not that happy most of the time.*

The gift we receive from the people of Acornhoek is a great realization:

An abundance of money, material possessions, success and security can't bring lasting happiness. It is only through our connection with Spirit, with the Earth and with each other that we can find the real fulfillment and joy we seek. Through this authentic abundance we experience true happiness in life.

VICTIM-SAVIOR PROCESS

We do not see the people of Acornhoek as victims or ourselves as rescuers. That old-paradigm polarity leads only to perpetuation of the problem. If we were to view the people we serve as victims or ourselves as saviors, it would be disempowering to those we strive to empower and support. Over the years of working in Acornhoek, we have processed this issue.

The role of the savior is tempting because it feels good to rescue someone. Giving someone a handout and having them look up to you as a savior can provide the feeling of being needed, helpful, important and powerful; however, it can create a cycle of dependency that locks the recipient into the opposite side of the polarity: needy, helpless, unimportant, powerless and downtrodden, essentially trapping them in the victim role.

Polarity lists, squares and practicing other forms of self-inquiry are important to clear the shadow processes that maintain a cycle of dependency and victim-savior consciousness. By clearing this polarized patterning it is possible to serve others and to practice generosity without creating a cycle of dependency or disempowering those receiving the gift. Serving from the place of unity consciousness helps birth a new paradigm of non-separation, non-duality and heart-centered consciousness.

We are not claiming to be perfect at this; however, we have discovered that it is important to be conscious of the process and to hold the intention to serve from this place of unity consciousness. Although it is rarely possible to start from this place or live this way at all times, it is a goal to strive for. It is also critical not to use our own imperfect consciousness as an excuse not to practice generosity. We have discovered that just by making the attempt to give, to serve others and to practice putting love into action, Spirit meets us more than half way.

This leads to the question of handouts: *If giving handouts creates a cycle of dependency and disempowerment, then should I or shouldn't I, for example, give money to homeless people?* The answer is: Yes, absolutely, give money to homeless people—or anyone else for that matter. Give whenever your heart tells you to. If your heart tells you to give a handout of money or goods, then it's vital to do it. Perhaps that person really needs whatever you've got, and you're the angel that Spirit has sent to fulfill that need. There is no way to quantify the immeasurable love, joy and gratification that gift-giving can provide the giver, the receiver and everyone else involved. Give and give and give—and then process the emotions that arise around the act of giving. Akin to the '60s aphorism, *If it feels good, do it,* perhaps a new version for our times is: *If it makes love, do it.*

Learning how and when to give is as simple as learning to follow your heart. This game without rules is really a process of discernment that develops with time and practice. As we practice listening to the heart, we learn to discern more and more what it's telling us. Like learning a sport or a musical instrument, the more we practice, the better we become at the skill.

In general the guidelines for practicing generosity and putting love into action include both following the heart and processing any limiting consciousness that accompany the giving, such as a savior mentality. By giving with a cleared consciousness, we create a win-win both for ourselves and for the recipient. Like the domino effect, practicing love in action is contagious. This is how a new paradigm of heart-centered conscious is birthing on the planet.

Part Four
Remembering

CHAPTER 20

The Resurgence of the Feminine

❦

It is time for the ancient feminine wisdom and energies that are trapped in the Earth to be freed, brought back into the world and remembered so that a balancing between masculine and feminine can take place on Earth.

In 2005 Archangel Michael, one of Leslie's primary spiritual guides, spoke to her in a vision in which he was working with another radiant being to push a large, bullet-shaped stone off a hole in the ground. As the vision became clearer, Leslie recognized the second being as Apollo, the Greek sun god, who had once appeared to her in a quiet olive grove in Delphi in the 1970s.

Archangel Michael had originally introduced himself to Leslie in the early 1980s, and had explained to her then that in the pre-Christian era he had been known as Apollo. In essence they were one and the same being, with different names in different places during different cycles. It is relevant that both are associated with the sun and both subdued, or slayed, a serpent.

This is the omphalos *stone. It has covered the hole of the Python at Delphi for the past age, trapping feminine energies in the Earth, and now it is time for it to be removed.*

And with this final message from Archangel Michael, the vision faded into a mist.

Leslie recognized the omphalos, meaning *navel* in Greek, because she had seen it in the Delphi museum in the 1970s. Shaped like the head of a snake, the stone originally resided at the Temple of Apollo, close to the spot where the Delphic oracle sat. It was considered to be the Greek *axis mundi,* the place where Heaven and Earth meet.

Delphi was originally established as a sacred site during the Neolithic civilization which existed between about 10,000–2,000 BCE. During this era, Gaia the Earth Mother ruled Delphi and was worshipped at the sacred site, which was the center of the Greek world. Her oracular priestesses were known as *Pythia,* derived from Python, the great Earth serpent son of Gaia.

During the first millennium BCE, Apollo's arrival marked the birth of a new era. Here, according to legend, Apollo the sun god, the patron of male beauty, order and harmony, conquered and slew Python with golden arrows and buried him in his lair at Delphi by placing the omphalos stone over his hole.

Apollo brought in priests to care for the sacred site. Temples were built in Apollo's honor, and Delphi grew increasingly popular as a pilgrimage destination. Although priests replaced the priestesses, the omphalos and Pythia remained in the temple's inner sanctum, where in ecstatic trance she uttered prophecies and guidance.

The omphalos myth represents the turning of the ages, from Neolithic to Patriarchal. Worship of the great Earth Mother goddess and her fertility were the focus of life for the Neolithic peoples, which gave rise to a settled, agricultural civilization.

Earth energies, symbolized by the serpent, were respected by the ancients. They were attuned to the natural flows of energy (ley lines or meridians) in the land and knew how to use the energy to help heal the physical body and maximize their crop yields. Reverence for Earth's life force was woven into every fabric of Neolithic culture.

The navel is of course the point from which we receive nurturance from the mother—our most primal connection to life support. By blocking this point with the omphalos stone, the male sun gods cut off our connection to the earth. This is the point where humanity became disconnected from the vital force that flows to us from Mother Earth. Instead we became *head/intellect* beings, further entrenching the system of separation and the Patriarchal Age.

THE SERPENT AND FEMININE POWER

The Greeks, in addition to many other ancient cultures, associated the serpent or dragon with the goddess, fertility and feminine power.[61] With its fluid, sinuous movements, one of its primary associations is with the flow of life force or kundalini, which in its dormant phase lies coiled like a snake at the base of the spine.

However, Python, the serpent son of Gaia, represents not only fertility, feminine power and the flow of life force in the Earth—but also yin-yang balance. Snakes are sometimes associated with the yang/masculine because of their phallic shape. Because Python is the son of Gaia, not the daughter, he integrates both the masculine and feminine. This symbolism takes on even greater significance in light of current anthropological research, which reveals that the Neolithic era was a time of greater equality and harmony between men and women, when yin and yang principles were more balanced.

Python's subjugation by Apollo was the metaphorical end of the era of Earth veneration, fertility worship, and yin-yang balance, and heralded the dawn of the Patriarchal Age. Beginning approximately 5,000–6,000 years ago, our modern era has been a time of dominating and controlling Earth's natural resources and the feminine. Like Python in his hole, the reverence for Earth energies and the yin principle have been relegated to the subterranean realms of human consciousness, and the memory of this power mostly forgotten.

Although Apollo and Archangel Michael are one essence, they were revealed as two entities in Leslie's vision. This accentuates the message that the collective male—*all* of the male/sun/son energy—needs to unite in moving this omphalos stone and releasing the python which they originally subjugated. The yang/masculine energy must undo what it originally did when it enslaved the serpent son of Gaia.

Little did Leslie and I know that her vision heralded a new chapter in our lives. Archangel Michael was beginning to guide us on a voyage of discovery deep into the mists of the past. We not only journeyed back in time to learn about the turning of the previous age but also took a physical pilgrimage to ancient sacred sites of Greece, France and the UK to explore and discover one of the Earth's primary meridians known as the Archangel Michael/Apollo ley line. The journeys, which are intimately intertwined, were, and continue to be, life-changing adventures.

FROM THE NEOLITHIC TO THE PATRIARCHAL AGE

At the time of her vision, Leslie and I were reading extraordinary books about the transition from the Neolithic to our modern Patriarchal Age.

Riane Eisler's *The Chalice and the Blade: Our History, Our Future* was an enormous help in putting Archangel Michael's message in context and significantly reframed the perspective of human history we had been taught in school. Through archeological and anthropological research, Eisler reexamines our traditional historical worldview and proposes an inspiring new theory, specifically from a more feminist perspective.

According to *The Chalice and the Blade*, over the course of a couple thousand years the peaceful, egalitarian Neolithic peoples were gradually wiped out by tribes who invaded from the north. Known as the Indo-Europeans (although they were neither Indian nor European), they poured through the Caucasus Mountains from the Russian steppes on horseback with iron weapons and decimated the Neolithic settlements in what is now the Balkans, Europe and the Middle East. Without fortifications or advanced weaponry, the Neolithic men were massacred, and the women and girls were taken as slaves and concubines. *It was a process that . . . entailed enormous physical destruction that continued well into historic times.*[62] . . . Furthermore, *Indo-European rule was imposed through the chaos of massive physical destruction and cultural disruption.*[63]

Eisler refers to writings by the ancient Greek poet Hesiod:

> *We have already seen that Hesiod's references to "a golden race," who lived "in peaceful ease" and to whom "the fruitful Earth poured forth her fruits," are memories of the more peaceful and egalitarian farming peoples of the Neolithic, who were even by this time [about 700 BC] only remembered in legend.*[64]

The Indo-Europeans subjugated the Neolithic culture and the women who had helped create it. From Eisler's research it is evident that in Neolithic times men and women shared a much more harmonious, egalitarian relationship than today, and both held positions of power in the culture—a dynamic she refers to as a *partnership model.*

As the Patriarchal Age developed, a new form of social organization which focused on power, domination and control replaced the Earth goddess culture—a new dynamic Eisler calls a *dominator model.*

With the subjugation of the Earth Mother came masculine dominance over the feminine. Neolithic goddess worship was supplanted by the cult of the Sky God, the white-bearded patriarch on his throne in Heaven. The war-like Indo-European tribes brought with them a completely different perspective on the worth of women. They revered the power of physical strength, and women could not compete in this arena. The intrinsic value of women and feminine energy was discounted, marginalized and rendered invisible.

With patriarchy came the birth of a more left-brained culture with a focus on logic, linearity and the development of technology. This shift also heralded the era of literacy, of alphabetic writing. Brought in by the Hebrews, alphabetic writing supplanted hieroglyphics and cuneiform writing and radically transformed consciousness.

Hieroglyphics and cuneiform were pictographic in form, meaning that the letters were shaped like the object to which they originally referred.[65] The Hebrew alphabet used symbols or characters to represent the individual sounds (vowels and consonants) of the language rather than objects or ideas.[66]

Perhaps more than any other invention, the alphabet assisted with the fundamental transformation in human consciousness and the turning of the age. The era of the feminine, right-brained, holistic, intuitive mindset gave way to the dominance of the left-brained, linear, logical masculine. Leonard Shlain in *The Alphabet Versus the Goddess* writes about the Greek myth, the *Rape of Europa,* a metaphor of this developmental shift.

> *Zeus and Typhon, the terrible serpent, were engaged in a battle to the death; the winner would rule the universe. Typhon had overcome*

Zeus by tearing out the Olympian's sinews, and the other Olympians fled in terror when they saw their leader disabled. Enter the puny mortal, Cadmus. Distracting Typhon with flattery and music, he allowed Zeus to regain his sinews, and then stood back while Zeus slew the monster with his awesome thunderbolts. Unprecedented in a Greek myth, a mere mortal, lacking the superhuman strength of a Hercules, intervened in a battle of Titanic proportions, saved the day for the Olympians, and earned for himself their respect and gratitude.[67, 68]

It was the mythical hero Prince Cadmus in this story who introduced the alphabet to the Greeks.

The Bible was the first book ever written to make use of an alphabet, and according to Shlain it was instrumental in establishing the dominance of men and the subjugation of women.

[I]n a seminal book over seven hundred pages long, the demolition of women's status begins on page 2 and is essentially completed on page 3. Gender relations is the first issue raised and settled after the creation of the universe, which suggests its priority for the author(s).[69]

The [Hebrew] innovations of monotheism and Rule by Law, combined with the abrupt repudiation of all female deities, created considerable confusion concerning the relationship between men and women.[70]

A sacred book that details how mischievous and worthless women are would be a powerful means of advancing, at women's expense, the fortunes of both the left brain and literacy.[71]

The Bible introduced the idea of sin, which had not existed in prior civilizations, and Eve (woman) and the serpent (feminine power) were effectively demonized.

The Egyptians, Babylonians, Greeks, and Romans had no word in their language for sin; the Israelites introduced both the word and the concept into the stream of Western civilization.[72]

The story of Adam, Eve and the serpent is an allegory so rich with meaning it is beyond the scope of this book to explore. In essence women were blamed for humanity's fall from grace. We are told that we were kicked out of Eden, a heavenly realm where all our needs were met (a possible reference to the previous era when life was more idyllic), and forced into a life of pain and suffering because of the sinfulness of women.

And it has been downhill for women ever since:

Western civilization's extraordinary continuity down through the ages with regard to the repression of the feminine can be summarized by the following set of quotations:

"Sin began with a woman and thanks to her we all must die." Ecclesiasticus 25:24 (second century BCE)

"Women are the gate of the devil, the patron of wickedness, the sting of the serpent." St. Gerome (fifth century CE)

"Men have broad shoulders and large chests and small narrow hips and are more understanding than women, who have but small and narrow chests and broad hips; to the end they should remain at home, sit still, keep house and bear and bring up children." Martin Luther (16th century)

"Husband and wife are one person in law; that is, the very being or legal existence of the woman is suspended during the marriage." William Blackstone (18th century).[73]

Over time women lost ground culturally, politically, religiously, and in every way imaginable. Their stature diminished until ultimately they became little more than chattel. During the Dark Ages, in Europe over the course of a century or more, a slaughter took place as part of the Inquisition, in which over ten million women were tortured and killed by the church for crimes such as practicing midwifery and herbal medicine. Feminine power was conveniently labeled as witchcraft and destroyed. Only in the past century or so have women begun to regain their rights. Although great strides have been made in that direction, women still struggle for recognition and rights to this day, and prejudice still reigns in the minds of both men and women. We still live in a world that reveres machismo, and in the minds of many, it is still *a man's world*.

THE FALL

Another remarkable book that reframed our worldview and helped put Leslie's vision into perspective was *The Fall: The Insanity of the Ego in Human History and the Dawning of a New Era*, by Steve Taylor.

> *For the last 6,000 years, human beings have been suffering from a kind of collective psychosis. For almost all of recorded history human beings have been—at least to some degree—insane.*

> *This seems incredible because we have come to accept the consequences of our insanity as normal. If madness is everywhere, nobody knows what sane, healthy and rational behavior is any more. The most absurd and obscene practices become traditions, and are seen as natural. It becomes "natural" for human beings to kill each other, for men to oppress women, for parents to oppress children, for small groups of people to wield massive amounts of power and dominate massive numbers of other people. It becomes normal for people to abuse the natural world to the point of ecological disaster, and to despise their own bodies and feel*

guilty for experiencing completely natural desires. It becomes "natural" for human beings to try to accumulate massive amounts of wealth that they will never need, and to endlessly chase after success, power and fame—and also somehow "natural" that, even if they do manage to gain wealth and status, they never find contentment and fulfillment anyway, but remain constantly dissatisfied.

All of this insanity was the result of an event which I call The Fall—a collective psychological shift which large groups of people underwent around 6,000 years ago.

We will see that before the Fall human life seems to have been fairly carefree and pleasant, even joyful. But after it, life became "nasty, brutish and short," so full of misery that countless generations could only endure it by convincing themselves that it was just a brief stopover—to grin and bear as best they could—before they ascended to an eternal paradise. But perhaps now...we are turning a full circle, and returning to a kind of sanity. Over the last few centuries—particularly since the eighteenth century—there have been signs of a re-emergence of all the old "pre-Fall" characteristics.[74]

An anthropologist and psychologist, Taylor spent years traveling the world researching *pre-Fallen* cultures, primarily indigenous tribes in very remote areas, such as the Trobriand Islands of Papua New Guinea and the rainforests of South America. Spending significant time with the tribes people, he learned details of the various aspects of their society, such as family, money, sexuality, the body, food, government and religion. Mostly untouched by the modern world and Western culture, the tribes were in varying degrees of *Fallen-ness* and *un-Fallen-ness*. Normally the more remote and untouched they were, the less Fallen the culture and the more carefree, pleasant and joyful their lives. In general the more they had become influenced by modernity, the less egalitarian the relationships between men and women, and the more suffering they seemed to experience.

Although it is not within the scope of this book to give a thorough analysis of *The Fall*, the important message Leslie and I took away is that *it doesn't have to be like this*. There is a way out of the mess.

> As humanity heals and clears the insanity of the ego and moves into the heart, the more balance we achieve between masculine and feminine—inside and out. We begin to live in love and joy and to establish a new paradigm on this planet.

The amazing evidence that Taylor presents is a hopeful reminder that another way is possible, that we have had it before and can have it again. *The last 6,000 years have been a schizophrenic nightmare from which we are finally beginning to awake.*[75]

A New Paradigm

Our world is tremendously out of balance. Because of the dominance of the masculine, the suppression of the feminine and our lack of reverence for our Mother Earth, we are destroying the web of life and making the planet uninhabitable. We must return to a balance between masculine and feminine—both in our culture and inside ourselves—if we are to survive as a species. As Riane Eisler explains in *The Chalice and the Blade*:

> [T]he present system is breaking down, [and] we must find ways to break through to a different kind of future.
>
> The chapters that follow explore the roots of—and paths to—that future. They tell a story that begins thousands of years before our

recorded (or written) history: the story of how the original partnership direction of Western culture veered off into a bloody five-thousand-year dominator detour. They show that our mounting global problems are in large part the logical consequences of a dominator model of social organization at our level of technological development—hence cannot be solved within it. And they also show that there is another course which, as co-creators of our own evolution, is still ours to choose. This is the alternative of breakthrough rather than breakdown: how through new ways of structuring politics, economics, science, and spirituality we can move into the new era of a partnership model.[76]

In Taoism the extreme of yang gives rise to yin. In Chinese medicine when an illness is due to an excess of yang energy in the body, the doctor tries to restore yin energy to create balance. As yang recedes, yin is birthed in the body, and the patient's health returns. And so it will be with the Earth. Many millions are working to restore the yin and bring balance back to our planet. However, as author Charles Eisenstein points out:

On a less cheerful note, in Chinese medicine there is also a condition called "the collapse of yang," which happens when maintaining a prolonged imbalance so depletes the body's resources that nothing is left to sustain the process of rebalancing. Then all intervention is useless. It is too late. The patient dies.

For civilization, the collapse of yang would mean that when we finally see the source of our crises, we will be too weak to do anything about it. Today we have not yet reached that point. Sufficient social and natural resources still exist to create a beautiful world for all of us. Yet we continue to deplete social, natural, cultural, and spiritual capital at an accelerating rate. How long until we so exhaust it that, when we wake up to the urgency of our condition, we find we lack the strength to create the beautiful world we can see clearly at last?[77]

Let us trust this will not be the case for our beloved planet and all her life forms. It certainly does not need to end this way. Although we may be facing possible extinction, there is a worldwide groundswell of sacred activists whose commitment and dedication can create miracles.

The inspiring book, *Blessed Unrest—How the Largest Movement in the World Came into Being and Why No One Saw It Coming,* by environmentalist and social activist, Paul Hawken, is the result of a decade of examining the worldwide movement for social and environmental change.

> *From billion-dollar nonprofits to single-person dot.causes, these groups collectively comprise the largest movement on earth, a movement that has no name, leader, or location, and that has gone largely ignored by politicians and the media. Like nature itself, it is organizing from the bottom up, in every city, town, and culture, and is emerging to be an extraordinary and creative expression of people's needs worldwide.*[78]

Hawken likens the Earth to the human body. When we contract a disease, our immune system initiates the healing process and a return to balance and wholeness. It is the same for the Earth. Because she is sick with pollution, climate change and social injustice, her immune system—the world's movement of sacred activists—is kicking in. The Earth's immune system is made up of everyone who is doing the work of restoring the environment and social justice around the world, and we are showing up in record numbers now.

The new paradigm of the heart is birthing, even as the old system is dying. Reading about the state of the Earth nowadays, we are challenged not to get sucked into a rabbit hole of fear, hopelessness and depression. It is critical to remember that in these so-called *end times*, we are not only witnessing the death of the old but also the birth of the new.

> *If you look at the science about what is happening on Earth and aren't pessimistic, you don't understand data. But if you meet the people who are working to restore this Earth and the lives of the poor and you aren't optimistic, you haven't got a pulse.*[79]

A LOT OF ENLIGHTENED WOMEN

In the early 2000s, just before Leslie and I discovered these powerfully transformative books, the world was entering a particularly dark phase. Events such as 9/11, the US war in Iraq, and the intensified rape of the environment left us reeling in the face of the world's insanity.

In a rare fit of anger and despair, Leslie screamed inwardly to the heavens, *What is it going to take to change this world?*

She said the answer from the guides came instantly and very matter-of-factly: *A lot of enlightened women.*

This unexpected, provocative response both stunned and intrigued us. *Why just women? Why not men, too?* We had often observed at our gatherings the disproportionate gender ratio, which on average was about 80% women to 20% men, and the response certainly spoke to that imbalance. Pondering the situation, we realized that the feminine has been *disempowered* for so long that it is essential that women step more into their power in order to balance the rampaging, imbalanced yang energy in the world. Furthermore, we understood that because men in general still hold the power, they do not have as much incentive to change as women do. Therefore, it is going to take a lot of women stepping into their enlightened power to create a tipping point for the Earth.

The response from Leslie's guides does *not* mean that it is *not* important for men to wake up too. On the contrary it is critical that men strengthen their commitment to their spiritual practice, step into their divine masculine power, develop their inner feminine and balance the two sides. It is also vital for men to support and hold space for women stepping into their power. When a man does all of this, he moves the omphalos stone and liberates the earth's creative energies. In so supporting the collective healing of the masculine-feminine relationship, he takes a major step forward on his own evolutionary journey.

It is never easy to face our dark shadows in human consciousness, and it is the rare person who chooses to make such a conscious journey. Both men and women, whether oppressed or oppressors, have a long road to walk, and we must walk it together.

> We are genderless souls having experiences in male and female bodies, which are on loan to us from Mother Earth for a few short years. Whether we have a male or female body this time around, there's never been a better time to create inner yin-yang balance, to help heal an imbalanced collective gender relationship and to step into our true power—our own inner Divinity.

Shortly after Leslie's guides offered this potent message and while we were reading these transformational books, we prayed deeply to be shown what more we could do for the Earth and how we could help birth a new paradigm of the heart. Intimating that a new adventure was about to begin, Archangel Michael put another book in our hands that launched a quest we never could have imagined.

CHAPTER 21

The Power of Pilgrimage

❧

This "river" of energy appeared truly dynamic as it interacted with the countryside through which it passed, being joined by other tributaries and streams of earth energy of varying qualities. The picture that was beginning to emerge was one of a vast interlinked flux of subtle energy, with sacred sites marking crossings and unusual energetic formations. We found it impossible not to compare this with the idea of the earth's nervous system, with the St. Michael Line as a main channel, but merely one part of a bewilderingly complex structure of subtle power spreading throughout the land.

Only after this tantalizing, if baffling, period did we start to come across references to the Wouivre, or Vouivre, the serpent energy of the Druids. To them, this was the animating power of the Earth which ran in sinuous currents through the land. It was linked with fertility, healing, inspiration and revelation and represented the vital Life force on which everything depended. Its universal symbol was the Serpent or Dragon.

As we researched further we became aware that a lost knowledge of the Serpent or Dragon Lines could be found in many cultures. One of the most notable was the extant tradition of the "Rainbow Serpent," a symbol of the primal routes walked by Australian aborigines, which linked their sacred sites and were said to have been dreamed into existence by the old Gods. They were created, according to legend, by song (resonance or vibration) and hence are known as Songlines. This, it could be construed, is an evocative mythic way of saying that the colours and sounds associated with these serpent energies have a certain vibration that gives them a form of "personality."

[T]his was, in effect, a signature that focused our attention as we worked with it, and we became aware, as our sensitivities increased, that the entire surface of the earth was covered in a web of these dragon lines of varying resonance, which often seemed to possess an interactive form of intelligence. Wouivre is very close to the old English word weaver *which may give a clue to the difficult concept of an animate web of subtle biomagnetic/spiritual energy that creates a matrix of vital force within the body of the Earth.*[80]

In an extraordinary act of divine synchronicity, we were given a book that added a whole new dimension to Leslie's vision of Archangel Michael and Apollo: *The Dance of the Dragon—An Odyssey into Earth Energies and Ancient Religion* by Paul Broadhurst and Hamish Miller, with Vivienne Shanley and Ba Russell. Its subject is the Archangel Michael/Apollo ley line, which is a straight line that runs from the southern tip of Ireland, through England, France, Italy, Greece and Israel. It is an axis 60 degrees west of north. Amazingly, along the line in Ireland, England, France and Italy, there are many churches and monasteries dedicated to Archangel Michael. In Greece, there are many temples and sacred sites dedicated to the god Apollo and to one of his sisters, Athena. Some of the major sites along the line are Skellig Michael in Ireland; St. Michael's Mount in Cornwall, England; Mont Saint Michel in Normandy, France; Sacra di San Michele, Assisi and Monte Gargano in Italy; Delphi, Athens and Delos in Greece; and Mount Carmel and Megiddo in Israel.

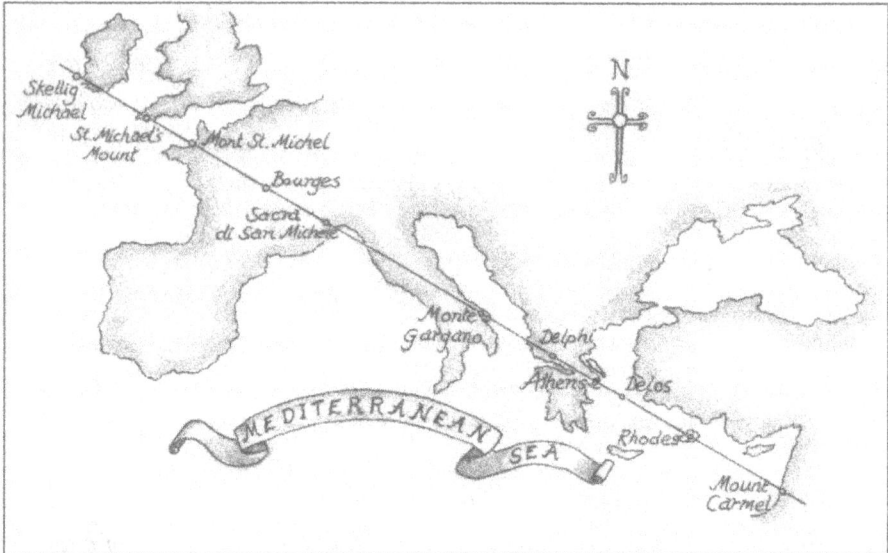

The Apollo/St. Michael Axis through Ireland,
Cornwall, France, Italy, Greece and Israel

Over the course of ten years, the authors traveled the line, approximately 2,500 miles, and dowsed it, mapping the Earth's energy currents that run along it. Dowsing is an ancient technique, still used today to trace the Earth's energetic pathways or more commonly to find underground water sources. Leslie and I sometimes use the method to track pathways of energy at sacred sites. Since reading *The Dance of the Dragon*, we have dowsed several sacred sites on the ley line and beyond.

The authors' journey was initially inspired by the book *Sacred Geography of the Ancient Greeks* by the distinguished French scholar, Jean Richer, first published in French in 1967, and later translated into English by Christine Rhone and John Michell and published in 1994. Richer was a well-known author and teacher with a deep interest in mythology and occult disciplines. He had a significant interest in Greek temples and monuments, studied their unique, sacred qualities and positioning on the landscape and suspected some underlying plan that determined their orientation. While living in Athens, he had an oracular dream in which the god Apollo alluded to a geographic connection between Athens and Delphi. On waking, Richer immediately got a map, a pencil and a straight edge, and traced a straight line between Athens and Delphi. Extending the line, he was amazed to discover that it also went through the island of Delos—Apollo's sacred birthplace. Athens was home to the goddess Athena (Apollo's sister), and because Apollo was the presiding deity in Delphi, he thus realized that there was a direct connection between the geographical location of the temples of the two primary deities of the Greek pantheon, Apollo and Athena.

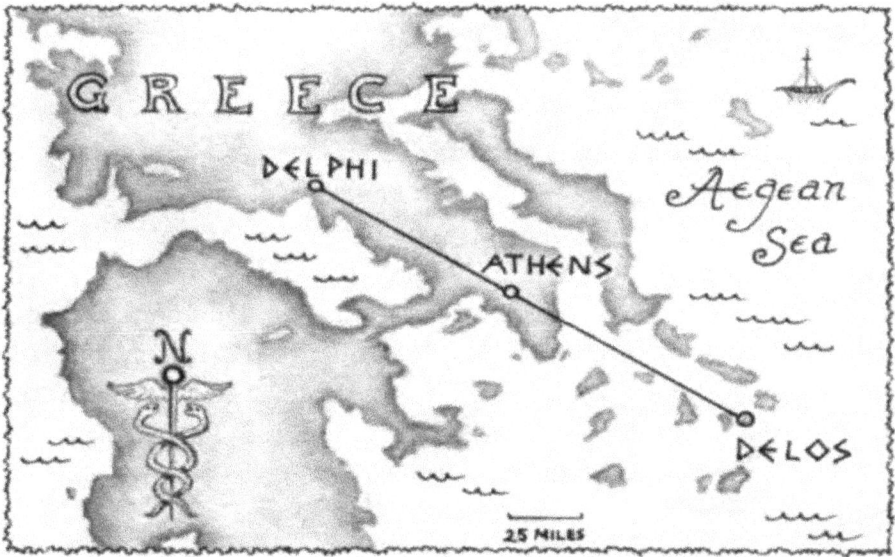

It was thus an "Apollo Line" that appeared to mark the career of the Sun God from birth to his prime, when he became the presiding spirit of the land at Delphi, the Greek center of the world. The tradition that Apollo took over Delphi from Gaia hinted that the legend of the Sun God overlaid an earlier understanding, where Delphi was the omphalos, or navel, of the fertile Earth Goddess.[81]

Richer's discoveries did not end with the Apollo line. In the years to follow, he continued his research and made many more fascinating discoveries about the geography of ancient Greece's sacred centers. Among other things, he uncovered astonishing zodiacal configurations formed by sacred sites and learned that Delphi was the center of an enormous zodiacal *wheel.*

Later, Jean Richer's older brother, Lucien, continued his work. He thought to extend the line further into Europe and discovered many sanctuaries of St. Michael along it, five of which are noted above. The degree of accuracy of the line is remarkable. All sacred sites on the 2,500 miles of the Archangel Michael/Apollo line are contained in a straight path, which is about 25 miles wide.[82]

As you will recall from the previous chapter, Archangel Michael and Apollo are the same essence. The female/yin counter balance to that yang principle is Athena. Archaeological evidence indicates that the churches and monasteries dedicated to Archangel Michael and temples dedicated to Apollo and Athena were built on top of Neolithic pagan sacred sites. Let's just pause for a moment and wonder at the extraordinary capacity of that pre-patriarchal culture, to recognize the earth currents and mark the sites in such a widespread area with such precision. We can imagine, too, the brutality of power used to stamp out this incredible knowledge from our collective memory.

THE MASCULINE AND FEMININE EARTH CURRENTS

The authors of *The Dance of the Dragon* discovered through dowsing that there are two ley lines crisscrossing the entire length of the Archangel Michael/Apollo line, forming a design which resembles that of the caduceus.

The caduceus is the ancient mystical symbol depicting two snakes twisting around a central staff. In the Egyptian pantheon, Thoth, the father of medicine, was the holder of the caduceus. In Greek mythology, Apollo, who is associated with healing and medicine, gave the caduceus to his brother Hermes. Today, a form of the caduceus is the symbol for medical professionals, including the American Medical Association,[83] and thus snakes—or kundalini (life force)—still have an association with healing energy.

Let's take a closer look at the important symbolism of the caduceus. Two snakes encircling a straight line are a direct mapping of how the life force moves within the subtle energetic form of the human body.

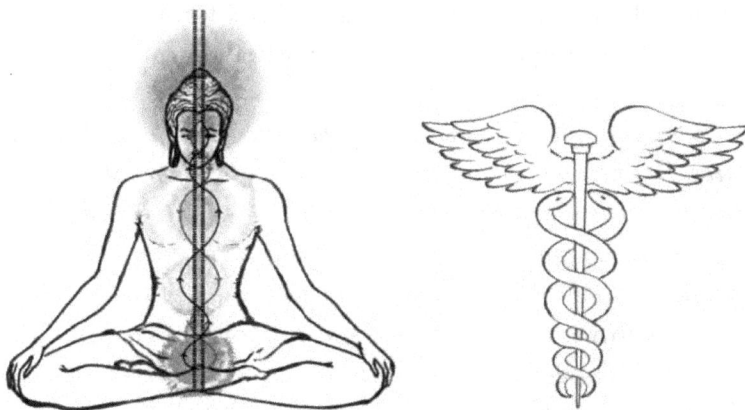

In meditation, clairvoyants and sensitives are able to see and feel this energetic movement inside the body. The straight line corresponds to our central core of subtle energy, the shushumna. The two energy flows, which wrap around the shushumna, are known in Sanskrit as the *ida* and *pingala*. Although it is beyond the scope of this book to explore their functions fully, they are electromagnetic fields of yin and yang energy. Consciousness flows in and through them as they wind their way around the shushumna in a double-helix form. The pingala is the yang upward flow of energy, and the ida is the yin downward flow of energy.

The ancient symbol of the caduceus maps the esoteric knowledge of the subtle human anatomy—the shushumna, ida and pingala—and presumes an understanding of the inner workings of our fundamental energetic flows of life force. When they are in perfect balance, we very naturally enjoy perfect health. Not only is a balanced, awakened life force the source of health in the human body, but so too in the body of Mother Earth.

While researching their first book, *The Sun and the Serpent,* which maps the ley lines of England, the dowsing authors found that one of the curving lines had yang qualities and the other yin qualities.

> *Where the Michael current was predominantly solar, fiery and positive, this new one, which we called Mary, was more attuned to the Moon, and was altogether more gentle. We later found that this line was particularly fond of churches dedicated to St. Mary. We should have predicted that there would be a second current of energy with the opposite polarity to the one we had become so familiar with. E. J. Eitel in his classic* Feng-Shui—The Science of Sacred Landscape in Old China *stated this explicitly when he wrote, "there are in the earth's crust two different, shall I say magnetic currents, the one male, the other female, the one positive, the other negative."*[84]

Just as the human body has its weaving flows of yin and yang subtle energy in the form of the caduceus, so does the Earth.

In their journey of discovery along the Archangel Michael/Apollo line through Europe, the authors named the masculine line Apollo, and the feminine line Athena.[85] The Apollo line often passes through large rocky outcroppings, towers and other masculine forms. The Athena line favors places with more feminine, watery, womb-like qualities, such as wells, springs or caves.

Where the two lines cross, or *mate*, is a point of creation, with connections deep inside the Earth. These nodes, like chakras, are places of great spiritual and energetic power, which were recognized by the ancients and chosen as significant sacred sites. There are many examples of these sites throughout Greece, Italy, France and the UK including the Temple of Apollo at Delphi, the Parthenon in Athens and the sacred island of Delos where Apollo and his sister Artemis were born.

HUMAN ACUPUNCTURE NEEDLES

Leslie's vision and our discovery of *The Dance of the Dragon*, coincided with an invitation to co-facilitate a retreat in France and with the launch of the Dutch translation of *The Marriage of Spirit* in Holland. Like our work on the Nilotic meridian in South Africa, Leslie and I realized we were being called to Europe to work on the Archangel Michael/Apollo ley line.

In between the Dutch events and the French retreat, we traveled to Greece to meditate on the ley line. Our intention was threefold: 1) to act as human acupuncture needles on the Earth, 2) to balance masculine and feminine within ourselves and 3) to help free the ancient feminine energies trapped in the Earth to balance the excessive yang, as Archangel Michael had instructed Leslie in the vision.

The extraordinary nature of our pilgrimage motivated a return visit the following year to lead meditation retreats exploring ancient sacred sites on the ley line in Greece and France. We had numerous incredible experiences, and in the interest of conciseness, I have summarized just a few of the highlights here.

Although the distant island of Crete is not on the ley line, we knew we needed to begin our pilgrimage there because the matrifocal[86] Neolithic culture endured there longer than anywhere else on Earth, until as recently as 1,500 BCE.

We landed in Crete on my birthday, which I took as a sign that our pilgrimage would be blessed by a rebirth in consciousness and by energetic renewal. Seeing the renowned Minoan snake priestess figurines at the archeological museum was a highlight. They are remnants of the Neolithic civilization that thrived there, tangible evidence of a time when the feminine and the serpent—representing life force, healing and earth currents—were revered, not demonized. Bare-breasted and wielding snakes, which wrap around the arms, waists and headdress, these small but mighty priestesses exude the power of the feminine. They left an indelible impression on us both.

Contemplating the fact that these sensual, snake-entwined priestesses presided at a time when the masculine served the great Earth Mother goddess, I recalled that the snake, due to its phallic shape, was sometimes used to symbolize the masculine. I wondered if perhaps these figurines represented much more than just the power of the feminine. Could they also represent the balance and harmonious collaboration of masculine *and* feminine, rather than a predominance of the feminine power? If so, these famous figurines are beautiful representations of yin and yang in authentic service of each other.

After leaving Crete, we visited many sacred sites on our earth-energy pilgrimage through Greece. Our most potent experiences were at Delos, Delphi and Dodona, where ancient goddess-worship sites are buried underneath the existing, Patriarchal-era temples to Greek deities. Praying and meditating on the ley lines, we focused especially on the nodes, where the masculine and feminine currents cross and form powerful energetic vortexes. In the twenty-four years of our relationship, I have rarely seen Leslie incapacitated from working with energy, yet at each of these three sacred sites, she experienced shifts in consciousness so profound she became physically debilitated for a day or so. She had difficulty describing these unparalleled experiences but explained they were about the dissolution of old structures and the reordering of energy.

Delphi

After meditating on the ley lines on the sacred island of Delos, we traveled to the most venerated shrine of the ancient Greek world, Delphi. As we drove from Athens up the foothills of sacred Mount Parnassus, Leslie unexpectedly entered a deeply altered state. Lying on the back seat with her eyes closed, she was so enveloped by the experience that she could hardly speak, occasionally whispering only a few unintelligible words. After a similar experience on Delos a few days prior, this second incapacitation was doubly rare.

Her dissolution and inability to speak reminded me of accounts of the Pythia of Delphi, who would induce a trance in the inner sanctum of the Temple of Apollo. There they allegedly mumbled prophecies, often incoherently, and uttered strange sounds, the meaning of which were interpreted by attending priests.[87] Leslie seemed to be reenacting ancient Delphic priestess rituals in the back seat of the car before we had even arrived.

As we drove up the steep mountain slope and approached Delphi, she slowly began to revive. Strangely, she returned from the inner journey with hardly any memory of what had transpired, an extremely unusual experience for her. Her conscious awareness was taken away as some part of her left the body to work with energy elsewhere. She only knew that something profound had transpired. If this foreshadowed the days ahead, we sensed we were in for an interesting and powerfully transformative ride.

As we wound around the twisting mountain road, there was a steep drop into an enormous gorge on our left and a breathtaking view of the valley below. Vast, pristine and intensely silent, the valley was host to a forest of pine trees which seemed to whisper their mystical secrets in the forceful, hallowed winds.

As we climbed the pass approaching Delphi, with the majestic Mount Parnassus rising dramatically on our right, Leslie slowly began to revive, and we entered the palpable Delphi vortex in a state of awe. On our left, Delphi was ringed by the gorge, a range of massive mountain peaks and a delta of olive groves, which flowed down to the shores of the Gulf of Corinth. It is no surprise the ancients chose this site. Surely such astonishing natural beauty must be graced with great spiritual power.

The Mother was tangibly present. Her tender, nurturing heart space was all around us, enveloping us with a blessed welcome. Considered the center of the known world in ancient times, the place where Heaven and Earth meet, it is no wonder one feels close to the Divine at Delphi.

Delphi retains many levels of energy from the devotions of countless pilgrims over millennia, from the worship of the Earth Mother in Neolithic times to Apollo's more recent reign during the pre-classical and classical Greek and Hellenistic eras. Its lengthy history as a world-renowned worship site reveals the great shift in consciousness that transpired at the turning of the ages.

The first oracle was dedicated to Gaia, the Earth Mother, and Poseidon, the "Earth Shaker." The serpent Python, the son of Gaia, inhabited a cave further up the mountain, but when Apollo came to claim the shrine for himself he used golden arrows or darts to slay the serpent and established his own sanctuary on a broad mountainous terrace. The radiant Sun God of harmony, order, music and prophecy thus initiated a new age that superseded that of former times, when the serpent Gods and Goddesses were omnipotent. Not for the first time, nor for the last, a new God of Light had taken on the characteristics of previous divinities, banishing them to the twilight realms of our collective consciousness where they still live.[88]

Following the map in *The Dance of the Dragon*, we went directly to the spots with the most Earth current activity. The Athena and Apollo currents form a unique node at the Temple of Apollo unlike any other in their 2,500-mile journey across Europe. Both currents enter the temple side-by-side along its central axis and occupy exactly the same location, flowing precisely together in a tight, concentrated path for some distance. The fusion of the masculine and feminine Earth currents creates an exceedingly powerful energetic effect.

I took the opportunity to pray for the balance of masculine and feminine energies in myself and on the planet and also practiced *Planetary Acupuncture.*[89] This simple yet potent technique can be done anywhere; however, it is especially powerful when practiced at sacred sites. Beneficial to the practitioner as well as to the Earth, you act as a human acupuncture needle and assist with raising the vibration of love on the planet. It involves sitting quietly in meditation while performing breathing exercises to process celestial, terrestrial and personal energies through your body and the Earth. These consist of three different kinds of breath, each performed three times to form cycles of nine breaths, which are repeated.

As I performed repeated cycles, I found the most important part of the exercise was to add my love to the equation. By focusing on the love, I raised my vibration, and in time my sensitivity increased tremendously. Eventually I entered an altered state and could feel the subtle currents of love I was generating mixing with the Earth currents. They were being carried in a dynamic, higher vibratory flow of energy and moving out along the ley lines into the earth grid. I visualized Python himself—freed from his subterranean prison—receiving my love and positive intentions and carrying them out into the world.

I became aware of an unusually strong masculine-feminine balance in the energy field at the Temple of Apollo. With each in-breath I could feel this potent yin-yang fusion permeating my body. While meditating there and in fact throughout the several days we spent at Delphi, I sensed an inner shift occurring. A deep layer of shadow left my body, an old patterning relating to masculine-feminine imbalance. Delphi's hallowed ground seemed to absorb the old layers of shadow and imbalance that I was ready to release to the gods. Offering gratitude to Apollo and Athena, I noticed that the ancient Hermetic axiom, *as above, so below*, applied perfectly here: As the masculine and feminine Earth currents flowed together in perfect alignment, balance and harmony, so my consciousness transmuted and began to reflect that orientation as well.

DODONA

After several days in Delphi, we drove to Dodona, which is the most ancient sacred site on the Greek mainland and has very few visitors due to its remote, mountainous location. Much older than Delphi, it too was an oracular, priestess site but dated back to at least 2,000 BCE. Eventually it succumbed to patriarchal influences and became a sanctuary of Zeus around 1,300 BCE.

About thirty miles from Dodona, Leslie was drawn deeply inward into a state of dissolution. The sensations became so intense that she could not continue to read the map, and we pulled off the main road to recline the front passenger seat so that she could lie down. Barely able to speak, she could not communicate what was happening and soon withdrew completely into an inner, subconscious realm to do energy work and receive a download. This was déjà vu. I had rarely seen her in such a dysfunctional state—and now it was for the third time in two

weeks. All she could convey was that primordial memories of matrifocal times were being awakened.

As I continued driving to Dodona, I pondered the situation and realized all three experiences had coincided with visits to key sacred sites
of ancient goddess worship. In a sudden *aha* moment, I got a clear
and spontaneous download that this was connected with the intention
of our pilgrimage! Later Leslie confirmed that during her dissolved
state at Dodona, she was helping to release the trapped feminine energies in the Earth. She was also shown that this had been the case at
Delos and Delphi as well. Acting as a human transformer, her body
was transmuting and balancing the excessive patriarchal energies and
assisting with the unleashing of Python, the great Earth serpent.

We pulled into the parking lot at Dodona and meditated in the car
for quite some time, until eventually she said the work was complete.
To help embody the energy, we meandered slowly through the ancient
ruins, where we felt a deep resonance with the goddess. Just being on
the land at this intensely powerful site had opened us both to receive
mystical downloads that took a long time to unpack and decode.

Our pilgrimage continued to the island of Corfu and then on to
France, where I co-led a meditation journey with Denise Lurton-
Moullé, our friend who had given us *The Dance of the Dragon*. Exploring
more sacred sites on the Michael/Apollo line, our little group of spiritual warriors performed profound meditations in the original church
at Mont Saint Michel. Like many other European churches that are
built on top of former pagan/Neolithic sacred sites, the original
church is found in the basement. Although *Notre Dame Sous la Terre*
is normally off-limits to the general public, through apparent divine
intervention, we were allowed access and found the ley line activity to
be very strong. Because it was the summer solstice, we were more sensi-
tized to the subtle energies of the Earth and her natural elements, and

we sensed a vast magnification of our prayers and loving energy field wherever we meditated on the mount. In fact, we discovered that the whole of Mont Saint Michel acted like an enormous electrical power station—transforming and amplifying energy along the Earth's grid.

When our energy work was complete, we celebrated like playful children. Wandering to the west side of the mount, we gazed at the sun slowly setting while the tide gurgled in. The wispy cloud formations filtered the light, creating crimson reds, florescent pinks, burnt oranges and golden yellows. Archangel Michael was painting a magical sky with his giant brush, a color-and-light show which shimmered mirror-like on the fast-moving tide below. We huddled together, awestruck by the vibrant spectacle. Spiritual energy filled us to overflowing, and high on the light, we surrendered in a rapturous embrace.

Our intimate band also spent a week on the exquisitely beautiful Chausey islands, a nature preserve off the coast of Normandy. Although the authors of *The Dance of the Dragon* had not visited Chausey, we brought our dowsing rods with us and discovered that the Michael/Apollo line runs through there. After all of the wonderful synchronicities on our journey of discovery led by Archangel Michael, we were astonished, yet not surprised, how the divine plan continued to unfold in miraculous ways.

Since our first pilgrimage in 2006, Leslie and I have continued to explore the energy of the Archangel Michael/Apollo ley line and are constantly amazed by its profound spiritual power.

THE POWER OF PILGRIMAGE

We have to be humble enough to learn to live with this mysterious question: Who am I? I am a mystery to myself. I am someone who is in this pilgrimage from the moment that I was born to the day to come that I'm going to die. And this is something that I can't avoid, whether I like it or not — I'm going to die. So, what I have to do is to honor this pilgrimage through life. And so I am this pilgrim . . . who's constantly amazed by this journey. Who is learning a new thing every single day. But who's not accumulating knowledge, because then it becomes a very heavy burden on your back. I am this person who is proud to be a pilgrim, and who's trying to honor his journey.

—*Paulo Coehlo*

Pilgrimage is as ancient as human memory; it is a tradition in all religions. The search for our origins, for a taste of our eternality, for the feeling of something holy. We seek places where we might touch Heaven, where the divine presence is more tangible than others.

Pilgrimage is a metaphor for the inner journey, the journey from ignorance to enlightenment. We take an expedition to a sacred site, but the goal is not about reaching the destination; it's about being present for the journey itself. Each step along the way offers its own awakening. Each adventure brings new insights, epiphanies and growth, resulting in raising our consciousness. Each experience improves and expands our sense of self, bringing us closer to the knowledge of who we truly are—the vast, eternal Self.

[T]o re-establish the harmony of the First State, all the great teachers— Buddha, Lao-tse, St Francis—had set the perpetual pilgrimage at the heart of their message and told their disciples, literally, to follow The Way.[90]

Some believe that the longer and harder the pilgrimage, the more spiritual growth occurs. Making full body prostrations every few steps or carrying extra weight are common techniques of adherents to this philosophy. Perhaps this arises from feelings of guilt and a need for atonement.

I believe that a primary purpose of a pilgrimage is to learn to enjoy the path. When we get caught up in the planning and the goal, we forget to cultivate the joy along the journey. True joy is an effect of spiritual awakening. It is therefore fitting we remember to pack a significant supply of it in our bundle when embarking on a pilgrimage.

Leslie and I have been on many pilgrimages, each one full of remarkable experiences, but it is important to recognize that everyone can do this work. Making a pilgrimage and meditating and praying for qualities such as peace, love and balance—both inner and outer—are for everyone. One's level of attainment in consciousness is not a prerequisite. Pilgrimage is an immensely worthwhile endeavor that can produce powerful results for anyone who feels drawn to it.

> One does not need to be an enlightened master—or even a great meditator—to do this work. Everyone is capable of visiting sacred sites and adding their love to the planetary equation. By setting an intention and making a commitment to heal oneself and/or the Earth, it becomes so. Everyone's love is amplified at sacred sites. It is as simple as that.

BALANCING MASCULINE AND FEMININE

Humanity has grown increasingly ignorant of its connection with the natural world and the web of life. Reverence for Earth energies and the invisible currents that sustain life have all but disappeared, and we are in the process of destroying the planet and her life-giving essence. Climate change, melting of the ice caps, destruction of the rain forests, rapid extinction of species, raping of Earth's natural resources, over-population, disease and war are all evidence of extreme imbalance in our relationship with Earth.

> The feminine must be given her proper place of equality with the masculine. Yin and yang need to be brought into harmony in order to facilitate the healing of the Earth. It is time for humanity to return to the laws of nature and to reawaken the understanding of her life-giving properties. We must re-learn how to use them to heal ourselves. It is time for humanity to come back into balance with Earth, to honor and revere her and help her heal as well.

The balancing of masculine and feminine in each of us is essential for the opening of the global heart. We have come once again to the turning of the ages, where humanity stands on the threshold of a great shift in consciousness. This shift requires the conscious awareness of each individual as they enter into the heart. Archangel Michael has made it clear that he is helping humanity facilitate the movement into the heart and that the new paradigm will be a time of equality, peace, harmony and balance, ushering in a time of vast change in human consciousness.

In *The Myth of the Goddess* by Anne Baring and Jules Cashford, Sir Laurens van der Post writes in the Foreword:

> *Here for the first time to my knowledge, the story is told in full. It is the awful, yet at the same time strangely inspiring story of the feminine, still unvanquished and undismayed, which we are all called to honour and obey if we are not also to vanish, like so many other cultures in the labyrinth of the past. . . . The horizon behind us is littered with*

the rubble of civilizations which have failed to renew themselves, have failed a challenge somehow to transcend their opposites in something that will combine in balance both the masculine and the feminine and, in their union, create something greater than the sum of their parts. (ix–x)

CHAPTER 22

Piercing the Veils

❧

Are you Leslie Temple-Thurston?

Yes.

Wow, I just came from Brazil, and the people there love you.

I'm sorry, you must have the wrong person. I've never been to Brazil.

Are you a spiritual teacher?

Yes.

And your name is Leslie Temple-Thurston?

Yes.

Well, there can't be many out there with that combination. It's definitely you. I have just come from Brazil, and you are very well known and loved there.

In the early 2000s, at a hair salon in Santa Fe, an American woman sitting next to Leslie engaged her in this conversation. Later that day, still confused yet amused by the strange circumstance, she told me the story. I remembered that sometime in the 1990s we had received a parcel from Brazil with audio tapes of a Brazilian Portuguese translation of Leslie's *Marriage of Spirit* recordings. Apparently the English audio had made its way to Brazil, where some dear people appreciated the information enough to transcribe it, translate it and re-record it in Portuguese. They were requesting permission to disseminate it in Brazil. We had given permission with gratitude, but years had passed, and we had heard no more about it—until this day in the hair salon in Santa Fe, of all places.

I went through my files, found the old correspondence and contacted the Brazilians. They confirmed the success of the audio recordings and asked permission for the book version to be translated into Portuguese and published in Brazil—again we were happy to give permission. In 2006, in support of the book launch, we went to Brazil and offered events in Rio de Janeiro, Brasilia and two other cities. We fell madly in love with the country and our new heart-centered friends there. Full of love, joy and passion for life, they welcomed us with such warmth and gracious hospitality that we never wanted to leave.

At an event in Rio, a woman named Nirupa, who had traveled from the rainforest to see Leslie, approached us in tears. Through our translator, Ivana, she explained that in her area, the remote state of Acre, the rainforest was being decimated by loggers, cattle ranchers and soybean farmers. She had opened a meditation and yoga center in the capital city, Rio Branco, but was struggling to bring the light into a very dark area. She begged Leslie to join her in some meditations at her center, Gaia, in Acre in an attempt to lift the dense consciousness which was exploiting and destroying the rainforest.

Thank you for the kind invitation. If you think my coming will help, then I'm happy to support you. Nature and forests are very precious to me.

As Ivana conveyed Leslie's words, Nirupa's eyes lit up, and she started nodding vigorously. No translation was needed to decipher her response; nevertheless, Ivana diligently interpreted each word with appropriate intonation.

Yes, please come! I'm sure you can help bring in the light.

In 2007, we returned to Brazil and added several more cities to our two-month itinerary, including Rio Branco, Acre, where we sat in meditation at Gaia with a lovely group of participants. We met hundreds of beautiful souls deeply devoted to the spiritual path and to living in love. It became clear to us that Brazil was one of the world's leading centers for the birth of the new paradigm of heart-centered consciousness. The love and joy we experienced there, especially through their exquisite singing and dancing, was contagious and full-bodied.

THE RAINFOREST AND THE TEA

At the end of the trip, we were invited to fly deep into a remote part of the rainforest to meet an Indian tribe, the *Ashaninkas,* who had had very little contact with the outside world. However, after arriving in the small town of *Cruzeiro do Sul* (Southern Cross), we received word that they could not meet with us after all. Trusting that the significance of this change of plan would become apparent, we took pleasure in having some free time in the heart of the beautiful Amazon rainforest.

Before long our attention was drawn to the plight of the *Katuquina* Indians, who were struggling to keep their land and culture in tact as the Western world ineluctably encroached further and further into their territory. The drive to their village took several hours along a new dirt road, and on the way we witnessed numerous clear-cuts, like raw wounds in the forest, with cattle ranches and farms springing up. The leader of the Indian village spoke to us, via Ivana, about the overwhelming changes the new road had brought. The road yoked them to the Western-world farmers, ranchers and consumerism. The tribe was relying increasingly on supplies from Cruzeiro do Sul, and as a result its youth were leaving to find jobs in town. The loss of traditional skills and the erosion of their tribal ways were devastating. An increase in pollution, the introduction of diseases and a decrease in unspoiled land were also causing ongoing problems and contributing to a less sustainable lifestyle.

We could feel the grief of the tribal leaders. However, they were open to new ways of increasing their sustainability, including selling beautiful handicrafts made by the tribe, producing boots from latex harvested from the local rubber trees and extracting oils from rainforest nuts. In an ideal world they would not have to be involved in the money system at all, which is in itself unsustainable, and they could continue to rely on their own sustainable relationship with the forest and nature as they had for thousands of years. We joined in prayer, asking that their tribal ways and environment could remain intact.

We sang and danced with the Indians and purchased some of their lovely crafts in support of their efforts towards sustainability. Just before we were set to leave, we were engulfed in a sudden deluge of rain so dense we couldn't see more than a few feet in front of us. The dirt roads, which were bad on our way into the forest, were almost impassable leaving. With visions of spending the night stranded in the car in the middle of nowhere, I learned my first Portuguese phrase, *Não se preocupe, seja feliz*—Don't worry, be happy—which became our mantra on that leg of the journey. Despite many tense moments, our stalwart driver, Luis, miraculously managed to get us home that night.

One of the highlights of our time in the forest was an unexpected invitation to join Luis and his local spiritual community for a private *Ayuhuasca* ceremony. Prepared from rainforest *teacher-plants*,

Ayuhuasca is a sacred medicinal tea that takes one on a journey in consciousness. Deeply honored yet having no idea what to expect, we accepted the kind invitation.

A couple of days before the ceremony, we were given a general orientation about Ayuhuasca. Considered a traditional medicine by many South American indigenous peoples and a religious sacrament by some Brazilians, Ayuhuasca is also known by other names, such as *Santo Daime*, which literally translates as *Saint Give-me*. It is believed that the guiding spirit of the plants used in making the tea will *give you* an experience based on whatever intention you set beforehand. For example, people may ask for a specific physical healing experience, for spiritual revelations, for insights into how to be a better person or for answers to questions about the nature of the universe.

After two days of deep meditation and prayer around our specific intention, Leslie asked to be shown the mystical nature of the forest, and I requested an experience of my spiritual enlightenment.

Arriving around dusk, Leslie, our small group of friends and I took seats in comfortable, reclining, patio chairs, which were arranged outdoors in a circle on a cement platform in the midst of the forest. With only a tin roof over our heads and no walls to separate us from the trees and wildlife, we were surrounded by countless hues of green and the vibrancy of nature. Chirping cicadas, singing crickets and a symphony of other insect and bird life serenaded us. As the heat and humidity of the daytime gave way to evening, a cool, moist breeze caressed our skin, and we savored the sweet scent of the damp forest and the magic of the twilight.

As the ceremony began, we stood in a circle, singing and praying together. I felt an overwhelming connection with the loving hearts of each soul present. The leader of the ceremony, a friend of Luis's, walked around with a pitcher of the tea, gazed into each person's eyes and in turn intuited how much tea to put in each glass. I noticed that Leslie got a small dose, about 1/10 of a glass. The next person got a little bit more. It seemed as though in general each person got no more than a quarter of a glass. However, after gazing into my eyes and a brief hesitation, he poured until the glass was full. *This must be because I'm so much taller and weigh so much more than everyone else,* I assumed.

After another prayer, we drank the sacred brew and waited quietly in meditation. About twenty minutes later the effect of the tea began to kick in, and I felt a warm, tingly sensation as my body started to melt into my reclining chair. A great physical discomfort slowly enveloped me. Waves of extreme nausea, churning sensations in my stomach, burning fever and other severe body pains grew in intensity.

Simultaneously, an equally agonizing mental-emotional equivalent was escalating. Dark, shadowy thoughts and feelings erupted with mounting frequency. Extreme fear, paranoia, guilt and a host of other negative emotions built and began to sweep through me like raging wildfire.

> *Oh my God! Please help me! I want out of this! Please make it stop. I can't deal with this. I'm losing control. This will never stop. I'll always be this way. I'm going insane. I can't believe I did this. This is the worst thing that's ever happened to me!*

Pulling every tool I could think of out of my spiritual toolkit, I was glad I had spent the previous fifteen years practicing shadow-clearing techniques. The first was the neutral witness.

> *I am not these emotions. They are passing through me. I am the pure awareness. None of this is real. I am the perceiver, feeling these*

uncomfortable feelings move through me. I am pure consciousness, light and love. This too shall pass.

This refrain became my mantra.

Next I put my attention in the *Cave of Brahman,*[91] which is a mystical place in the center of the head. Meditating on this location creates a powerful, conscious connection with the spiritual realms.

> The cave of Brahman is a location in the subtle body, a few inches behind the third eye.
>
> It holds great mystical power and corresponds to the pineal gland, pituitary gland and hypothalamus. By holding our attention here in meditation, a doorway into higher dimensions opens.

As I repeated the witness mantra and focused on the Cave of Brahman, the physical, mental and emotional pain intensified so much that I was forced to put one hundred percent of my attention on the pain. The fear and paranoia were especially overwhelming. Witnessing the emotions and physical pain pass through me became in itself a very powerful meditation in which total concentration was required. Like driving at top speed along a freeway, I felt that if I moved a milli-meter physically or let my mind stray for one second, I would die or go insane.

As the meditation deepened amidst the agony, I noticed that my heart rate and breathing were slowing down considerably. Slower, slower, slower, until my heartbeat was barely detectable and I was hardly breathing. Even though a torrent of toxic emotions and physical pain raged through my entire being, the meditation was calming me physically—helping me to find a certain acceptance in spite of the horrendous passing parade.

I'm dying. I'm going to die tonight in the middle of the Brazilian rainforest. Well, you know, I've actually had a really good life. I have absolutely nothing to complain about. It's been such a great ride, and I wouldn't change a thing. If I have to die, I can't think of a better place to go.

Then my heart stopped beating completely and I stopped breathing.

I must be dead now. Am I dead? No, I know I'm not dead because I'm still conscious of horrific pain. But how can I be alive if my heart is not beating and I'm not breathing?

I was reminded of a similar experience I once had in meditation. But this was different—this was accompanied by a massive wave of the worst emotions and physical pain imaginable.

Just as the darkest, most intense and awful shadow reached its crescendo with no apparent end in sight, I suddenly popped into a world of bright white light, and in an instant the pain vanished. Although my eyes were closed, I looked around my inner reality and saw an extraordinary, vast and expansive realm of luminosity. Surrounding me in all directions was nothing but golden white light. Gazing out at the far-distant horizon, I noticed a slight curvature, as if I were high above the surface of the Earth. From my bird's-eye view I looked down on luminous grid lines, which formed a matrix or web of light that extended far beyond me and encircled the planet as far as I could see. To my right, a few feet away, was a being I recognized. With the body of a man and the head of a hawk, he was the Egyptian god Horus, and he communicated with me telepathically.

I am your guide here. I will take you on a tour of this realm and show you things you must know.

At supersonic speed we zipped along the gridlines. On either side of us, I noticed beautiful, brightly colored mandalas, like billboards on the side of the road. We stopped to look at a few.

At this level of consciousness, these colorful, kaleidoscopic forms are representations of things on Earth. In fact anything you can name on Earth has a mandala here—on the Causal plane. For example, this one is the mandala for birds. And this one is for cats.

Each mandala was beautiful in its way, and as I gazed at them, I received an inner, telepathic knowing of what aspect of Earth they represented. Among other things, one was a war, some were people, and one was my relationship with Leslie.

When the journey ended, I thanked Horus for his guidance and support. Slowly I opened my eyes and saw that the rest of the group was also emerging from their experiences. Several hours had passed, and we were all gradually becoming re-accustomed to the physical surroundings. Feeling completely reborn and marveling at my experience, I realized I had successfully endured the ordeal. It was surreal, and I lived to tell the tale. Knowing I would never be the same again, I sensed I had left some old egoic baggage behind forever. Jubilant and free, I joined with Leslie and our new Brazilian friends in the end of the ceremony, which involved joyful singing, dancing, music and many *abraços e beijos* (hugs and kisses), a Brazilian specialty. We thanked our hosts profusely for a life-changing spiritual experience and said tearful goodbyes.

I learned much that night, and although Horus disclosed things which are too personal to reveal here, I can share one of the most important lessons, which relates to finding one's core of spiritual illumination. Leslie often describes the path of clearing egoic shadow as a voyage through the subtle-physical body. The shushumna—the column of light corresponding to the spine—is the luminous core of enlightenment inside each one of us. However, seeing it clairvoyantly, the radiant core is covered over by a thick, black, tarry substance, which is the egoic shadow blocking us from becoming conscious of our enlightenment.

> The process of clearing the ego involves peeling away layers of black, tarry matter from the shushumna, eventually revealing our core of spiritual illumination.

That was the journey I made with the Ayuhuasca.

The tea catapulted me through the black, tarry stuff in a very short amount of time to suddenly pop into the core of enlightened consciousness, which is the shushumna. My intention for the journey was to be given an experience of my enlightenment, and that is exactly what the teacher-plant gave me. However, I hadn't bargained on having to go through all of that shadow first. (Do we ever?)

That experience had been an excellent metaphor for my journey of Self-discovery. It reminded me that when I feel stuck in the shadow, I can persevere with hopeful tenacity, knowing that the luminous core is just beyond the dark, heavy stuff. As I experienced viscerally that night, the darkest hour is just before dawn.

> Despite the intensity of our shadow experiences, we never know when it might be time to pierce the veils and enter the realms of golden white light.

We have only tried the tea a couple of times since being in the rainforest. Now, if I choose to do it, I take a very small amount[92] and am a bit more circumspect about the intentions I set. The spirit of the plant does give you exactly what you ask for.

Our experiences in the rainforest and in many other parts of Brazil hold a special place in our hearts. Almost every year we have returned to Brazil to offer events and have continued to fall ever deeper in love with this country and its beautiful, heart-centered people. Leslie's books, audio and courses have been translated into Portuguese, and now there are Brazilian graduates of CoreLight's training programs who facilitate the courses there.

DEATH AND REBIRTH

Sharing insights with Leslie about my Ayuhuasca journey, I asked her why it was Horus who greeted me as my guide on the Causal plane.

Leslie, I've always heard that you are met on the other side of the veil by a being with whom you resonate the most. For example, a Muslim might be met by Mohammed, or a Christian might be met by Jesus or the Virgin Mary. I don't really know Horus—why did he meet me?

You've had so many Egyptian lives, and your deeper soul nature resonates with Horus. Christianity is relatively new in the grand scheme of things. You've had many lives before the Christian era, and you've spent many incarnations in the ancient Egyptian mystery schools.

Of course, Horus is also linked to Jesus, and scholars have drawn parallels between the Horus mythology and the birth, death and resurrection of Jesus. Perhaps you should look into that.

Researching this ancient Egyptian creation myth, I discovered that Horus is the son of the goddess Isis and the god Osiris. Before Horus was conceived, Osiris was dismembered, and his parts spread throughout the country. In love, Isis gathered his bits together and conceived Horus. Osiris' dismemberment represents our fractured self in this paradigm of separation. We experience ourselves as disparate parts, apart from the Creator. We need to collect all our scattered pieces to become whole again. This journey of Self-discovery is the process of re-collection (collecting our parts) or re-membering who we truly are. Horus was born of this remembering, which required the feminine principle of Isis. Her union with Osiris (the conjoining of our masculine and feminine parts), produced Horus, the radiant god of light.

In my initiation, Horus (the rebirth/unification principle) gave me a bird's-eye/hawk-eye view of reality so that I could recognize the true interconnected/unified nature of our reality. What died in that experience was the last vestiges of a self who believed that I was somehow separate from Source. What was reborn was the Self who remembered my true nature as being one with the Creator.

It took several years to understand all that had happened in my experience with the tea and to integrate the change, but in retrospect I see that in facing some of my worst fears around loss—loss of control, loss of sanity, loss of life—egoic knots dropped away. Although this shedding of egoic shadow may not be complete or permanent, it was enough to experience a taste of enlightenment. And in that moment of egoic detachment, a new me was born—a resurrected me if you will.

Of course this rebirth was not simply the result of one encounter with a cup of tea—no matter how powerful the plants may be. Rather, it was the culmination of many years of disciplined practice. The experience in the rainforest can be viewed as an exam at the end of a course.

I was given the opportunity to put my accumulated knowledge and skills to the test. In casting off the mass of egoic baggage, a new level of Self-awareness was born, which then took several years to integrate and mature.

Perhaps it is no coincidence that Horus is symbolized by the all-seeing eye and certainly, as a guide, he gave me a view of reality that goes far beyond physical sight. Like a hawk, seeing the curvature of the horizon from the Causal plane, I am aware of having gained altitude in my perspective on what it means to be an immortal spirit in a human body on this beautiful blue planet. From that vantage point, our troubles, worries and burdens don't hold so much weight and no longer fill the screen of our awareness. Through the eyes of Horus it is easy to see that we are not the ego or the physical body, that there is no such thing as death and that in truth we are the cosmic, timeless Self.

As Brad, I began to experience more expanded and consistent states of calmness, equanimity and detachment, even amidst the stresses and hurly burly of our busy work and travel schedule. I became aware of a deeper level of discernment and intuitive ability emerging. I felt a new level of my heart opening into love, compassion and courage. My relationships started changing, and a stronger, more mature self began to emerge. The mirror of my interactions with people reflected this new me, which was gratifying and brought me great joy.

My relationship with Leslie began to change as well, and gradually over a number of years our old way of serving each other gave way to a new form. She had always been the spiritual teacher, and I had held responsibility for the worldly manifestation. Her yin was held and supported by my yang capacity, and my yang was nurtured and fed by her beautiful, loving flow of yin. During our first fifteen years together, I primarily focused on developing yang qualities of strength and manifesting form. Now, although we still serve each other unconditionally, the greater balance of yin and yang within me has empowered me to take on a more active teaching role. A welcome confirmation that I'm on the right track is the flow of more administrative support into the CoreLight office so that I am freed up to do this.

The teacher in me was born as a result of the insights Horus imparted in the rainforest. As such, my dedication is to help others re-member their true nature as the Self.

The journey of becoming is ongoing. The pilgrimage is not over. In many ways it feels like the adventure is just beginning.

Moving Beyond Victim Consciousness

❧

Please magnify any remaining shreds of ego, so that I can process them and become free before I leave my physical body.

Leslie made this incessant plea to her spiritual guides in the years leading up to December 21, 2012—the date the ancient Mayans predicted humanity would begin to birth a new cycle of human evolution.[93] Knowing that one of the highest forms of service to others and to the Earth is to clear your own consciousness, she wanted to make the biggest difference possible at this pivotal moment.

Her guides asked, *Do you want to ascend?*

I'm not sure what you mean by "ascend." I want to ascend in consciousness, but I don't want to drop my body yet.

Given your current level of evolution, it might be better to drop your body.

But I still have work to do on Earth. There are people I can help here.

We will do what we can, but if you choose to ascend to the next level and keep your body, we can't promise anything. It is not normally

*done. You will be a sort of trial—a pioneer. We don't know what will
happen.*

Leslie had always been a pioneer and agreed to the experiment. It was
during this time that she began to experience memory loss.

Her guides have informed her that it is not Alzheimer's disease but
rather part of the *experiment* to which she agreed. Health care professionals have also told us that she *doesn't fit the profile* of someone
with Alzheimer's. While there are physiological and neurological
components to the memory loss, it is clearly a spiritual process. She
describes it as entering a *whole-brain state* and as an evolutionary
step for herself and humanity—part of the work she has come here
to do.

Meanwhile we have been exploring various practical, physical pro-
tocols to help her improve the left-brain function and to ameliorate
the short-term memory loss, all of which have helped slow down its
progression.[94]

Her guides have told her that the changes to her brain are facilitating her movement into the fifth dimension and that those who follow
will not necessarily have to experience memory loss. We know she is
paving the way forward in consciousness even though we don't fully
understand the process yet.

At a soul level Leslie chose this—a great soul accepting a great challenge. While much of her journey has involved processing collective
shadow through her own body, the most recent process in paving
the path for collective evolution in consciousness came at a price—
memory loss. However, we know that she is not a victim or a martyr
in this situation. It is an opportunity for growth that she chose. We
all choose our degrees of challenge at a soul level, based on our own
level of evolution.

EMOTIONAL PROCESS

As Leslie goes through her changes, I too face major transformation in what feels like the greatest challenge of my life. Since her memory loss began, it has been a raw and intense emotional roller coaster. Recently I had a dream that reflects some of the emotional trauma being processed.

Leslie and I were in a campground with a large, extended group of friends in the middle of the forest. There was a small village of tents, and everyone was busy in some form of camp-related activity. I was chopping wood when I heard the news that there was a bear approaching the village. People scrambled wildly in a panic.

Oh no! Leslie is near where the bear is approaching.

As this realization dawned on me, I ran to find her and saw the bear at the edge of the forest. Menacing and dangerously close to Leslie, it was just about to lunge and maul her. In horror, I tried to run to her so I could fight off the bear and rescue her, but my feet were anchored to the ground. Despite using every ounce of my strength and willpower, I was unable to move. Immobilized and powerless, I watched helplessly as the bear attacked her.

Suddenly I woke up, sweating, terrified and with my heart pounding.

The dream reflects the fear, helplessness and pain I have been experiencing for the past five years. Over the course of our relationship I have embraced my role—always nurturing, supporting and protecting my beloved, yet I cannot shield her from this process. I stand on the shoreline helplessly watching her drift slowly out to sea, powerless to do anything to bring her back. As I grieve, the shattering, loss and hopelessness have been almost unbearable at times. Utterly bereft, I have learned that perhaps the hardest thing in the world is to watch a loved one suffer.

However, at another level I'm sure the dream was reminding me of the fact that there are no victims when we leave the system of duality. The symbol of the bear is important and is strongly associated with the primitive aspects of humankind. One of the bear's most notable features is that it hibernates and spends much of its existence in an *unawakened* state. Because of the hibernating aspect, they are also strongly associated with cycles and rebirth. In the dream Leslie is devoured in her process of awakening the hibernating consciousness of humanity. However, the symbol of the bear is not merely about destruction; it conveys creation and nurturance as well. So the bear is not only destroying Leslie but also facilitating a rebirth.

This is the most challenging experience I have ever faced, and I have had to call on every ounce of spiritual wisdom in order to get through the darkness. I rely on a strong witness and processing skills and am supported by caring and compassionate friends. All of this helps enormously, but the process is by no means complete. This challenge is a work in progress.

Recently my friend Lina posed a question that I have found invaluable:

> Who is it that you are loving when the memories and the personality fall away and when the person no longer acts in accordance with your perceptions?

I invite you to pause and reflect deeply on this question. Getting to the truth will require significant self-inquiry and surrender. Ultimately we see that we are not our memories, the personality or the body; that there is no death and that we are the timeless, immortal Self.

Even with this understanding and with all my spiritual tools, I still struggle with the loss of the Leslie I have always known and loved. As

I helplessly watch her experience the pain and indignity of memory loss, it is tempting to fall into the drama of victimization.

However, the role of victim keeps us locked into the system of separation more than any other egoic shadow process. The victim drama is ubiquitous in everyone's life whether we are conscious of it or not; therefore, let's take a closer look at the dynamics involved so that we can move beyond it.

> Victim consciousness, inextricably linked to its polarities, is the primary egoic knot the world is working through now. We are all being given an opportunity at this time to transcend it and move into the heart.

TYRANT, VICTIM, REBEL, SAVIOR ARCHETYPES

Throughout the book we have discussed the polarities of victim-tyrant and victim-savior. Now we can connect the dots between the opposing roles of victim, tyrant and savior, and introduce the role of the rebel. These four archetypes constitute a dynamic quartet, locking each other into egoic games of power and powerlessness. Thoroughly examining the complex, bidirectional flow of power in the victim-tyrant-rebel-savior archetypes is beyond the scope of this book; for now an overview is offered.

These four central archetypes form the underlying structure of all egoic processes. By bringing to conscious awareness the underlying patterns that keep us stuck, we can exit the system of separation.

All egoic processes, whether involving money, sex or survival, at their root, are power issues. This is the nature of third-dimensional ego. Power in this dimension is synonymous with control and is always polarized against powerlessness and lack of control. If stuck in any kind of attraction-repulsion reaction, we can be sure that a power dynamic needs to be resolved.

The dynamic of authority and subservience is usually implicit in any drama. The person in the position of power is the authority, and the person who appears powerless is subservient. The two sides may flip flop, and often each side does a little of both.

Frequently the drama doesn't involve another person. We may feel powerless in the face of life circumstances, such as accidents or natural disasters. When faced with illness, we may feel disempowered and oppressed by the body. Perhaps the government, corporations or banks are at fault. Sometimes allergies can leave us feeling that the very air we breathe is to blame. All of these situations involve feeling powerless and oppressed by a force beyond our control.

In any victim drama it's essential to identify and witness the archetypes, and these can easily be recognized by following the power.

In the system of separation, there are only four power roles that can ever be played:

* The **tyrant** occupies a position of power, authority and control, and is seen as negative. The tyrant's agenda is to exploit, win and control.
* The **savior** occupies a position of power, authority and control, and seen as positive. The savior's agenda is to rescue those who seem helpless and powerless.
* The **victim** occupies a position of powerlessness, suppression and lack of control, and appears to be weak and helpless. The victim feels tyrannized and wants to be saved.

    ♦   The **rebel** occupies a position of powerlessness, suppression and lack of control, and reacts against this. The rebel resents outside authority and desires to regain power and control.

The game of power and powerlessness played by these four archetypes is as old as time itself. The battles of Horus and Set, Zeus and Typhon, Apollo and Python, Archangel Michael and Satan and every ancient myth and modern Hollywood movie—are the eternal dance of duality. Day vanquishes the night, night triumphs over day, and then day is victorious again the next morning. In an endless cycle, light and dark and good and evil continually vie for supremacy. The same is true with these four archetypes. In *The Hero with a Thousand Faces,* Joseph Campbell wrote about a universal motif of adventure and transformation that runs through all of the world's mythic traditions. Tyrant, victim, rebel and savior are aspects of that universal motif.

Recognizing how limited our options are within this simple, underlying structure of the system of separation—especially given the countless permutations of human dramas—is tremendously empowering. It is a giant step towards leaving the separate system and entering the new paradigm of the heart.

Tyrant, Victim, Rebel

The four roles are inextricably bound to each other. We dance between them so quickly that, without a strong enough witness, we are unlikely to even realize that we are reacting and choosing to play out one of the roles.

There may be a situation or person acting as a petty tyrant—perhaps a boss, coworker or parent. From the level of duality, we have two choices:

We can play the victim or the rebel role. When we play the victim, we resist expressing our objection or anger at the tyrant. Instead we keep it in and feel helpless, powerless, subservient and lacking in control. However, playing the role of the victim has its pay offs, and we may even revel in it for a while, feeling sorry for ourselves and gaining sympathy and attention from friends. On the other hand our suppressed anger leaves us seething with self-righteous indignation and covert rage. We rebel inwardly against the authority of the other, and this offers us some subjective sense of control of the situation. Even mild resentment is a form of inner rebellion. On the surface we present the victim, but *sub rosa* is the rebel. However, because these rebellious, unexpressed responses are antagonistic in nature, they are attacks, and through them we become an inner tyrant. Our thoughts and feelings, although hidden, have an enormous impact on others around us, especially those who become the object of our projections; we can even make others sick with our unexpressed projections. Thus, unconscious rebelling has flipped right into tyrannizing, and the former tyrant has become our victim, even though the person may not know it consciously.

Rebelling against the tyrant through overt eruptions of emotion and anger, in an attempt to prevent the victimization, may briefly help us feel a little more powerful and in control. However, in doing so, we have become the tyrant, and the other person the victim. The cycle repeats itself ad infinitum in the realm of egoic power dynamics. It is a win-lose every time.

No matter how frequently we try on the different costumes of tyrant-savior-victim-rebel, we won't find lasting happiness. The only way out is to witness the polarized dynamic, process it and offer it up. Grace creates the healing, and we move into a healthier, more balanced relationship without the dramas and power games. From this unified place our relationships are more heart-centered and fulfilling.

Victim, Savior

When you love you should not say, "God is in my heart," but rather, "I am in the heart of God."

—*Kahlil Gibran*

Each of these four archetypes has its own form of power, including (and especially) the victim. Most think the victim is powerless—subjugated by an outside authority—yet the victim wields tremendous power, usually in an *unconscious and covert* manner. The victim's power includes: 1) manipulating through guilt or pity, 2) leaching energy (like a vampire), and 3) controlling the rescuer.

> The hidden nature of the victim's power is the key to the game. Once we recognize the behaviors—either in ourselves or others— we can witness them, process them and let them go.

As discussed in the beginning of the book, a common game people play in the dual system is to give away their power and project it onto a savior/rescuer figure—often in the form of a charismatic leader. Instead of taking responsibility for their own evolution, victims idealize the savior and place the burden of their growth on the savior's shoulders. When they begin to lose their path to salvation, as they inevitably will, they feel victimized and project their failings onto the savior, who is demonized and ripped off the pedestal.

Leslie's guides told her when she awakened in 1988, that her role in this life is to be a bridge between the old and new paradigms and to help people find their own inner divinity. This is why she has always stressed that she is not a guru or a savior, that people should not project their own divinity onto her and that she should not be put on a pedestal. A polarized model which promotes power and powerlessness between teacher and student, between leaders and followers, is obsolete and belongs in the old paradigm. Of course, teachers and leaders are still necessary for our growth and development. However, the time has come for us to take full responsibility for our thoughts and actions, and not simply believe what is imparted. Rather we must weigh all teachings and guidance against our own hearts and minds, and decide for ourselves what is true.

> Our teachers are not saviors, and it is time to leave the polarized archetypes behind. There is no savior outside of us. We are the saviors we've been waiting for.
>
> We can stop projecting our power onto others and step into our own power and inner divinity—the Self. The new paradigm of the heart awaits humanity when enough of us make this leap in consciousness.

LEARNING TO LOVE WHAT IS

Even when we have physical hardships, we can be very happy.
—The Dalai Lama

How we handle hardship determines our quality of life. Or as someone succinctly affirmed, *Attitude determines altitude.*

Obviously a part of me is deeply attached to the Leslie I've always known and loved. My expectation was that we would continue on our evolutionary trajectories, in a manner that was complementary, supportive and familiar. Having that expectation dashed felt like a breach of trust. My initial response was to feel betrayed by life and by God, and the resultant feelings of victimization soon segued into rebellion.

A mixture of anger and outrage at life's unfairness colored my grief as I moved through the normal, egoic stages of grief (denial, anger, depression, bargaining and acceptance).[95] However, witnessing my broken trust and the tyrant-victim-rebel-savior consciousness (or *victim consciousness* for short) were the first steps of the healing process. Remembering that victim consciousness is the primary egoic knot we are trying to unravel right now has been helpful.

The heart must have its due and express its own rhythm—so I continue to allow the grieving process to unfold in its own way. However, two methods of transcending victim consciousness have also been especially helpful. Both are part of the journey of learning to love what is. The first is to find the gift and the opportunity in the challenge. The second, forgiveness, leads on from the first.

> In every situation—no matter how painful and traumatic—there is a gift and an opportunity. Finding them begins the process of learning to love what is and to move beyond victim consciousness.

This is not about having a Pollyanna attitude, suppressing the emotions and playing *the glad game*. It is essential not to be in denial but rather to feel, allow and witness all the painful emotions—while simultaneously seeing the positive side beyond apparent victimization.

In finding the gift and the opportunity, I have realized that without this change, neither Leslie nor I would have stepped into the next stage of our souls' evolution. We would have maintained the status quo because we were enjoying life so much the way it was. Having been thrown into this test, we see the opportunity to rise to the occasion—to change and grow in a whole new way. For Leslie it is an opportunity to pioneer and embody a new state of consciousness, which she recognizes as a challenge her soul has chosen. Because memory loss is changing the nature of her work, I am being called to step beyond my support roles. By reminding myself of these gifts, which we would not have received without the change, I am moving beyond victim consciousness and learning to love what is.

Seeing the gift and the opportunity in the challenge leads to another stage in moving beyond victim consciousness—forgiveness.

> When we can forgive life, Spirit, others and ourselves for putting us through challenges, we transcend victim consciousness and move into the paradigm of the heart. Learning to forgive may be life's greatest challenge, yet it is our next evolutionary step.

Psychologists generally define forgiveness as *a conscious, deliberate decision to release feelings of resentment or vengeance toward a person or group who has harmed you, regardless of whether they actually deserve your forgiveness.*[96] In addition to *a person or group*, this would also apply to forgiving life or Spirit for the challenges presented to us.

Forgiveness is about overcoming our sense of betrayal. We feel betrayed and victimized when the trust we had in something is damaged. Whether we trusted that life would continue unchanged, but it didn't, or that someone would behave loyally, but they didn't, it is natural to feel victimized and betrayed because the trust was broken.

Betrayal and victimization causes pain and the heart shuts down. This is the ego's way of protecting us from getting hurt again. The heart remains closed towards whatever we feel betrayed us—a person, life itself or Spirit. However, shutting down the heart to every one of life's ubiquitous betrayals inevitably results in a very closed heart and a life of spiritual loneliness and suffering. Keeping the heart closed in protection keeps us locked into separation. At some point we may recognize this and choose to take the journey beyond it into the heart. This is the journey into forgiveness.

Finding forgiveness is not an easy journey, but it is the hero's quest—the path of any aspiring spiritual warrior. Two primary qualities are required: 1) warrior courage—willingness to risk the self, and 2) yielding yin—willingness to remain vulnerable in our love. Risking vulnerability is scary, but as we discussed in the Prologue, there is immense power in it. We need only look to the likes of Gandhi, King, Mandela and Malala Yousafzai to see that those who discover the power of vulnerability and the open heart—forgiving their oppressors and moving beyond their own victim roles—often become the greatest heroes and world leaders.

To be clear, we are not talking about naively laying down all protection before an enemy. It is important to practice discernment and to be prudent about our actions in the face of tyranny. Knowing how to draw a boundary and say no to the oppressor are essential skills on this journey. It is equally important, however, to move beyond hatred of our enemies and of that which oppresses us. By learning to love and forgive, we discover the power of the heart, which far exceeds the polarized power of victims, tyrants, rebels and saviors.

> The power of the heart is transcendent power and is the doorway out of victim consciousness.

My daily prayer and meditation practice now includes forgiving life, Spirit, Leslie—and my own soul—for putting us in this challenging situation. While I still don't fully understand why it has to be this way, every day I forgive and surrender all of it to the Self.

The root of the word *forgive* comes from the Old English *giefan*, which means to give, and the prefix *for*, which means completely—to give completely. *Forgiefan* also means to give in marriage, i.e., unity. This suggests that to truly forgive we need to give ourselves back to unity with Spirit and no longer feel separate and/or victimized. Forgiveness cannot happen from a position of separation, from one of the roles— victim, tyrant, rebel or savior—only by embracing the unity.

Giving forgiveness its full due is beyond the scope of this book; however, practicing the steps discussed in this chapter is a good start.

To me, the journey out of victim consciousness into forgiveness feels like a continuum—a pilgrimage without final destination. Maybe this journey is one step at a time, taken each day of our lives.

Processing Collective Victim Consciousness

What is true for an individual (microcosm) is true for a collective (macrocosm). The principles we have discussed in this chapter can also be applied to collective consciousness—the mass mind. When enough individuals transcend victim consciousness, the macrocosm will make the shift as well. This is when we will begin to see major change take place in the world.

Tyrant-victim-rebel-savior power games are being played out on the world stage as never before. Potential tyrants and saviors include: the patriarchy, the deep state, governments, politicians, corporations, banks, the military-industrial complex, the media, science, technology and religions. Potential victims and rebels include: women, people of color, LGBTs, indigenous people, sensitive men, Mother Earth, the environment and animals.

The spiritual warrior sees beyond the surface of unfolding world dramas and remembers that humanity is at the turning of an age when extreme yang is giving rise to yin. We experience the dramas with a witness and recognize that our role is to move beyond hating the tyrant. We stand in our authentic spiritual power, balance yin-yang qualities within and move into the heart—this is our journey in transcending victim consciousness

> We recognize that facing our opponent is how we develop our warrior spirit and that there is no growth without a villain. As the 6,000–year cycle of patriarchy comes to a close, we continue to be offered no shortage of opportunities for processing and growth. The potential outcome for humanity is a new paradigm of heart-centeredness and inner and outer peace.

A CALL TO ALL SPIRITUAL WARRIORS

At this turning of a great age, Spirit is calling us to move beyond victim consciousness and into our authentic power—the power of the Self. There has never been a better time to grab this evolutionary brass ring. We are in a time of extraordinary challenge—*and opportunity for soul growth*—and we have all the tools we need for success. We know how to balance yin and yang, inwardly and in the world. We know how to open the heart and to put our love into action.

Now is the time for all men and women on a conscious spiritual path to transcend the limitations of the ego and to choose love. This is what brings both personal fulfillment *and* Self fulfillment. When enough of us step up into our authentic spiritual power, the world will reflect this change to us. We will create a new paradigm of balanced, heart-centered consciousness and find lasting inner and outer peace.

Never doubt that a small group of thoughtful, committed people can change the world. Indeed, it is the only thing that ever has.[97]

CONCLUSION

Although the stories in this book have been about my own spiritual journey, they go beyond the personal and reveal underlying, universal principles that apply to all those on a path of Self-discovery. In this sense it is a transpersonal story—as much about Spirit as it is about Leslie and me. My hope is that the following summary may provide an overview—a quick-reference map, together with compass and tools—to help guide the way.

MAPPING THE JOURNEY OF THE SPIRITUAL WARRIOR

Our conscious spiritual journey often begins with an epiphany, possibly sparked by pain, trauma or a *wake-up call* of some kind—an accident, illness or loss. As we seek healing and understanding, the desire to know ourselves deeply begins to emerge, and we begin walking the path of Self-discovery. We realize that the more we can be true to ourselves and let our uniqueness shine, the happier and more fulfilled we become. We usually move from religious dogma to a path of spirituality. Trusting increasingly in the support of the invisible realms, we develop the skill of following the heart and discover that our worldly life *is* our spiritual life.

Spiritual warriors learn to manage energy impeccably—we eliminate addictions, manage our thoughts, journal our processes, offer our service selflessly, and in every way do less of that which drains us and more of that which feeds us. These practices, which become our lifelong companions, help us to build our light and eventually to realize the Self.

Through meditation and shadow clearing, we can learn to still the mind, find inner peace and surrender to spirit. We learn how to shed egoic conditioning and release old identities, and we progressively discover that we are not the personality. We become masters of our thoughts, realize their power to ameliorate the world around us and recognize that all thoughts are shared and universal. Beyond the limitations of the self, we begin to glimpse the truth of who we are—the vast, eternal, timeless Self.

By placing our attention in the Cave of Brahman, that mystical place in the center of the head, we stop thought, open doorways to higher dimensions and deepen our conscious connection with the Self. Recognizing that our inner core of light is masked by egoic shadow, we discover that peeling the darkness away with spiritual practices such as meditation and egoic clearing work reveals the light. When we experience the most challenging shadow, it is helpful to remember the darkest hour is just before dawn.

The path of generosity catapults us into the realms of love, and as we move beyond the limitations of the self, we begin to recognize that there is nothing in this world that is not love. This is one of the most challenging concepts for the mind to grasp. In essence it is the paradoxical discovery that the Divine is in everything: in horror and in beauty, in war and in peace, in destruction and in creation, in death and in life. The path of loving leads to a state of objectless and unconditional love and ultimately to becoming love itself.

Those on the path of Self-discovery cultivate humility, which empowers them to look squarely in the mirror. It takes great courage, insight and sensitivity to see ourselves clearly, and it allows us to grow and to become established in the heart. We learn not only to receive truth without defensiveness but also to speak truth with love, which further fosters our sensitivity and empathy.

Spiritual warriors develop their intuition and receive guidance from the invisible realms. Realizing there is no such thing as randomness or coincidence, we recognize the value in synchronicity. We develop trust, overcome fears, live more spontaneously and learn to follow our heart, dreams and passion. Living on faith, we open the door to a seamless flow of grace, which leads to greater joy and fulfillment.

When we choose to take the position of the neutral witness, we can observe life from outside the personality and can practice being neither attracted nor repulsed. By using this lens and understanding the principles of non-duality, we recognize that there is no such thing as separation. We begin to fully appreciate that we are not part of the world but rather the world is part of us. We witness the dance of duality and recognize that our hidden opposite is the part of us that we suppress into the unconscious and project onto others, who act it out relentlessly until we are able to grasp it consciously. Once we name the unconscious opposite side, making it conscious, the egoic game is over, and we no longer feel blindsided and victimized by life's apparent randomness. In our relationships we see the mirror of our own unconscious self, find balance within, feel less separate and reclaim our wholeness.

The spiritual warrior practices clearing egoic shadow, using methods like polarity processing and squares, to discover that by holding the tension between pairs of opposites, we allow room for a third option to manifest. By naming the opposites, seeing the shadow dynamics and making an offering of them to Spirit, grace comes in to create healing and to bring us into unity consciousness. This is the middle way.

As our sensitivity develops, the subtle body anatomy becomes familiar territory. We begin to feel our chakras and the shushumna—the luminous core of enlightenment within. We access our kundalini energy and use it to ascend in consciousness and enter samadhi—an experience of the peace that passes all understanding.

A spiritual warrior embodies Spirit in every facet of life—including relationships, sexuality, work and money. We enter into relationships consciously, lovingly and with the intention to serve our partners as well as to be true to ourselves. We do not manipulate, dominate or compete with each other. Balance and empowerment are the result. Realizing that the fulfillment we seek is within us, we don't depend on our partners for fulfillment.

We recognize that lovemaking is a sacred act. We devote our sexual lives to the worship of the divine essence in each of us, which becomes an initiation into a heightened embodiment of the Self. We realize that in terms of masculinity, femininity, sexual orientation and gender identity—we are infinitely more than a biological definition.

A spiritual warrior's relationship with work and money is balanced and heart centered. We offer ourselves generously and strengthen our faith in the support of the invisible realms through practicing the art of skywalking. We live in a financial flow and strive to share rather than hoard money. If the flow is blocked, we first look inwardly to clear our own money shadows. We come to fully recognize that we do not own or possess the flow of money and that we are required to be responsible, loving and generous stewards of it.

Resources, money and support pour in, often in unfathomable ways, when love is put into action. Eventually, our generosity and selfless service lead to the dissolution of the separate self and to the realization of the Self. This is the meaning of *selfless*—being beyond the old, limited egoic self and awakening to the vast, cosmic Self. This way of life can heal the unprecedented inequality in our global village and help move humanity into the new paradigm of the heart. Practicing love in action is contagious and opens hearts all around us. It is encapsulated in the South African principle of ubuntu: *I am a person through other people. My humanity is tied to yours.* One of the most important spiritual messages of our times, ubuntu speaks to our common humanity and our unity. It involves practicing loving kindness, generosity and sharing, and is the heartbeat of any sustainable community.

As the age of patriarchy draws to a close, there is a collective resurgence of feminine energy. It is going to take a lot of enlightened women to create the shifts humanity and Mother Earth need to balance and heal 6,000 years of rampaging yang dominance. Whether we have a male or female body this time around, there's never been a better time to help heal an imbalanced collective gender relationship and to step into our true power—our own inner divinity.

We can assist with the balancing of yin-yang—both personally and collectively—through pilgrimage. By visiting sacred sites with this intention and by adding our love to the flow of Earth energy, we facilitate inner and outer peace, balance and healing.

Moving beyond victim consciousness is central to our spiritual development. The game that tyrant, victim, rebel and savior archetypes play keeps us locked into the system of separation. By witnessing and processing our roles of power and powerlessness, we can stop projecting onto others, release it all and step into our own authentic power and inner divinity. When we can see the gift and opportunity in our difficulties and forgive that which oppresses us, we transcend victim consciousness, and we move into the paradigm of the heart.

Entering the Mystery

We are all walking a mysterious path. Life in a human body on planet Earth is about facing the unknown, dealing with constant change and meeting challenges we don't understand and can't explain. Each of us on our journey of becoming is learning how to meet this mystery, this formless unfolding of consciousness. We are called to love what is— to love our circumstances and ourselves. We are learning to respond authentically, to witness what life gives us and eventually to be at peace with the mystery. Our experiences teach us how to let go, surrender, have the courage to continue and not to fall away from Spirit.

So often when facing the unexpected we get angry with God and life because of dashed expectations. In those moments we somehow believe that in committing to a spiritual life, we struck a bargain with the Divine to ensure that things would be easier somehow. Of course, in many ways, life does improve enormously when we are on a conscious, committed spiritual journey. But when life doesn't meet our expectations (perhaps expectations we didn't even know we had) and especially when it feels like we are stepping backward, we suspect the sting of God's betrayal. These are the most critical crossroads, and in these moments we can choose our response.

It is through our willingness to face loss, unfairness and change with a spirit of courage and commitment that we evolve beyond feelings of persecution. Instead of indulging in victimhood and blaming the outside, we can take responsibility and look instead for the gift and the opportunity in each situation. This is the choice we all face.

Now more than ever, as we confront monumental world issues, we are being given the opportunity to balance yin and yang, to move out of the system of separation, to grow beyond the paradigm of tyrant-victim-rebel-savior consciousness and to enter the realm of the heart. By making these changes within ourselves, we will change the world together. At this pivotal moment in human evolution, we are learning to feel unafraid of the great, formless mystery called life—fearlessly letting go and surrendering over and over again in each present moment, opening and deeply relaxing into the joy of this exquisite human adventure.

We are entering the great mystery. And it is love.

My wish and prayer for all of us embodied on planet Earth at this time is that we may know and become love.

Bless you on your journey.

THE CONTINUUM OF ENLIGHTENMENT

> The journey of enlightenment is a never-ending continuum of spiritual evolution. Although there are milestones along the way, there is no fixed goal or endpoint. On this journey we are always learning, growing and becoming.

When Leslie experienced her awakening in April 1988, her old self and egoic structures completely dissolved. However, because being on this planet as a human requires some degree of separation, she assumed a *care-taker personality*, a kind of minimal structure to allow her to stay in a physical body. Passing this milestone, she moved out of the third dimension.

Over the last few years as she has transitioned through yet another phase of her soul evolution, she has taken on so much light that it has becoming increasingly difficult for her to retain her human body. When one holds so much light, the desire to have a physical body becomes more and more insignificant.

LANGUAGE AND THE ETERNAL PRESENT

Recently Leslie's guides shared more information with her about her new role:

> *You will not be teaching in the same way anymore. You will be like an umbrella, over-lighting the spiritual evolution of many souls and spending much time in meditation. When you speak now, it will be short, succinct and impactful.*

Leslie knows her opportunity for growth is to continue her inner work and maintain the witness even through the challenge of the memory loss. She says that like the painter, J. M. W. Turner, who bound himself to the mast of a ship and sailed through a raging storm so he could paint the experience, she secures herself to the neutral witness while a storm rages around her.

Leslie continues her role as a bridge for others as she observes the self through a lens less clouded by the structures of memory. She is using this opportunity not just to learn and grow but to continue translating into language the transcendent nature of her experience. In a recent conversation, she explained:

> *I feel like a student again, and the memory loss offers me lessons in humility. In the beginning I experienced reactions to it, such as fear, but when I moved beyond that and just surrendered, I saw I was being given deeper teachings, not just about humility, but also about living in the present moment.*

> *Losing the memory is one way of completely dropping the ego. When you lose the memory, you enter the eternal present, the eternal "now" moment. It is an experience of the Divine. For me, being in it is like entering vast, interstellar space; a cosmic, immeasurable state of oneness—a beautiful energetic field of unity, divinely conceived and exquisite.*

> *Words are so limited in trying to describe this experience! (Laughing.)*

> *Interestingly, I find it is language that brings me back into the world and allows me to stay here.*

> *Now, in between words or thoughts, I go into the void, into transcendent awareness. When I drop language, I'm "gone." Out into the cosmos. Then I really struggle to come back again. I lose my train of thought.*

Words are my feet, and my feet are walking through the cosmos, one step at a time.

Language is peripheral really. But I'm trying to hold onto it because when I put words to paper, I can come and go between the two worlds.

I committed to be a bridge. That is why I hang onto language, so I can come back. I feel like an angel flying between the worlds, sometimes touching down between heaven and worldly life—a go between.

Words are stepping-stones into the cosmos. That's my job, and it's fun! I'm helping bust open the cosmos to bring awareness and understandability to it instead of it just being vast, empty, higher-dimensional consciousness.

This language could be called wisdom. This work is about teasing wisdom out of empty space. It's not really empty; it just seems that way when you're in the third dimension.

What an ascension we are in! An ascension into the knowledge of the Self.

Leslie's teachings of non-duality and unconditional love still remain in the form of books and audio, imbued with the vibration of enlightenment.

EMERGENCE

In the pupae stage of a caterpillar's transformation, it completely liquefies within its protective chrysalis. Its former self dissolves completely before it can metamorphose into a butterfly.

As Leslie and I let go of old roles, we are experiencing a similar process of dissolution before we can emerge as entirely new beings. Sometimes we feel liquid. At other times more formed, our wings beginning to unfurl, still wet and drying.

In writing this transpersonal autobiography I have recognized that my story is both unique and universal. The act of telling the story has been profoundly healing, helping me learn what I have learned, so to speak—to fully grasp and move through and beyond it. Writing the stories with the intention of releasing them, not holding onto them, has been a powerful method of letting go of an old self.

Nowadays I am constantly reminded we are not our memories. Memories are only a story of the former self, which is in the process of transcending and awakening to awareness of Self.

However, our stories are still powerful tools for transformation. Just as Leslie's story of spiritual development was incredibly healing and empowering for me, my hope and prayer is that my story has made a positive difference in your life.

AN INVITATION TO READERS

I invite you to write your own transpersonal autobiography. This empowering exercise is an effective way to reclaim and release your own memories as you metamorphose.

I also invite you to join me by participating in CoreLight's events courses, phone bridges, online forums, meditation retreats and sacred sites pilgrimages. CoreLight's teachers and I offer guidance and support with processing, healing and releasing the story of the egoic self as we each emerge into the awareness of Self.

Every soul's journey of becoming, evolving and discovering is a celebration.

Please let me know how we can support you on your spiritual journey.

Thank you. I look forward to hearing from you.

www.CoreLight.org
brad@CoreLight.org
+1 (505) 424-8844

CANYONLAND DREAMTIME
BY LESLIE TEMPLE-THURSTON

After three decades of teaching, Leslie is returning to her first passion—art. Painting and creating works of art bring her enormous joy and provide yet another vehicle for her to channel love and healing into our world. Her painting on the book cover, Canyonland Dreamtime, evokes the luminous, mystical landscape of the American Southwest, specifically Santa Fe, New Mexico, where we lived for almost twenty-five years. The seated yogi/yogini—half man, half woman—represents the balance of masculine and feminine in each of us. The original painting, metallic gold acrylic on canvas (5.5' x 3'), has a numinous quality, radiating and reflecting golden light.

We invite you to visit our web gallery of Leslie's sacred art, available as *giclees* (museum-quality prints on canvas).

When Leslie woke up, her spiritual guides taught her to infuse her art with a transmission of healing energy, which holds seeds of transformation. Buddhists call this type of artwork *Termas*—hidden treasures esoterically embedded in an object by a spiritual master.

Each painting and collage is imbued with a specific vibration, calibrated to support the Earth and humanity at this pivotal moment in our evolution. The owner of the piece becomes sponsor and steward of the shakti transmission, which radiates into the home of the steward and out into the world.

www.CoreLight.org

Seeds of Light's projects continue to blossom and support a growing number of children and adults in South Africa's marginalized community of Acornhoek, Limpopo. Please visit www.SeedsOfLight.org to donate. I invite you to join me on a retreat to South Africa where we visit the projects and meet the people we serve.

IMAGE CREDITS

Page number	Image credit
Dedication	Dan Piburn for CoreLight, Santa Fe, NM, Juy 7, 2017
Page 123	Rider-Waite Tarot Card "the Devil" December 1909 by William Rider And Son. Public Domain.
Page 136	Leslie Temple-Thurston for CoreLight, Santa Fe, NM 2018
Page 234	Omphalos in Delphi Archeological Museum. 15 August 2009, Юкатан CC-BY-SA-3.0
Page 250	*Dance of the Dragon*, by Broadhurst, Miller, Shanley and Russell
Page 251	*Dance of the Dragon*, by Broadhurst, Miller, Shanley and Russell
Page 253	Leslie Temple-Thurston and Patti Blair for CoreLight, Santa Fe, NM 2018
Page 256	Heraklion Archaeological Museum, Crete. Photo by Brad Laughlin, September 19, 2017
Page 257	Heraklion Archaeological Museum, Crete. Photo by Brad Laughlin, September 19, 2017
Page 257	Heraklion Archaeological Museum, Crete. Photo by Brad Laughlin, September 19, 2017

ENDNOTES

1. The German mathematician and philosopher Gottfried Leibniz coined the term *theodicy* in 1710 in his work *Théodicée*, in an attempt to justify God's existence in light of the apparent imperfections of the world.

2. The New Oxford Annotated Bible with the Apocrypha, Revised Standard Version (Oxford University Press, 1977).

3. Ibid.

4. The Nag Hammadi Library is a collection of thirteen ancient books ("codices") containing over fifty texts and includes a large number of primary "Gnostic Gospels"—texts once thought to have been entirely destroyed during the early Christian struggle to define "orthodoxy." Other important, primary Gnostic texts, such as The Gospel of Mary, were discovered in the century *before* the recovery of the Nag Hammadi Library. See http://www.gnosis.org/naghamm/nhl.html (accessed November 13, 2016).

5. Leslie Temple-Thurston, *Impeccability* audio recording (CoreLight, 1990), available at www.CoreLight.org.

6. Ibid.

7. Ibid.

8. Ibid.

9. Ibid.

10. Ibid.

11. Ibid.

12. Leslie Temple-Thurston with Brad Laughlin, *The Marriage of Spirit—Enlightened Living in Today's World* (Santa Fe, CoreLight Publishing, 2000), p. 28.

13. *Yoga* is a Sanskrit word that means *union* and refers to our union with the Divine. It is a derivative of the word *yoke*, which is the harness that connects an ox and a farmer—the physical device that allows their union. There are many forms of yoga, each of which is a particular practice that helps one advance on the spiritual journey of discovering unity with the Divine. Nowadays most people use the word yoga to refer to *hatha* yoga, the popular form of physical stretching and exercise. In Hinduism the four main branches of yoga are traditionally considered to be 1) *Bhakti* yoga, which is the path of *love and devotion* to the Divine; 2) *Karma* yoga, which translates as *action*, and involves finding union with the Divine by performing acts of selfless service or good deeds; 3) *Raja* yoga, which literally translates as *royal* yoga, the main practice for which is meditation; and 4) *Jnana* yoga, which is the path of union with the Divine through *knowledge, discernment and wisdom*, and involves self-inquiry and the philosophy of non-dualism. All the yogas are valid and important, and usually people are drawn to a particular branch of yoga based on their personality. A person who is very heart-centered by nature may feel inclined towards the path of bhakti. Someone who is more mentally oriented may have a predilection for jnana yoga. I personally have found great rewards in all four of these yogas and continue to devote time to all of them.

14. When Leslie's spiritual guides gave her these techniques, they told her the information was to go out unobstructed. We have therefore always offered Marriage of Spirit workshops by donation, and

the e-book is now available on our website on a choose-your-own-price basis, including free sample chapters.

15. 1 Corinthians 15:31.

16. Leslie Temple-Thurston, *The Heart of the Matter* audio recording (CoreLight, 1990), available at www.CoreLight.org.

17. Spiritual Warrior Training course is available as an online correspondence course at www.CoreLight.org.

18. The heart chakra is part of the subtle body anatomy and resides in the center of the chest. Chakras are discussed in more depth in upcoming chapters.

19. Op. cit., Temple-Thurston, *Heart of the Matter.*

20. Ibid.

21. Many years later Leslie also shared some of this information with her closest students and has given me permission to share it here.

22. Leslie Temple-Thurston with Brad Laughlin, *The Marriage of Spirit—Enlightened Living in Today's World* (Santa Fe, CoreLight Publishing, 2000), p. 82.

23. Ibid., p. 83.

24. Much of this chapter is excerpted from the Squares chapter in our book, *The Marriage of Spirit—Enlightened Living in Today's World* (Santa Fe, CoreLight Publishing, 2000).

25. *Darshan* is a Sanskrit word that means the giving of a blessing.

26. Sexuality is a topic well beyond the scope of this book, so the focus here will be limited to a general discussion. If it's of interest to you, I highly recommend Leslie's audio recording, *Sexuality, Spirituality and Kundalini—Non-dual Teachings for Couples and Singles,* which is available at www.CoreLight.org.

27. The term *sexual orientation* typically refers to how one self-identifies with the terms heterosexual, homosexual, bisexual or asexual. The term *gender identity* refers to how one self-identifies with gender, which may or may not correspond to the biological sex assigned at birth.

28. C. G. Jung, "Marriage as a Psychological Relationship" in CW 17: The Development of the Personality (1925), p. 338

29. C. G. Jung, "The Relations between the Ego and the Unconscious," in CW 7: Two Essays on Analytical Psychology (1957), p. 309.

30. See: https://kinseyinstitute.org/research/publications/kinsey-scale.php. Research showed that sexual behavior, thoughts and feelings towards the same or opposite sex were not always consistent across time. An official Kinsey *test* does not exist, which is contrary to popular belief and many tests across the web. The original Kinsey research team assigned a number based on a person's sexual history. The Kinsey scale is not comprehensive enough to cover all sexual identity issues. Newer scales suggest that sexual identity involves not just sexual orientation but also biological sex and gender identity.

31. Paramahansa Yogananda, *Autobiography of a Yogi* (Self-Realization Fellowship), chap. 10.

32. Lorin Roche, *Radiance Sutras*, as quoted in *Evolutionary Love Relationships: Passion, Authenticity and Activism*, by Chris Saade and Andrew Harvey (chapter 9).

33. Barbara Marx Hubbard, *Emergence: The Shift from Ego to Essence* (Hampton Roads, 2001), p. 23.

34. Spiritual Warrior Training is a correspondence course which provides spiritual guidance, tools and inspiration, and is available at www.CoreLight.org.

35. Leslie Temple-Thurston, *For Love and Money* audio sets, available at www.CoreLight.org.

36. A Dutch- and Flemish-derived language brought to South Africa by its early settlers.

37. *Elohim* translates as *gods* in Biblical Hebrew. It is used throughout the *Torah* (the Five Books of Moses in the Old Testament), referring especially to their acts as creator gods.

38. Pronounced *Mo-dee'-mo-lay*.

39. Meridians are integral to the system of Chinese acupuncture and are part of the subtle body anatomy, or non-physical anatomy. The Earth also has a subtle body, just as humans do. The Earth's meridians, also known as ley lines, are akin to the meridians of the human body. Just as an acupuncturist can heal a patient by placing needles at key points on certain meridians, so humans can affect the health and wellbeing of the planet by praying, practicing meditation and performing sacred ceremonies at key points on the

Earth's meridians. For more information on *Lulungwa Mangakatsi,* see *The Mystery of the White Lions*, by Linda Tucker.

40. The Earth grid is a network of meridians crisscrossing the planet. Like a spider's web, all meridians in the grid are connected.

41. Although it seems like magic, it is no hocus-pocus. We know money manifests through the universal laws of flow and through grace when we are in alignment with divine guidance and are willing to practice the principles of skywalking, as described in Chapter 16.

42. Desmond Tutu, *No Future Without Forgiveness* (Doubleday, 1999).

43. *Oxfam Report*: www.oxfam.org/en/pressroom/pressreleases/2016-01-18/62-people-own-same-half-world-reveals-oxfam-davos-report. Accessed July 10, 2016.

44. *11 Facts about Global Poverty*: www.dosomething.org/us/facts/11-facts-about-global-poverty. Accessed July 10, 2016.

45. *Poverty Facts and Stats*: www.globalissues.org/article/26/poverty-facts-and-stats. Accessed July 10, 2016.

46. *State of the World Report*, The New Internationalist Magazine: https://newint.org/features/1997/01/05/keynote/. Accessed July 10, 2016.

47. Richard Lee, *The Dobe !Kung*, p. 101.

48. Marshall Sahlins, *Stone Age Economics*, p. 209.

49. Charles Eisenstein, *Sacred Economics: Money, Gift, and Society in the Age of Transition* (Random House, Kindle Edition), pp. 244–245.

50. *Vulnerable* means children with at least one parent ill, absent or deceased.

51. Creating a paid position was a big decision at the time, and we made it reluctantly, since it has always been important to us that all of the money we raise go directly to support the children and the projects. However, we had reached a threshold and could see that paying someone a stipend would enable us to help so many more in Acornhoek. Leslie and I have never taken any money for our work with Seeds of Light, and although Seeds of Light now has employees, the original spirit of our intention remains, and the administrative overhead is kept very low.

52. Judith Baker Miller, *Hand Spun Hope: Making a Difference in Rural South Africa.* Judy's inspiring experiences with the Mapusha Weavers.

53. Maude Barlowe, *Blue Gold: The Fight to Stop the Corporate Theft of the World's Water* (New York: The New Press, 2002), p. 10.

54. Deep gratitude to the facilitators, David Patient and Neil Orr.

55. The other three main yogas, described in Chapter 4, Who Am I?, are bhakti/devotion, raja/meditation, jnana/knowledge.

56. Leslie Temple-Thurston, *Impeccability,* audio recording, www.CoreLight.org.

57. A home in which the adults are deceased or absent, and the older children raise the younger ones.

58. Thank you to Nina Cohen, David Patient, Neil Orr, Builders' Warehouse and Spring of Hope.

59. A drop-in center is different from an orphanage in that there is no overnight accommodation. Although our original intention was to build an orphanage with overnight accommodation, the South African government passed a law making it very difficult to provide this service. Their intention—for better or worse—was to encourage local communities to assume more responsibility for the care of orphans and to discourage the institutionalization of raising children. Drop-in centers are especially important in areas where there are large numbers of child-headed households.

60. Statistics as of 2012 at http://www.avert.org/children-orphaned-hiv-and-aids.htm (October 2015).

61. To name a few: Egypt (Wadjet), China (Kuan Yin riding the dragon), Mesopotamia (Inanna, and primordial dragon goddess of creation, Tiamat), India (Manasa).

62. Riane Eisler, *The Chalice and the Blade: Our History, Our Future* (San Francisco: Harper, 1988), p. 83.

63. Ibid., p. 107.

64. Ibid.

65. Leonard Shlain in *The Alphabet Versus the Goddess* references Bill Bryson, *The Mother Tongue: English & How It Got That Way*, (New York: Morrow, 1990), p 117.

66. Leonard Shlain in *The Alphabet Versus the Goddess* references John Bowker, *The Complete Bible Handbook* (New York: DK, 1998), p. 165.

67. Leonard Shlain, *The Alphabet Versus the Goddess: The Conflict Between Word and Image* (New York: Penguin, 1999), p. 121.

68. Zeus is Apollo's father and they both slay a serpent in a very similar fashion. It is interesting that like Python, Typhon is a serpent son of Gaia. So Zeus and Apollo—arguably the two primary patriarchs of Greek mythology—were complicit in slaying Gaia's offspring. Furthermore, these two parallel myths reinforce the fact that this patriarchal pact was to be passed down through the generations.

69. Op. cit., Shlain, p. 112.

70. Ibid.

71. Ibid., pp. 115–6.

72. Ibid., p. 76.

73. Bernard Lietaer and Stephen Belgin, *New Money for a New World* (Qiterra Press. Kindle Edition, Locations 4064–4081).

74. Steve Taylor, *The Fall: The Insanity of the Ego in Human History and the Dawning of a New Era* (O Books, 2005), pp. iii–iv.

75. Ibid., p. iv.

76. Riane Eisler, *The Chalice and the Blade: Our History, Our Future* (San Francisco: Harper, 1988), p. xxiii.

77. Charles Eisenstein, *The Ascent of Humanity: Civilization and the Human Sense of Self* (North Atlantic Books, 2013), p. 197.

78. Paul Hawken, *Blessed Unrest—How the Largest Movement in the World Came into Being and Why No One Saw It Coming* (Penguin, 2007), back cover.

79. Paul Hawken, http://www.goodreads.com/quotes/350509-when-asked-if-i-am-pessimistic-or-optimistic-about-the (November 5, 2015).

80. Paul Broadhurst and Hamish Miller, et al., *The Dance of the Dragon* (Cornwall, UK: Mythos, 2003), pp. 48–49.

81. Ibid., p. 8.

82. Christine Rhone and John Michell in *Twelve Tribe Nations and the Science of Enchanting the Landscape* report on Lucien Richer's discoveries. The *degree of error* was calculated by drawing a straight line on Mercator's projection of the globe between Skellig Michael in southern Ireland and Mount Carmel in Israel and by measuring the distance from that *rhumb line* to each of 13 of the primary sacred sites on the alignment.

83. Op. cit. Broadhurst. It is interesting to note that the logo of the AMA is a caduceus with only one snake instead of two wrapped around the center line, which closely resembles the symbol for the US dollar ($)—an apt metaphor.

84. Ibid., p. 50.

85. Apollo's twin sister, Artemis, can also be considered his yin counterpart; however, because the ancient Greeks primarily built temples dedicated to Athena along the ley line (possibly because she was the patron goddess of their capital city, Athens), the dowsing authors call the feminine line Athena, not Artemis.

86. *Matrifocal* means a focus on the feminine. Traditional historians have referred to the Neolithic period as a *Matriarchy* because of widespread worship of the great Earth Mother goddess and

because the spiritual leaders were priestesses. The word *Matriarchy* implies an opposite to Patriarchy, which infers that women were in control of the culture and dominated men, the inverse of our modern, male-dominant culture. Rather, according to Riane Eisler's research in *The Chalice and the Blade*, it was a time when men and women experienced greater equality than they do today, and therefore perhaps a more accurate term than *matriarchal* is *matrifocal*.

87. Some researchers claim that this prevailing theory is not true and that the Pythia prophesized coherently. If so, it would be one more example of a patriarchal rewriting of history which includes feminine disempowerment and masculine empowerment.

88. Op. cit., Broadhurst, p. 302.

89. Martin Gray's Planetary Acupuncture technique can be found here: sacredsites.com/sacred_places/sacred_sites_meditation.html.

90. Bruce Chatwin, *Anatomy of Restlessness: Selected Writings 1969–1989.*

91. One of the names of God, *Brahman,* is a Vedic Sanskrit word, which in Hinduism means the ultimate reality underlying all phenomena.

92. After my first experience, I learned why I was given such a large amount of tea. The *curandeiro* (shaman/healer leading the ceremony) intuits how much you need to achieve your intention and pours the glass accordingly. In retrospect I'm certain the spirit of the plant guided his hand due to my lofty intention. I had detected a surprised look in his eyes when he'd realized how much he'd given me, but I dismissed it and rationalized that he'd given me much more because of my size.

93. It is also when the Earth aligned with the Sun and the exact center of the Milky Way galaxy. An excellent book on the subject is John Major Jenkins, *The 2012 Story: The Myths, Fallacies and Truth Behind the Most Intriguing Date in History.*

94. For example, switching to a diet that includes daily intake of a small amount of animal protein and lots of vegetables, is low in carbohydrates, sugar-free and gluten-free, and includes plenty of Omega-3 oils. New research demonstrates that the hippocampus (which is responsible for short-term memory) can be healed and *re-grown* by adhering to this diet and twenty minutes per day of cardiovascular exercise. For more information, see the work of Dr. Perlmutter: www.drperlmutter.com, *Grain Brain: The Surprising Truth about Wheat, Carbs and Sugar—Your Brain's Silent Killers.*

95. Elizabeth Kubler-Ross, *On Grief and Grieving: Finding the Meaning of Grief through the Five Stages of Loss.*

96. From the Greater Good website (accessed January 13, 2014), based on forgiveness expert Fred Luskin's essay, What Is Forgiveness? and the work of Jack Kornfield.

97. Margaret Meade, as quoted in Donald Keys, *Earth at Omega: Passage to Planetization* (Branden Books, 1982).